DONALD DAVIDSON

D1453326

Donald Davidson

A Short Introduction

Kathrin Glüer

OXFORD

UNIVERSITY PRESS

OXFORD
UNIVERSITY PRESS

Oxford University Press, Inc., publishes works that further.
Oxford University's objective of excellence
in research, scholarship, and education

Oxford   New York

Auckland   Cape Town   Dar es Salaam   Hong Kong   Karachi
Kuala Lumpur   Madrid   Melbourne   Mexico City   Nairobi
New Delhi   Shanghai   Taipei   Toronto

With offices in

Argentina   Austria   Brazil   Chile   Czech Republic   France   Greece
Guatemala   Hungary   Italy   Japan   Poland   Portugal   Singapore
South Korea   Switzerland   Thailand   Turkey   Ukraine   Vietnam

Published by Oxford University Press Inc.,
198 Madison Avenue, New York, New York 10016

www.oup.com

Library of Congress Cataloging-in-Publication Data

Glüer, Kathrin, 1966–
[Donald Davidson zur Einführung. English]
Donald Davidson : a short introduction / Kathrin Glüer.
p.   cm.
Includes bibliographical references (p.   ).
ISBN 978–0–19–538296–9 (hardcover : alk. paper) —
ISBN 978–0–19–538297–6 (pbk. : alk. paper)
1. Davidson, Donald, 1917–2003.   I. Title.
B945.D384G5813   2011
191—dc22   2011006715

ISBN 978–0–19–538296–9 (Pbk.)
978–0–19–538297–6 (Hbk.)

1 3 5 7 9 8 6 4 2

Printed in the United States of America
on acid-free paper

CONTENTS

PREFACE

This book aims at providing a short and crisp introduction to the philosophy of one of the twentieth century's deepest analytic thinkers: Donald Davidson. It is based on an earlier, shorter book written in German: *Donald Davidson zur Einführung* (Hamburg: Junius Verlag, 1993). What most clearly remains from the earlier version is the basic idea of the overarching shape and design of Davidson's wide-ranging but highly interconnected work. Using the radical interpreter as a guide results in the rather straightforward, systematic structure of both books. I have substantially rewritten and updated large parts of the original, however. Of course I have also corrected mistakes—and no doubt made some new ones.

Of all the people who have helped me along the way, I would like to especially mention these: Donald Davidson was always there and most generously answered all my questions when I was working on the German version. Daglinm Føllesdal was a most discerning early reader and thoughtful critic. John Perry not only rediscovered the book, but also most kindly helped with getting the present version on its way. And Peter Pagin provided most valuable comments and support at all times.

DONALD DAVIDSON

Chapter 1

Introduction

Donald Davidson was one of the twentieth century's greatest philosophers. When he died in 2003, at the age of eighty-six, he had not only lived a wondrously rich life, but also made important, often seminal contributions to most of the core areas of philosophy. A plane-spotter on an American aircraft carrier during World War II, he put on plays by Aristophanes in college—in the original Greek, and with musical scores by Leonard Bernstein. Later, he taught at some of the greatest American universities, amongst them Princeton, Stanford, and Berkeley. He loved to play music for two pianos with his wife, and enjoyed all sorts of outdoor activities including surfing, skiing, and mountain hiking. His philosophical interests ranged from general theory of meaning and content to formal semantics, the theories of truth, explanation and action, metaphysics and epistemology. Davidson was one of those rare figures who simply could not enter any discussion without significantly reshaping it; contemporary philosophy of mind and language in particular would not at all be the same without him.

An analytic philosopher of great rigor and originality, Davidson presents us with arguably the most systematic and coherent vision of the human mind and its relation to the world offered by any philosopher since the great system builders of centuries past. The profound humanism of this vision brought Davidson fame well beyond the circles of analytic philosophy and the Anglo-Saxon world. His singular ability to fruitfully combine an analytic perspective with its emphasis on logic, argument, and a scientific stance, with aspects of humanistic thought, gives Davidsonian philosophy its distinctive character.

The history and present gestalt of twentieth century philosophy of mind and language cannot be fully appreciated without at least a basic understanding of Davidson's work. The interest of this work, however, is by no means limited to the historian; even though few share Davidson's grand vision today, the arguments behind his often radical views remain eminently relevant to present interests and discussions. A basic familiarity with these arguments is a must for anyone interested in reading or doing philosophy of mind and language today: You simply have to know your Davidson.

Minded creatures, Davidson held, are essentially rational animals. And rational animals are *interpretable animals*. Their minds are essentially public; they are in principle accessible to their interpreters, other rational animals understanding what they say, think, and do. The interpreter thus is the hero, the main character of Davidson's philosophy.

Mental states such as beliefs and desires never come alone; according to Davidson, they always form whole systems, systems possessing a basic, internal coherence and rationality. This rationality extends to actions as well; the actions of a rational animal can be explained by the reasons provided for them by its mental states, its beliefs, and desires. At the same time, there are systematic, foundational relations between mind, behavior, and the surrounding world of objects and events. The contents of a creature's mind depend in systematic and observable ways on these objects and events, as well as on its behavior. And the same holds for the meanings of such a creature's words.

Indeed, Davidson most provocatively claimed the circle of rational animals to be quite select: Only creatures with language belong to it. Language and thought are interdependent; no thought, and thus no mind, without language. Davidson held many very controversial doctrines. He argued for the veridical nature of belief; in any whole system of beliefs, any particular belief might be false but the vast majority of background beliefs is bound to be true. Hence, Davidson thought that no general philosophical skepticism, be it skepticism about the external world, one's own or other minds, can even get off the ground. Davidson defended semantic holism, but disputed the conventional nature of linguistic meaning. He held that no solitary creature can have a language, but was at the same time convinced that the idea of communally established, shared meanings is philosophically utterly uninteresting. Rather, he conceived of meaning in not only individualistic, but even occasional terms; the meanings of words are established anew in any particular communicative exchange, be it ever so short-lived. Davidson revolutionized the theory of action explanation by showing how reasons explanations can be conceived of as causal explanations. He pioneered a sophisticated, decision-theoretically informed belief-desire model of practical reasoning. At the same time, Davidson conceived of the mental and the physical as irreducible realms each possessing their own right and value. While large parts of analytic philosophy were in the grips of naturalistic reductionism—the idea that the mental in some sense can be reduced to the physical—Davidson firmly held on to a more humanistic anti-reductivism. While retaining the thought that there is just one neutral ontology of objects and events, Davidson resisted physicalism in all its forms, holding no one way of describing the world to be privileged above, or more basic than, the others. The foundational relations between the semantic and the non-semantic, the mental and the nonmental, the rational and the nonrational, Davidson concluded, have to be conceived of as holistic relations of global supervenience.

Disparate as they may initially appear, from a Davidsonian perspective all of these semantic, epistemic, and metaphysical claims are intimately connected. There is a sustained vision behind them all. Knowing your Davidson thus requires seeing these connections and getting a sense of his vision.

Due to the character of his writings, however, knowing your Davidson might easily seem a rather daunting task. Davidson's work consists almost entirely of essays of rare elegance, style, and density. A true master of the form, Davidson seldom exceeded twenty pages. Today, these essays are readily accessible in five volumes of *Collected Essays* published by Oxford University Press between 1984 and 2006, and there is also the smallish *Truth and Predication* (Harvard University Press, 2006) containing two series of lectures. But Davidson's oeuvre is thematically tightly interwoven and holistic to a point where understanding only gradually dawns upon the whole. Full of references and allusions, to anything from the classics to modern analytic philosophy, his papers fully tax the reader's Bildung and analytic acumen. Be they ever so witty and stylish, easily penetrable they are not.

Any introduction to Davidson's philosophy must provide the reader with a guide that maps out an extensive, multileveled and intricately structured philosophical edifice. This is a short introduction to the whole of Davidsonian philosophy. It aims at crispness and clarity in the rather bold lines and connections it draws for the reader, but without sacrificing a satisfying level of detail and critical discussion. We shall therefore hold ourselves to the main routes and passages of the Davidsonian construction, emphasizing its unity and systematic nature. We shall not deny ourselves visits to some of its particularly intriguing and consequential side galleries, but many of them will be left to the reader's own explorations. The guiding idea of this introduction is simply this: There is a key to the Davidsonian structure, and this key is held by its main character, the interpreter. Once his central role is recognized, most other things rather easily fall into place. From this perspective, it is the theory of meaning and content that is at the very center of Davidson's philosophy.

I said that it is the interpreter that is the hero in the Davidsonian story. More precisely, it is the *radical* interpreter. Davidson adopted this notorious figure from another giant of twentieth century philosophy of language, his Harvard teacher Willard Van Orman Quine. Quine was first with the idea of exploring the nature of linguistic meaning by sending an imaginary field linguist out into the remotest of jungles. His task is the construction of a translation manual for a radically alien language—a language, that is, that he does not know anything about in advance. His data consist of nothing but the observable behavior of the speakers, linguistic and otherwise, and its observable circumstances. According to Quine, the extent to which the field linguist can radically translate the alien language is the extent to which meaning is a scientifically respectable notion. The rest remains indeterminate. According to Quine's (in)famous doctrine of the indeterminacy of translation, this rest is considerable. The Davidsonian interpreter, by contrast, does not produce a translation manual, but rather a theory of interpretation for the alien language. This is a formal semantic theory allowing him to understand, or interpret, any utterance a speaker of this language might make. Like

Quine, Davidson is convinced that the data available to the radical interpreter are the data ultimately determining meaning. This shared foundational doctrine amounts to a weak version of what might well be called *semantic behaviorism*. Quine thought that behaviorism was the latest and best science at the time, but this is no part of Davidson's motivation for adopting it. For Davidson, the public nature of meaning provides sufficient reason for semantic behaviorism. This venerable doctrine, the doctrine of the essential publicness of meaning, Quine and Davidson share with a long line of great philosophers stretching from Dewey to Wittgenstein. If Davidson can make good on the claim that what results is semantic behaviorism, such behaviorism cannot be considered outdated just because behaviorism has long lost its paradigm status in psychology or just because other forms of externalism have recently dominated the philosophy of mind and language.

The radical interpreter is a truly ingenious device illustrating the Davidsonian take on the public nature of meaning and its metaphysical foundations. The data available to the radical interpreter are precisely those facts that determine meaning. But at the same time, meaning is by its nature accessible, or knowable, on the basis of the facts determining it; these very facts provide the radical interpreter with empirical evidence for his semantic theory. In Davidson's hands, meaning thus shows its epistemico-metaphysical double nature. According to him, meaning is an evidence-constituted property. Given this double nature, what better way could there be for vividly dramatizing the very metaphysics of meaning than the epistemic scenario of radical interpretation?

The radical interpreter cannot merely interpret linguistic utterances, however. Whatever he interprets an alien speaker as saying, he at the same time necessarily ascribes a belief to him.

If he takes the speaker pointing at a familiar animal as sincerely saying that there is a rabbit there, for instance, he by the same token ascribes that belief to him. Ultimately, the radical interpreter even has to interpret whole persons; their speech, mental states, and actions only come in 'package deals'. Moreover, he needs a principle relating the behavior he observes, and its circumstances—such as the salient presence of rabbits—to contents and meanings. This is the *principle of charity*. Its Davidsonian version counsels the radical interpreter to interpret his speakers as having true and coherent beliefs where plausibly possible. Extending all the way to the speakers' actions, charity becomes in the end a principle of basic, overarching practical as well as theoretical rationality. Consequently, such rationality is built into the very metaphysics, as well as the epistemology, of the mind; from a Davidsonian perspective, charity is the constitutive principle of the mind. At the same time, it foundationally links not only the semantic and the non-semantic, but the mental and the nonmental, the rational and the nonrational in general.

Thus, we begin to see how the radical interpreter unifies all the prima facie diverse and disparate themes and doctrines of Davidsonian philosophy. The claim of the irreducibility of the mental, for instance, ultimately derives from the foundational ideas codified in radical interpretation: Charity, with its requirement of a basic internal coherence and rationality in systems of mental states, is a constitutive principle of such a radically different nature from those operative in physics, Davidson argues, that reduction becomes impossible. Another example is his work on action theory, with its emphasis on action explanation. This is often seen as forming a side of his philosophy rather disconnected from the philosophy of language. But now, it naturally finds its place in a comprehensive theory of the interpretation of whole persons.

Nevertheless, there *are* two sides to Davidson's philosophy. Not because of any disconnect between the topics he is interested in, but because of the very nature of the question at the core of his philosophy: The question of what meaning, or content, *is*. This question is not exhausted by the foundational ideas the radical interpreter embodies. We also need to know more about the theory the radical interpreter is supposed to construe. What does it look like, what form does it take? Davidson's idea was that we have in fact answered the question what meaning is, a question as old and seemingly intractable as philosophy itself, if we can provide answers to both the "foundational" question—what determines meaning?—and the "formal" question: What form does a theory take that describes our linguistic competence, and ultimately even the structure and contents of our mind?

For starters, the radical interpreter is supposed to construe a formal semantic theory for his alien language. Such a theory, Davidson was one of the first and foremost to argue, has to be compositional: It has to enable us to derive the meanings of complex linguistic expressions such as whole sentences from the meanings of their parts, and the way these are combined. Alfred Tarski, the second great influence on Davidson's thinking, showed how an extensionally correct definition of a truth predicate can be recursively given for certain formal languages. Davidson pioneered truth-conditional formal semantics by arguing that a semantic theory for natural language could take the form of a Tarskian truth-theory. Such a truth theory, or "T-theory" for short, specifies the conditions under which whole sentences of its object language are true, and it does so compositionally. The radical interpreter's task thus becomes constructing a T-theory for the alien language, and he does so by applying the principle of charity. That is, he tries to find the (or at least a) T-theory that renders his speakers optimally correct, coherent, and rational in their beliefs and actions. The formal side of Davidsonian philosophy is not exhausted by formal semantics, however. A correct T-theory would allow the interpreter to interpret any sincere assertion and ascribe the belief expressed by it. But to get at the inner reaches of theoretical language, and at the links to desire and action, degrees of belief and preference are required, Davidson claims. Therefore, some formal decision theory needs to be employed in the interpretative project as well.

In the chapters that follow, I will begin with the formal aspect, with the question of how linguistic competence can be theoretically captured or modeled. Once we know a little more about the theory the radical interpreter is supposed to construct, we are naturally led into questions pertaining to its empirical nature and justification, and, thus, to radical interpretation. Here is an outline of how I shall proceed.

Chapter 2 presents Davidson's philosophy of language. In section 2.2, the basics of truth conditional semantics are explained. We take a quick look at Tarski's project of defining truth for formal languages. Then, we see how Davidson 'turns Tarski upside down' in order to use T-theories as formal semantic theories for natural languages. (See also the Appendix, where a T-theory for a small fragment of English is worked out in some formal detail.) Prospects and problems of the project of using such theories as formal semantic theories for natural language are discussed: Is it possible to construct T-theories for whole natural languages such as English? In what sense does such a theory capture our linguistic competence? And can we place enough criteria on its correctness to capture an intuitive notion of meaning? We shall see that formal criteria alone are insufficient. To come even close to singling out correct T-theories, empirical criteria need to be incorporated into the account. The scenario of radical interpretation dramatizes this aspect of T-theory construction.

In section 2.3, we see the radical interpreter in action. Employing charity, he seeks the T-theory that achieves the best overall fit with the data he collects. Thus, empirical constraints impose considerable limits on what counts as an acceptable T-theory. Nevertheless, the possibility of there being more than one "best" theory has by no means been excluded. Some significant indeterminacy thus remains. However, in striking contrast to Quine, Davidson does not think this indeterminacy any more harmful to the notion of meaning than the fact that we can measure it in degrees Celsius or Fahrenheit is to that of temperature. One may well wonder, however, whether indeterminacy really has been contained that effectively. In the last section of this chapter (section 2.4), we shall follow one immediate spin Davidson takes on the radical interpretation approach to meaning: his anti-conventionalism. The primary object of study for the radical interpreter is the individual speaker and his idiolect. For such interpretation to succeed, no pre-established, shared meanings are required. Davidson generally takes notions such as language, meaning and reference, and expression and sentence to be purely theoretical notions. Their only purpose is to account for successful linguistic communication. Such communication, however, can be an entirely momentary affair; meanings can be fleetingly established between two speakers for the moment of their interaction and no more, and philosophically it does not matter how 'wrong' we speak, by conventional standards, as long as we make ourselves understood. What results is a notion of meaning that is not only speaker- but also utterance-relative. We will take a closer look at this notion of meaning and explore its compatibility with the original scenario of radical interpretation.

Chapter 3 is devoted exclusively to the principle of charity. In the first section, we look at what Davidson later called the "principle of correspondence" and the "principle of coherence" (section 3.1). These two aspects of charity counsel the radical interpreter to interpret the alien speaker such that his beliefs are true and coherent where plausibly possible. But Davidson believed that these two principles alone were not sufficient to determine meaning and content on the basis of observable behavior. We need to integrate the interpretation of nonverbal behavior, the interpretation of intentional action, into the project. Accordingly, we need to widen our notion of interpretation from the understanding of linguistic utterances to the understanding of whole persons (section 3.4). Before we follow Davidson down this road to action, however, we shall pause and inquire into the status of the principle of charity (section 3.3). As the foundational principle of meaning determination, it should hold by necessity. But what kind of necessity does charity possess? And what kind of knowledge do we possess of charity? As we shall see, Davidson himself more and more tended towards conceiving of charity as an a priori principle of conceptual necessity. In the course of discussing these claims, we shall learn a bit about Davidson's version of naturalism, and investigate how well his take on charity fits into his Quine-inspired epistemology.

Chapter 4 unfolds Davidson's theory of action. Using the radical interpreter as our key here as well, we ask what it means to interpret nonverbal action: How are intentional actions described and explained? And how can the explanation of action be integrated into the project of radically interpreting whole persons or minded creatures? In this chapter, we familiarize ourselves with the action theoretic elements required by what Davidson called his "unified theory of meaning and action". In section 4.1, we learn about Davidson's revival of the Aristotelian practical syllogism, and his claim that reasons are causes. We then explore the compatibility of rational or reasons explanation with the idea of causal explanation; Davidson, and many philosophers after him, thought that these two modes of explanation are compatible, and, more precisely, that reasons explanation in fact is a form of causal explanation (section 4.2). For Davidson this crucially involves a neutral ontology of events, events that can be intentional actions under one description, but not under another. In this context, the first tricky questions regarding the relation between the mental and the nonmental arise: Davidson holds both that causal explanations require covering laws of a "strict" nature, and also that such laws are not forthcoming in intentional psychology. Because of the possibility of so-called "deviant causal chains", intentional action can neither be defined by means of the notions of reasons and causes, nor can its occurrence be codified by strict, natural law. This is part of the Davidsonian doctrine of the anomalism of the mental (more on which in chapter 6). In the last section of this chapter (4.3), we then return to reasons explanation and Davidson's pioneering contribution to developing a model of practical reasoning—a model not only allowing for weighing conflicting reasons and desires, but also for countenancing practical irrationality, most notably weakness of the will.

In the last two chapters, some of the most striking and important metaphysical and epistemological consequences of the core ideas in Davidson's philosophy are further explored. In chapter 5, the main theme is that of mind and world. We look first at Davidson's famous attack on the idea of radically different conceptual schemes. Davidson argues that there cannot be languages encoding radically different conceptualizations of the world; rather, all rational creatures inhabit a single, shared world. This is a world inhabited by quite ordinary material objects, objects to which minded creatures have a rather direct cognitive access. According to Davidson, there cannot be any "epistemic intermediaries"—such as sense data or perceptual experiences—providing evidence or reasons for our beliefs about the external world. We shall look at Davidson's epistemology for perceptual belief in section 5.2. By doing without intermediaries, Davidson further hoped to spoil the prospects of any radical skepticism of the senses. Much of his later writing is centered in one way or another around different scenarios of what he called "triangulation". Empirical content, as Davidson came to conceive of it, requires situations of "triangular" interaction between two creatures and (an object in) the world. Triangulation thus not only allows for further developing and modifying the reasons behind the foundational status of charity, and the possibility of radical interpretation. According to Davidson, it also supports a general anti-skepticism. Section 5.3 explores these later ideas, and at least some of the rather radical claims Davidson based on triangulation.

In chapter 6, we turn to the topic of the mental and the physical. As we saw earlier (in chapter 4), Davidson does not believe in the existence of any strict psychological laws. Moreover, he does not believe in the existence of any strict psycho-physical laws, either, thereby excluding the possibility of any nomological reduction of the mental to the physical. Nevertheless, Davidson combines the anomalism of the mental with a firm belief in the identity of mind and body. There is, he claims, but one neutral, monistic ontology of objects and events underlying these different classifications. Consequently, even though there cannot be identity between mental and physical *types* of events, any one mental *token* can very well also be a token of some physical event type. This ingenious construction, known as "anomalous monism", allows Davidson to combine the irreducibility of the mental with a peculiar version of the identity theory of mind and body: a token identity theory. After careful exposition of the intricacies of this position and the arguments supporting it (section 6.1), we shall spend the rest of the chapter exploring some critical questions (section 6.2). Davidson is very keen on the causal character of action explanation and the causal efficacy of the mental in general. But if the mental is indeed anomalous, all the explanatory power of citing a mental event would seem to derive from its physical, not its mental nature. Does anomalous monism thus reduce the mental to a mere epiphenomenon of the physical? Davidson argued that anomalous monism—even though compatible with epiphenomenalism—does not imply it. The principle of charity underwrites the very irreducibility of the mental, but there nevertheless might be room for a plausible relation of supervenience between the mental and the physical, a relation guaranteeing the causal efficacy of the mental. Thus, we round off our presentation with a final touch to Davidson's picture of the interpretable mind in its world.

Chapter 2

Radical Interpretation: Davidson's Philosophy of Language

2.1 The Basic Question

"What is it for words to mean what they do?" (Davidson 1984b, xiii). Ever since his seminal paper *Truth and Meaning* appeared in 1967, Davidson's work in the philosophy of language has, in one way or other, pursued this question. Over the years, he fine-tuned and developed his answers. He defended, elaborated, and corrected elements of his position, but the most central and basic elements of this position were in place early on.

"What is it for words to mean what they do?" is the most fundamental question of the philosophical theory of meaning. It is the question what meaning *is*, of its very nature and essence. The answer, however—or so Davidson tells us—we will find only if we place the question in its primary and original context: that of everyday communication by language. If we want to know what linguistic meaning is, we must not immediately fly off into abstractions such as the idea of particular languages such as English, German, or Swahili. Nor must we immediately start thinking in terms of sentences and words, their meanings and the things they refer to. There is a great deal of abstraction in even the seemingly most innocent talk about meaning and language. It is highly theoretical to talk about the meanings of sentences and words of any particular language: "In the end," Davidson says, "the sole source of linguistic meaning is the intentional production of tokens of sentences. If such acts did not have meanings nothing would" (Davidson 1993a, 298). What is meaningful, that is to say, are *utterances*, and utterances are particular actions: Actions directed at particular hearers by particular speakers at particular times. Moreover, even the concept of meaning itself is a theoretical concept: "The notion of meaning depends entirely upon successful cases of communication" (Davidson and Glüer 1995, 81). It derives all the content it really has from its contribution to an explanation, or an account, of successful linguistic communication. Meaning, Davidson argues, therefore is of a fundamentally intersubjective nature; what is meaningful are first and foremost certain utterances—those utterances where the hearer understands what the speaker wants to say. It is successful communication that concepts like meaning, language, word or sentence are there to explain.

In the late 1960s and the early 1970s, Davidson suggested an unconventional approach to the basic questions in the theory of meaning, an approach taking precisely the perspective just sketched. Communication is successful where we understand what someone else tries to say. But what is it to understand a linguistic utterance? "Central to my argument is the concept of *an interpreter, someone who understands the utterances of another*", Davidson writes (Davidson 1975, 157, emphasis added). This sentence might well form the motto of all his early papers in the philosophy of language. It introduces the main character of this philosophy, the interpreter. He is the prototypical participant of everyday discourse, characterized merely by his ability to understand what others say. Whether these others tell him about the weather, the nearby wildlife, or their weekend activities, the interpreter is there to decode their utterances; for Davidson, "interpretation" simply designates the process of understanding, or trying to understand—nothing more and nothing less. And it is this ability, the ability to interpret utterances of natural language, that Davidson suggests we look at in order to approach the question of meaning. In an age of deep distrust towards the philosophical analysis of concepts, this was an ingenious move. It combined a naturalistic attitude and scientific rigor with the pursuit of questions concerning the nature and essence of things like meaning.[1]

Our linguistic ability or competence, the ability to produce and understand linguistic utterances, is very complex. It is an ability that delivers knowledge: Knowledge of what someone said, knowledge of what the uttered expressions mean, knowledge of how to express thoughts in language. Linguistic competence, we can say, results in knowledge of meaning. Concentrating on the interpretive side of this ability, Davidson suggests approaching the question "What is it for words to mean what they do?" indirectly: by means of two others. Classically, these are formulated in the course of the opening paragraph of

---

1. Early on, Davidson comments on his own methodology:

> In philosophy, we are used to definitions, analyses, reductions. Typically these are intended to carry us from concepts better understood, or clear, or more basic epistemologically or ontologically, to others we want to understand. The method I have suggested fits none of these categories. I have proposed a looser relation between concepts to be illuminated and the relatively more basic (Davidson 1973b, 137).

Nevertheless, Davidson insists, the whole investigation is philosophical in the traditional sense of being "a conceptual exercise" (Davidson 2005, 73).

"Radical Interpretation", one of the most central papers in this context:

> Kurt utters the words "Es regnet" and under the right conditions we know that he said that it is raining. Having identified his utterance as intentional and linguistic, we are able to go on to interpret his words: we can say what his words, on that occasion, meant. What could we know that would enable us to do this? How could we come to know it? (Davidson 1973b, 125.)

What could we know that would enable us to do this? An answer to this first question amounts to a theoretical description of the ability to interpret utterances of natural language, a theory modeling this ability. Davidson calls such a theory a "theory of interpretation". Its task is the following: "Its subject matter is the behavior of a speaker or speakers, and it tells what certain of their utterances mean" (Davidson 1974a, 142). If the interpreter had such a theory for the utterances—that is, the linguistic behavior—of a speaker or a group of speakers, and if he knew that it was a theory of interpretation, he could use it to understand these speakers. Davidson explains: "You might think of this system as a machine which, when fed an arbitrary utterance (and certain parameters provided by the circumstances of the utterance), provides an interpretation" (Davidson 1986, 95). Such a theory is a theory in the formal sense. It consists of a system of axioms and inference rules by means of which the input of utterances is turned into an output of interpretations, an output of meanings or semantic values. Today, we call formal theories with this ambition "formal semantic theories."

At this point, a remark on terminology might be in order. Davidson himself uses the expressions "theory of meaning" and "theory of interpretation", but he does not speak of "formal semantic theories". "Theory of meaning" is, of course, a much more traditional term than "theory of interpretation". The former usually designates a whole philosophical discipline: All those philosophical considerations the object of which is the nature of linguistic meaning. Formal semantics clearly falls into this area, but does by no means exhaust it.[2] I shall use "theory of meaning" or "meaning theory" exclusively for the wider philosophical area, and use "formal semantic theory," or "formal semantics" for formal theories assigning semantic values to the expressions of given languages.

In Davidson's hands, construing a formal semantics is construing a theory by means of which we could interpret the utterances of a speaker or group of speakers. Moreover, such a theory is supposed to provide a model for the linguistic competence of these speakers. But precisely what form is such a theory to take—most importantly, what exactly are its outputs?

Davidson is a proponent of what is called "truth-conditional semantics". Truth-conditional semantics takes off from the observation, first found in Frege and Wittgenstein, of the close connection between meaning and understanding: Meaning is what you know when you understand an utterance. The basic idea of truth conditional semantics then is that what we know when we understand an utterance is when, or under what conditions, the uttered sentence is *true*. Hence the idea that a formal semantic theory is a theory that assigns *truth conditions* to the sentences of a given language.

Naturally, truth-conditional semantics is not the only option on the market. One influential alternative family of ideas about what the meanings, or "semantic values", of sentences consist in

<hr />

2. For more on the relation between formal semantics and philosophical meaning theory, cf. Glüer 2011.

is verification conditions, or conditions of warranted assertibility (for a little more on this, see Section 2.2). What is important right now, however, is only the connection between the form of a semantic theory and general meaning theory: By determining what the correct output of a formal semantic theory is, we make a contribution to meaning theory. For instance, if we knew that the correct theory is indeed a theory specifying truth conditions, we would know something very important and essential about what meaning is: It is truth conditions. So, construing a formal semantics is in the business of 'analyzing' meaning.

For this reason, it is crucially important to Davidson that the basic meaning theoretical questions not be begged when answering the second of his initial questions: How could we come to know it? How could we come to know a theory by means of which a speaker or group of speakers can be interpreted? How could we come to know of our particular theory that it not only has the right general form, but is the correct one for some particular language such as English? These questions need to be answered without presupposing knowledge of meaning.

What the correct interpretation of a speaker is, is an empirical question. That you speak English, I German, and my husband Swedish is something we can know only on the basis of experience. It could have been different; I could have been a native speaker of Swahili instead. These are matters of empirical truth about the world, and they do not hold by necessity. Moreover, we each speak our language with our own personal idiosyncrasies. We each, that is, speak what philosophers and linguists call "idiolects"; individual variants of our native language (and of any other language we have learned). A theory of interpretation for a speaker, or group of speakers, thus is an empirical theory, a theory formulating empirical knowledge about a particular part of the world: Knowledge about what the utterances of a speaker (or group of speakers) mean. Empirical theories are both built upon, and justified by, empirical evidence or data. It is very important that Davidson's second question is *not* a question concerning language acquisition. It is *not* about how we manage to acquire our first language, or to learn others. Rather, it is a question about the data and the justification we have for our knowledge of what others mean by what they say. In terms of formal semantic theories, it is the question of the data, or evidence, justifying such theories: These theories describe or model our linguistic competence, a competence that results in empirical knowledge. So what are the data supporting them?

To learn something about what meaning is, we must be able to formulate these data in terms not presupposing meaning or any other semantic notions; we must be able to formulate the data for it in non-semantic, nonlinguistic terms (cf. Davidson 1974a, 142f). To learn something about what meaning is, we thus are after the "ultimate evidence" (Davidson 1973b, 128) for any correct theory of interpretation. What *kind* of data is there that could do this job?

The question is completely general: It does not only concern speakers of a foreign language such as Kurt, but those of our own language just as much. For any speaker whatsoever we want to know: What justifies my knowledge of what she says?

The problem of interpretation is domestic as well as foreign: it surfaces for speakers of the same language in the form of the question, how can it be determined that the language is the same? Speakers of the same language can go on the assumption that for them the same expressions are to be interpreted in the same way, but this does not indicate what justifies the assumption. All understanding of the speech of another involves radical interpretation (Davidson 1973b, 125).

The quest for the ultimate, the "radical" evidence concerns the ability to interpret—regardless of who it is we interpret.

Some years after the publication of the cluster of papers I shall call "the radical interpretation papers". Davidson wrote an introduction to the collection containing them.[3] Here are the very first words of this introduction, summarizing his basic meaning theoretical strategy:

> What is it for word to mean what they do? In the essays collected here I explore the idea that we would have an answer to this question if we knew how to construct a theory satisfying two demands: it would provide an interpretation of all utterances, actual and potential, of a speaker or group of speakers; and it would be verifiable without knowledge of the detailed propositional attitudes of the speaker (Davidson 1984b, xiv).

We have already seen how providing a formal semantics contributes to answering the basic meaning theoretical questions, but we still need to make the connection when it comes to the evidence for, or the justification of, a formal semantics: Why do we learn something about what meaning *is* from learning how to justify semantic knowledge? Isn't the first a metaphysical question, while the second belongs to the theory of knowledge? Why would the epistemology of meaning tell us something about its metaphysics?

---

3. The radical interpretation papers are: Davidson 1973b; Davidson 1974a; Davidson 1975; Davidson 1976b.

Davidson's answer to this question is very much inspired by his teacher, W. V. O. Quine. It is encapsulated in the following claim: "What a fully informed interpreter could learn about meaning is all there is to learn" (Davidson 1983, 148). The metaphysics of meaning cannot, so to speak, 'outrun' or transcend its epistemology. There are no meaning facts beyond those that can be known on the basis of evidence available to the interpreter; the interpreter who possesses *all* the evidence has, ipso facto, all that is relevant. *That* is the ultimate significance of taking the perspective of the interpreter; that is why he is the key to the basic meaning theoretical question:

> Quine revolutionized our understanding of verbal communication by taking seriously the fact, obvious enough in itself, that there can be no more to meaning than an adequately equipped person can learn and observe; the interpreter's point of view is therefore the revealing one to bring to the subject (Davidson 1990b, 62).

But such epistemico-metaphysical double significance of the available evidence is quite unusual; for many, maybe even most objects or properties we do not think that the facts about them are exhausted by the evidence available to us. Why would meaning be different?

Because meaning is *essentially public*, Davidson argues: "The semantic features of language are public features. What no one can, in the nature of the case, figure out from the totality of the relevant evidence cannot be part of meaning" (1979, 235). The line of thought condensed into this relatively early passage is spelled out in some more detail in *Truth and Predication*, a small book based on two lecture series. In what originally was the third and final of the *Dewey Lectures* he gave at Columbia University in

1989, we find the most explicit motivation Davidson ever provided for his account of the foundations of meaning:

> What we should demand ... is that the evidence for the theory be in principle publicly accessible. ... The requirement that the evidence be publicly accessible is not due to an atavistic yearning for behavioristic or verificationist foundations, but to the fact that what is to be explained is a social phenomenon. ... As Ludwig Wittgenstein, not to mention Dewey, G. H. Mead, Quine, and many others have insisted, language is intrinsically social. This does not entail that truth and meaning can be defined in terms of observable behavior, or that it is "nothing but" observable behavior; but it does imply that *meaning is entirely determined by observable behavior*, even readily observable behavior. That meanings are decipherable is not a matter of luck; public availability is a constitutive aspect of language (1990b, 56, emphasis added).

Language is essentially social: Meanings are such that they can be understood. This, for Davidson, is the most fundamental thing about language. Remember that for Davidson the study of meaning is a theoretical enterprise directed at understanding communication—more precisely, communication by language. Linguistic communication is naturally something that involves more than one speaker. It is quite uncontroversially a social phenomenon. And meaning is nothing more than a theoretical notion used to explain this phenomenon. So, Davidson argues, there cannot be more to meaning than what we can know about it. Moreover, this knowledge is empirical knowledge, therefore it must be justifiable on the basis of empirical data. These data must, in principle, be accessible to any ordinary speaker and interpreter. But at the same time they must be such that they can be described in non-semantic, nonlinguistic terms. According to Davidson, this implies that the data must consist in behavior, "even readily observable behavior."[4]

Thus the significant double nature of these data. They justify the theory, but at the same time, Davidson tells us, they "entirely determine" the very thing the theory is a theory of: These data determine what linguistic expressions mean. The data thus form the metaphysical basis determining the phenomenon itself: Meaning, we could put it, is an evidence-constituted property. Davidson thus subscribes to what I shall call a *weak semantic behaviorism*:

(SB)   Meaning is entirely determined by observable behavior.

Weak, because there is no ambition to 'reduce' meaning to behavior, no claim that meaning is 'nothing but' behavior (cf. Davidson 1970b, 216f; Davidson 1982c, 100). But behavior, readily observable behavior, forms the foundation, the metaphysical basis on which meaning is determined. To this much behaviorism, Davidson simply saw no alternative in the theory of meaning—at least not for anyone sharing the belief in the essentially public nature of meaning, the belief that successful communication by language is the proper object of explanation and study for the philosophical theory of meaning.

In recent years, it has become fairly standard to distinguish between what is called "foundational semantics" and what is called "descriptive semantics".[5] Foundational semantics is the theory of meaning determination, while descriptive semantics concerns questions of the particular semantics for certain types of expressions in particular languages, for instance the semantics of

---

4. For discussion, see for instance George 2004.

5. The terms 'foundational semantics' and 'descriptive semantics' are Stalnaker's; see Stalnaker 1997, 535ff.

proper names like 'Aristotle' or 'Gustav Lauben', or that of indexicals like 'I' or 'here' in English. But if we try to apply this distinction to Davidson's two basic questions we see that it cannot be exhaustive. Davidson's second question—"How could we
come to know something that would enable us to interpret a
speaker?"—is indeed his version of the basic foundational question: What determines meaning? Since meaning, for Davidson,
is an evidence-constituted property, the quest for the data justifying the correct formal semantics for a language L is the quest
for the foundational basis of the meanings of L. What is it that
determines that words mean what they do? And how does this
work, what principle governs this determination? But his first
question—"What can we know that would enable us to interpret
the utterances of a speaker?"—is *not* a question of the particular semantics of particular kinds of expressions, be they names,
indexicals, or even simply all the expressions of a particular language. Rather, it is the general question of the form any semantic
theory as a whole should take. Should it take truth conditional
form? Or should it take some other form? To *this* question, we
need to have already given an answer before we can go on and
provide specific theories for particular kinds of expressions or
languages.[6] Moreover, answering this question does make a contribution to general philosophical meaning theory in telling us
something about the nature of meaning. It is, thus, a foundational
question just as much as the question of meaning determination.

In the next two sections, we shall investigate Davidson's
answers to these questions in turn. We shall start with the form
a formal semantic theory for natural language should take. Such

---

6. This is a bit oversimplified; of course, these two inquiries can interact. Should it, for
instance, turn out to be impossible to give an adequate semantics for proper names in truth
conditional semantics, this would provide some evidence against the claim that meaning
consists in truth conditions.

a theory is supposed to provide a theoretical description of our everyday linguistic competence, our ability to understand what others say. It is very important here that Davidson formulates the question hypothetically. He asks: "What *could* we know that would enable us to do this?" (Davidson 1973b, 125, emph. added.) This is important because Davidson does not claim that ordinary speakers in fact possess (explicit or implicit) propositional knowledge of such a theory. What ordinary speakers possess is simply linguistic competence, a complex ability to understand what other people say. When put into practice, this ability results in knowledge; ordinary speakers usually know what others mean by their utterances. The theory is supposed to *model* this ability:

> To say that an explicit theory for interpreting a speaker is a model of the interpreter's linguistic competence is not to suggest that the interpreter knows any such theory. ... Claims about what would constitute a satisfactory theory are not ... claims about the propositional knowledge of an interpreter, nor are they claims about the details of the inner workings of some part of the brain. They are rather claims about what must be said to give a satisfactory description of the competence of the interpreter. *We* cannot describe what an interpreter can do except by appeal to a recursive theory of a certain sort. It does not add anything to this thesis to say that if the theory does correctly describe the competence of an interpreter, some mechanism in the interpreter must correspond to the theory (Davidson 1986, 96).[7]

So, what form should a theory modeling linguistic competence take?

7. Commentators that take issue with this include Larson and Segal 1995, 10ff; Lepore and Ludwig 2005, 31ff; 212ff. For a defense of the Davidsonian stance, see Pagin 2011b.

2.2 Truth and Interpretation

2.2.1 From Frege to Tarski: Truth-Conditional Semantics

Davidson's idea is that a *Tarski-style theory of truth* can be used as a formal semantic theory for a natural language like English, Swedish, or Swahili. To thus give Tarski's work on truth a meaning theoretic turn is one of Davidson's most original contributions to the theory of meaning. Tarski had shown how to recursively define truth predicates for certain kinds of formal languages. Amongst those working in the Davidsonian tradition, it has become standard to call the systems of axioms and inference rules used to provide such definitions "T-theories."

Davidson's idea to use T-theories as semantic theories can be seen as the result of fusing some fundamental insights due to Frege with Tarski's work on truth—once a semantic perspective is brought to bear, Tarski and Frege seem to be simply made for one another. Gottlob Frege, a German logician and philosopher of mathematics, was strictly speaking even less concerned with natural language semantics than Tarski was. Frege was mainly interested in the idea that mathematics can be reduced to logic. In the course of his work on this idea, however, he made contributions that, in effect, laid the foundations for analytic philosophy of language as we know it today.[8]

A line of thought going back at least to Frege and the early Wittgenstein locates the primary unit of meaning in the sentence and connects sentence meaning with *truth conditions*. This connection essentially involves the idea that the meaning of a sentence is what a competent speaker of the language in question understands, or knows, when she understands the sentence, or an

8. For more on Frege's contribution to the philosophy of language, see Heck and May 2006.

utterance of it. And what such a speaker knows, the thought continues, is when, or under what conditions, a sentence is true. This idea finds its first explicit formulation in Wittgenstein's *Tractatus*: "To understand a proposition means to know what is the case if it is true" (TLP 4.024).[9]

There are basically two ways to go from here: We can try to understand meaning in terms of a realist notion truth. On such a notion, truth is something non-epistemic, something that we might not be able to attain or know. Realist truth conditions can be 'verification transcendent.' Or we can relate meaning to something more humanly accessible such as the conditions under which we can prove a sentence to be true, or more generally the conditions under which we can verify or falsify it. The philosophers of the Vienna Circle were meaning theoretical verificationists. Neo-verificationism, as pioneered by Michael Dummett (cf. Dummett 1976) and Dag Prawitz, is based on the notion of proof. Weaker versions of verificationism are held by philosophers such as Dewey, Putnam, Brandom, or Habermas, who try to understand the meaning of a sentence in terms of the conditions under which it is justified to assert it.[10]

Davidson, however, adopts truth conditional semantics without any verificationist restrictions. According to him, *truth* is what we can call "the basic semantic concept":

> To give truth conditions is a way of giving the meaning of a sentence. To know the semantic concept of truth for a language is to know what it is for a sentence—any sentence—to be true, and this

---

9. The German original has: "Einen Satz verstehen heisst, wissen was der Fall ist, wenn er wahr ist." Note that the German has "Satz" which is better translated as "sentence", not "proposition".

10. For more on this, see for instance Wiggins 1997; Segal 2006; Glüer 2011.

amounts, in one good sense we can give to the phrase, to understanding the language (1967, 24).

Davidson here speaks of the "semantic concept of truth for a
language"—this is the kind of truth predicate Tarski showed how
to define: A predicate of the form 'true-in-L', where L is the language the predicate is defined for. This is a predicate that truly
applies to all and only the *true* sentences of a particular language.
Therefore, Davidson claims, you know the truth conditions of
the sentences of that language if you know the semantic concept of truth for it.[11] For Davidson, that is, understanding a sentence is knowing under which conditions it is true. And to know
this I do not need to know whether it is true, or how I would
verify it.

---

11. Tarski conceived of his definitions as making a substantive contribution to the general
theory of truth. He saw them in an Aristotelian light, as giving precise form to the view
that truth consists in correspondence with the facts. Davidson, too, originally thought that
Tarski-theories in fact provided some sort of correspondence theories of truth (cf. Davidson
1969b), but later argued that this was a mistake (cf. Davidson 2005, 38ff, esp. fn. 4). He came
to think that truth cannot be defined at all, and that the only way to say something revealing
about the concept of truth is by tracing its relations to concepts equally fundamental and
beyond definition (cf. Davidson 1996, 20f). He suggested that even though often beyond
recognition, truth is essentially related to the propositional attitudes: The truth predicate gets
interpreted only through the 'pattern' truth makes amongst the attitudes, including speech
and action, and their causes. It has empirical content precisely because T-theories can be
applied to intentional creatures, can be correct or incorrect for a speaker, or group of speakers:
"If we knew in general what makes a theory of truth correctly apply to a speaker or group of
speakers, we could plausibly be said to understand the concept of truth" (Davidson 2005,
37). Given our overall meaning theoretical project, we cannot take meanings for granted in
characterizing truth, however. We must, that is, find a way of relating truth to the very same
non-semantic data about speakers' behaviour in observable circumstances that according to
Davidson provide the determination base for meaning, or content in general: "I therefore see
the problem of connecting truth with observable behaviour as inseparable from the problem
of assigning contents to all the attitudes" (Davidson 1996, 37). Ultimately, then, belief and
truth are part of a set of basic, irreducible, and interdependent concepts capturing what's
essential to intentional minds. For more on Davidson on truth, see below 5.1.2. See also
Lepore and Ludwig 2007a, 315ff.

But there is an enormous variety, a seemingly limitless supply of sentences with different meanings that natural language has on offer for its speakers. Competent speakers possess an astounding capacity to efficiently and speedily produce and understand these sentences, even if they have never heard them before. To model the linguistic competence of such speakers, the theory we are looking for must specify the truth conditions of a possibly limitless number of sentences. But the theory cannot consist of an infinite list pairing sentences and truth conditions—that would not provide much of a model for a capacity like ours.[12]

To model an ability creatures like us can possess, Davidson therefore submits, we need to provide "an *effective method* for determining what every sentence means" (1965, 8). An effective method is one that is *computable*; from a finite basis of elements, it delivers the desired result in a finite number of steps, and it can be carried out by a human or a machine. To provide a model of our linguistic ability, a semantic theory thus has to consist of a computable system of axioms and inference rules.

The need for providing a finitely axiomatized theory for an unlimited domain of sentences results, of course, from locating the primary unit of semantic significance in the sentence. This, however, is not a matter of choice. Rather, Davidson argues, it is only at the level of sentences—more precisely, at the level of *utterances* of sentences—that the abstractions used in theorizing about language connect with use, with the purposes and activities of speakers:

---

12. This modeling problem is often put in terms of the contrast between infinitely many meaningful sentences (in any natural language) and our finite capacities (cf. Davidson 1965, 8f). But the problem does not really depend on the assumption that there are infinitely many meaningful expressions. For even if we limited the meaningful expressions to those that human beings can parse or interpret, the number of these expressions will be too large for a mere list of sentences to model the ability to understand—or learn—them all (cf. Grandy 1990).

The semantic features of words cannot be explained directly on the basis of non-linguistic phenomena. The reason is simple. The phenomena to which we must turn are the extra-linguistic interests and activities that language serves, and these are served by words only in so far as the words are incorporated in (or on occasion happen to be) sentences. But then, there is no chance of giving a foundational account of words before giving one of sentences (Davidson 1973b, 127).

Again, it is an idea of Frege's that is at work here: He formulated what came to be known as the "context principle." It tells us "never to ask for the meaning of a word in isolation, but only in the context of a proposition" (Frege 1884b, X).[13] Davidson goes beyond this; for him, it is first and foremost utterances that are meaningful and can be evaluated for truth and falsity.[14] This is mainly because utterances of sentences containing indexical elements such as 'here', 'now', or 'I', or demonstratives such as 'that' do have truth conditions only once these elements have been assigned referents. And what they refer to varies with the speaker and the extra-linguistic context of the utterance. Ambiguous expressions such as 'bank', too, need to be disambiguated before definite truth conditions can be assigned, and anaphoric uses of pronouns and scope ambiguities need to be resolved.

But the context principle not only puts the emphasis on the sentence—it also provides an instruction for dealing with subsentential expressions, for instance words. We are not to deal with words in isolation, but in the context of whole sentences. Why?

13. The original German reads: "Nach der Bedeutung der Wörter muss im Satzzusammenhange, nicht in ihrer Vereinzelung gefragt werden" (Frege 1884a, X). Again, the German has "Satz" which is better translated as "sentence", not "proposition".

14. More precisely, Davidson understands truth as a three-place relation between a sentence, a person, and a time (cf. Davidson 1967c, 34). See also Davidson 2005, 49f.

Sentences, Frege tells us, have a semantic structure; they consist of semantically significant parts. In a famous letter, Frege writes:

> But a proposition consists of parts which must somehow contribute to the expression of the sense of the proposition: so they themselves must somehow have a sense. Take the proposition "Etna is higher than Vesuvius." This contains the name "Etna", which occurs also in other propositions, e.g., in the proposition "Etna is in Sicily". The possibility of our understanding propositions which we have never heard before rests evidently on this, that we construct the sense of a proposition out of parts that correspond to the words (Frege undated [1914], 43).[15]

It is sentences that have truth conditions, but sentences consist of parts, or words, and precisely what a sentence means, which truth conditions it has, seems to depend on these parts and on the way in which they are put together.[16] Frege was thus the first to formulate a modern version of what is called "the principle of compositionality":[17]

(Compositionality)   The meaning of a complex expression is determined by the meanings of its parts and its mode of composition.

---

15. The German original, again, has "Satz" (sentence) where the translation has "proposition": "Der Satz aber besteht aus Teilen, die zum Ausdrucke des Sinnes des Satzes irgendwie beitragen müssen. Nehmen wir den Satz 'Der Aetna ist höher als der Vesuv'. Wir haben hierin den Namen 'Aetna', der auch in anderen Sätzen vorkommt, z. B. in dem Satze 'Der Aetna ist in Sizilien'. Die Möglichkeit für uns, Sätze zu verstehen, die wir noch nie gehört haben, beruht offenbar darauf, dass wir den Sinn eines Satzes aufbauen aus Teilen, die den Wörtern entsprechen" (Frege undated [1914], 43).

16. That the way a sentence is put together, its syntactic form, plays a role for what it means over and above the meanings of its parts can be seen by comparing 'John loves Mary' with 'Mary loves John'.

17. For more on the principle of compositionality, including a short history, see Pagin and Westerståhl 2010b.

If natural language is in fact compositional, accounts of linguistic competence can systematically exploit this feature. Compositional accounts start with simple expressions, specify their meanings or semantic values, and then specify the meanings of complex expressions by means of recursive rules for 'building them up' on the basis of those of the simple expressions (and the way the simple expressions are combined).

This way of thinking of meaning, Davidson stresses, is ontologically completely neutral: To think of the meanings of subsentential expressions in terms of compositionality does not carry any commitment to the idea that for any subsentential expression there must be some *entity* that is its meaning. There is no commitment "that parts of sentences have meanings except in the ontologically neutral sense of making a systematic contribution to the meaning of the sentences in which they occur" (Davidson 1967c, 22). And in fact, Davidson thinks that there simply is no need to abandon this ontological neutrality: The systematic contributions of subsentential expressions to the meaning of the sentences in which they occur can, he claims, be adequately characterized without assigning entities to each and every simple expression. Such entities are therefore simply redundant in the theory of meaning:

> Paradoxically, the one thing meanings do not seem to do is oil the wheels of a theory of meaning—at least as long as we require of such a theory that it non-trivially give the meaning of every sentence in the language. My objection to meanings in the theory of meaning is not that they are abstract or that their identity conditions are obscure, but that they have no demonstrated use (Davidson 1967c, 20f).

It is at this point that Tarski comes into the picture. Davidson saw that the formal apparatus used by Tarski to define truth for certain formal languages could be used to put these two Fregean ideas—compositionality and truth conditions—together. We can, he suggested, use T-theories to ascribe truth-conditions to natural language sentences in a compositional way: A semantic theory for a language L "shows 'how the meanings of sentences depend upon the meanings of word' if it contains a (recursive) definition of truth-in-L. And, so far at least, we have no other idea how to turn the trick" (1967c, 23).[18,19] In the next section, we shall have a look at Tarski's project defining the semantic concept of truth for formalized languages. In section 2.2.3, we shall come back to Davidson's project of applying Tarski's machinery to natural language.

2.2.2 Tarski's Semantic Definition of Truth

The philosophical work of the Polish logician Alfred Tarski basically consists of the essay *The Concept of Truth in Formalized Languages*. It first appeared in Polish in 1933 and is of rather technical character. Easier access to Tarski is provided by his paper "The Semantic Conception of Truth" (1944). *Concept of Truth* starts with a description of its central problem: "The present article is almost wholly devoted to a single problem—*the definition of truth*. Its task is to construct—with reference to a given

---

18. Truth-theoretic semantics is not the only way of doing compositional semantics for natural language. Possible worlds semantics is another, arguably more comprehensive approach. Both types of semantics, however, proceed by way of recursive truth definitions.

19. In Davidson, it often sounds as if recursivity and compositionality were one and the same thing. They are not; not every recursive semantics is compositional. T-theories are both. And while recursivity is sufficient for ensuring computability, and, thus, effectiveness in a purely computational sense, it is not sufficient for ensuring efficiency in a different sense: A computation that, given some reasonable assumptions, would take a year does not capture the efficiency with which natural language speakers can understand sentences. Pagin 2011b argues that only (certain kinds of) compositional (and 'generalized compositional') semantics (including T-theories), account for this kind of complexity theoretic efficiency.

language—*a materially adequate and formally correct definition of the term 'true sentence'*" (Tarski 1933, 152).

The extension of 'true sentence'—that is, the set of true sentences—varies depending on the language in question; the same string of sounds or signs can be a true sentence in one language, a false one in another, and completely meaningless in a third. Therefore, Tarski does not aim at providing a single, general definition of truth: "The problem which interests us will be split into a series of separate problems each relating to a single language" (Tarski 1933, 153). A Tarskian definition defines a predicate of the type 'true-in-*L*' for a particular language *L*: the *object language*. I shall call predicates of this type "T-predicates". The definition itself is formulated in a language different from *L*: the *metalanguage*.[20]

Whether such a definition is "materially adequate" can be determined by means of a criterion that Tarski calls "Convention T". In *Concept of Truth*, Convention T is formulated for the language of set theory. I shall here reformulate it in a way more congenial to the use Davidson is going to make of it:

Convention T:

> A formally correct definition of "true," formulated in the metalanguage, will be called an adequate *definition of truth* if it entails all sentences which are obtained from

(T)   *s* is true if and only if *p*

> by substituting for "*s*" a name of any sentence of the language in question and for "*p*" the expression which forms the translation of this sentence into the meta-language.
>
> (Cf. Tarski 1933, 187f.)

---

20. The metalanguage may however contain the object language as a proper part.

A truth definition satisfying convention T is *materially adequate* according to Tarski because particular instances of the T-schema—"T-sentences"—such as

(T_1) 'Snow is white' is true iff snow is white,

give precise expression to the intuitions behind a traditional correspondence theory of truth. And it is *formally correct* if it is an explicit definition (not using 'true' in the explanans) formulated for an object language L in a metalanguage M not identical with L. Convention T provides a test for checking whether a truth definition for L correctly determines the extension of the predicate true-in-L. Neither Convention T, nor particular instances of (T) such as (T_1) can be identified with the truth definition itself, however; Convention T is a criterion for testing whether the right consequences—that is, all T-equivalences—can be derived from the definition.

Truth definitions of the kind originally devised by Tarski can be construed only for interpreted formal languages. To allow for a Tarskian definition of truth-in-L, such languages have to satisfy another condition: They must not be "self-referential". That is, they must not contain expressions that can be used to refer to the expressions of L itself. Languages containing such expressions—for instance, languages in which it is possible to predicate truth of their own sentences—Tarski calls "semantically closed". Most notably, it is natural languages that have a "universalist tendency" towards such closure. Semantic closure is fatal for the possibility of defining truth-in-L, however. If a language is semantically closed, and the laws of classical logic hold for it, the so-called semantic antinomies—that is, antinomies such as that of the liar—can be derived. Truth cannot consistently be defined for such a language.

Another condition can be derived from the first: If the object language must not be self-referential, the *meta*language must be such that it cannot be interpreted in the object language. Otherwise, it would be possible to translate the truth definition, formulated in the metalanguage, into the object language—which, again, would generate antinomies such as the liar. As Tarski puts it: The meta-language must be "essentially richer" than the object-language. However,

> it is not easy to give a general and precise definition of this notion of "essential richness". If we restrict ourselves to languages based on the logical theory of types, the condition for the meta-language to be "essentially richer" than the object-language is that it contain variables of a higher logical type than those of the object-language (Tarski 1944, 351).

Many formal languages contain infinite numbers of sentences. Just as the natural language semanticist, Tarski thus needs to provide a finite axiomatization. He suggests solving this problem by means of *recursion*. A simple recursive method would be to start with atomic sentences, sentences containing nothing but a predicate and one or more singular terms such as 'John sleeps' or 'Paul loves Elsa'.[21] The number of atomic sentences is finite, and the first step of the truth definition consists in determining a truth value for each of them. In the second step, rules are provided for determining the truth value of complex sentences on the basis of the truth values of the atomic sentences they are built up from. For instance, 'John sleeps and Paul loves Elsa' is a conjunction of two atomic sentences. There would be a rule saying that such a

---

21. This is, of course, a bit of a simplification since predicates or singular terms themselves might be complex.

sentence is true iff both its conjuncts are. This simple recursive method fails, however, as soon as the object language contains quantifiers. A sentence like

(1)   Some trees are tall and slim

cannot be analyzed as a conjunction of two atomic sentences; it does not have the same truth conditions as

(2)   Some trees are tall and some trees are slim.

Very many of the non-atomic sentences that can be formed in a language with quantificational resources cannot be analyzed as composed only of atomic sentences and truth-functional connectives; many of them must be analyzed instead as containing open sentences (n-adic predicates with at least one free variable such as '*x* is tall'). And open sentences, just by themselves, do not have any truth values.

But open sentences have truth values relative to assignments of objects to the free variables they contain. Therefore, Tarski introduces the notion of *satisfaction*. Satisfaction is a relation between (ordered sequences of) objects and (open and closed) sentences. The basic idea is that a sequence $s = \, <s_1, s_2, \ldots >$ satisfies, for instance, the two-place atomic predicate 'x_1 loves x_2' iff s_1 loves s_2. Satisfaction can then also be defined for non-atomic open sentences and, finally, for closed sentences, whether they are closed by means of individual constants or by means of quantifiers. Moreover, truth can be treated as a special case of satisfaction: "It turns out that for a sentence only two cases are possible: a sentence is either satisfied by all objects, or by no objects. Hence we arrive at a definition of truth and falsehood simply by saying that a sentence is true if it is satisfied by all objects, and false otherwise" (Tarski 1944, 353).

In the Appendix, we shall have a more detailed look at the inner workings of the machinery Tarski provides for defining truth, especially that of satisfaction. There, a T-theory (for a fragment of English) is worked out in some formal detail. From a semantic point of view, this machinery is so interesting because it is supposed to satisfy Convention T. Convention T demands of a truth definition that it entails T-sentences for all sentences of the object language—and from a semantic point of view, T-sentences specify the truth conditions of the sentences quoted, or otherwise referred to, on their left-hand sides. From a semantic point of view, that is, Tarki's machinery is so interesting because it allows to derive *truth conditions* for all sentences of a (formal) language. Moreover, it allows us to derive truth conditions in accordance with the principle of compositionality: The truth conditions for any sentence S are derived as a function of the meanings of S's constituent parts and S's mode of composition.[22] And these are precisely the properties Davidson argued were needed in a formal semantic theory—of natural language:

> I hope that what I am saying may be described in part as defending the philosophical importance of Tarski's semantical concept of truth. But my defence is only distantly related, if at all, to the question whether the concept Tarski has shown how to define is the (or a) philosophically interesting conception of truth, or the question whether Tarski has cast any light on the ordinary use of such words as 'true' and 'truth'. It is a misfortune that dust from futile and confused battles over these questions

22. At this point, we can therefore also disregard all questions concerning the philosophical relevance of Tarski's work on truth. In our present context, it is irrelevant whether what Tarski defines really is in any interesting way connected to our intuitive understanding or conception of truth, but see note 11 above. For more discussion, see also Heck 1997; Etchemendy 1988.

has prevented those which a theoretical interest in language—philosophers, logicians, psychologists, and linguists alike—from seeing in the semantical concept of truth (under whatever name) the sophisticated and powerful foundation of a competent theory of meaning (Davidson 1967c, 24).

2.2.3 Tarski-Theories for Natural Languages

2.2.3.1 *Truth and Meaning*

For Davidson, natural language is the ultimate concern when it comes to studying meaning. According to him, we might learn all sorts of interesting things from studying formal languages, but nothing essential to meaning. We will not have understood the nature of linguistic meaning unless we can answer the basic meaning theoretic questions with respect to natural language:

> The main, if not the only, ultimate concern of philosophy of language is the understanding of natural languages. There is much to be said for restricting the word 'language' to systems of signs that are or have been in actual use: uninterpreted formal systems are not languages through lack of meaning, while interpreted formal systems are best seen as extensions of fragments of the natural languages from which they borrow life.
>
> The inevitable goal of semantic theory is a theory of a natural language couched in a natural language (the same or another) (Davidson 1973b, 71).

Thus the idea of using T-theories as semantic theories for natural languages.

Tarski, on the other hand, thought that it was impossible to provide truth definitions for natural languages. His main reason for this was the "universal" nature of natural language, its semantic closure, and the semantic paradoxes resulting from it. So, how could we have a T-theory for a natural language L if L is "universal" and, therefore, inconsistent? Davidson, following Tarski again, suggests using only *fragments* of natural languages as object languages, fragments that can be formed from, for instance, English by excluding expressions such as 'true' and 'satisfied' from it (cf. Davidson 2005, 149).

Even more significantly, there is an important sense in which Davidson needs to turn Tarski 'upside down': He needs to invert the direction of explanation or analysis of the whole project. For there is a sense in which Tarski explains truth *in terms of meaning*. As we just saw, Tarski's criterion of adequacy for truth definitions is Convention T. Convention T demands T-sentences the right-hand side of which is a *translation* of the object language sentence referred to on the left-hand side. And translation is a synonymy-relation, a relation of sameness of meaning (across languages). Davidson therefore describes Tarski's project as follows: "Tarski intended to analyse the concept of truth by appealing (in Convention T) to the concept of meaning (in the guise of sameness of meaning, or translation" (Davidson 1984b, xiv).

Davidson, by contrast, is after answers to the basic meaning theoretic questions. In the context of his project, appealing to meaning, synonymy, or translation would amount to begging the question. Therefore, he suggests doing things the other way around, to use truth in order to analyse meaning: "Our outlook inverts Tarski's: we want to achieve an understanding of meaning or translation by assuming a prior grasp of the concept of truth" (1974a, 150).

Accordingly, Davidson proposes to reformulate Convention T in terms of truth. Where Tarski had translation, that is, Davidson uses truth as a constraint on T-sentences. A T-theory for a language *L*, formulated in a meta-language *M*, will thus be required to entail all *true* T-sentences, all *true* sentences that can be obtained from

(T)   *s* is true if and only if *p*

by substituting an expression referring to a sentence of *L* for '*s*' and a sentence of *M* for '*p*'.

Using truth instead of translation here makes quite a difference. One good look at the T-schema shows very clearly that a T-sentence is true if, and only if, the sentences related by 'is true iff' are true (or false) under the same circumstances. This is all that Davidson requires of a T-theory.[23] As we shall see shortly, however, the demand is a lot more substantive than first meets the eye.

The Davidsonian strategy of 'inverting Tarski' also involves conceiving of the semantic concepts used 'inside' the theory, concepts such as those of reference and satisfaction, as purely theoretical concepts. No pre-theoretic understanding of these con-

---

23. Why not require instead that all M-sentences be derivable, i.e., all true sentences of the form (M)?

(M)   *s* means that *p*.

Using intensional vocabulary such as 'means that' inside the T-theory would mess up its neat extensional logic by creating intensional contexts. Moreover, trying to fix this would lead to a kind of regress: "It is reasonable to expect that in wrestling with the logic of the apparently non-extensional 'means that' we will encounter problems as hard as, or perhaps identical with, the problems our theory is out to solve" (Davidson 1967c, 22). Once we have a correct T-theory for a language *L*, we can of course *add* proof rules to it that license deriving M-sentences from the corresponding T-sentences. But to do this, we *first* need to make the traditional, extensional T-theoretic apparatus deliver the right T-sentences—T-sentences, that is, that do specify meanings. See also footnotes 46 and 47.

cepts is presupposed; they are interpreted (to the extent that they are) by means of being part of an empirical theory that gets its empirical content exclusively through its theorems and their connection with the data, the evidence supporting it. "This," Davidson explains, "allows us to reconcile the need for a semantically articulated structure with a theory testable only on the sentential level" (Davidson 1973b, 137).

And he illustrates the theoretical nature of terms such as 'reference' and 'satisfaction' by means of an analogy with physics:

> Within the theory, the conditions of truth of a sentence are specified by adverting to postulated structure and semantic concepts like that of satisfaction or reference. But when it comes to interpreting the theory as a whole, it is the notion of truth, as applied to whole sentences, which must be connected with human ends and activities. The analogy with physics is obvious: we explain macroscopic phenomena by postulating an unobserved fine structure. But the theory is tested at the macroscopic level. Sometimes, to be sure, we are lucky enough to find additional, or more direct, evidence for the originally postulated structure; but this is not essential to the enterprise. I suggest that words, meanings of words, reference, and satisfaction are posits we need to implement a theory of truth. They serve this purpose without needing independent confirmation or empirical basis (Davidson 1977a, 222).

To test T-theories, we need to test T-sentences. As we saw, Davidson reformulates Convention T in terms of truth. To use Convention T as a criterion of adequacy for T-theories, we need to be able to find out whether a given T-equivalence is true. The truth-predicate used in (T) therefore needs to be *interpreted*;

using a T-theory as a formal semantic theory thus does presuppose a prior understanding of the general, pre-theoretic concept of truth. According to Davidson, this is as it should be. Philosophically speaking, Tarski's project of understanding truth in terms of meaning is misguided since meaning is a much more obscure concept than truth, Davidson argues. Moreover, "truth is one of the clearest and most basic concepts we have" (Davidson 2005, 55).[24]

The claim then is that T-theories can be used as formal semantic theories for natural languages—but *only if they satisfy certain formal and empirical constraints*. The first formal requirement is that they satisfy the Davidsonian reformulation of Convention T. But is that enough? An adequate T-theory T for a language L must be such that an interpreter who knows T, and knows that T is such a T-theory (cf. Davidson 1976b, 175), knows what the sentences of L mean: "Someone who knows the theory can interpret the utterances to which the theory applies" (Davidson 1973b, 128). Let's call such T-theories, and the T-sentences they entail, "interpretive" (as suggested by Lepore and Ludwig 2005, 72). Prima facie its reformulation in terms of mere truth makes it seem at best unlikely that a T-theory satisfying Convention T delivers interpretive T-sentences: Why should a true T-sentence specify the truth conditions of a sentence s if there is no further requirement on the relation between s and p, in particular, no requirement whatsoever on the relation between the *meanings* of s and p?

One way of putting this objection is asking how we could prevent a T-theory for English from implying equivalences like (3):

(3) 'Snow is white' is true iff grass is green.

---

24. But see note 11 and note 47.

Such a T-sentence clearly is not interpretive. Despite being true, (3) does not specify the truth conditions of the English sentence 'snow is white'.

In this simple form, the objection does not take into account the *holistic restrictions* imposed by Convention T. Convention T requires a T-theory to entail *all* true T-sentences. Only if all the T-sentences we can get from the schema

(T) s is true if and only if p

are true, is the T-theory supposed to be interpretive. Moreover, T-sentences are derived from T-theories as determined by, or as functions of, the meanings of the constituent parts of sentences (and the sentences' mode of composition). The predicate 'is white', for instance, is a constituent of the English sentence 'Snow is white'. Plausibly, the contribution 'is white' makes to the truth-conditions of 'Snow is white' is *the same* as the contribution it makes to the truth-conditions of other sentences it occurs in, for instance the sentence 'This is white'. And it is at least very unlikely that a (reasonably simple) T-theory entailing (3) also entails a true T-sentence for 'this is white' (cf. Davidson 1967c, 26, esp. fn. 10).[25]

Davidson not only thinks that there are thus holistic restrictions T-theories have to obey. He goes on to further embrace full-fledged *semantic holism*. This is perfectly explicit in the following passage from "Truth and Meaning":

25. Presumably, it would entail something along the lines of

(i)   'This is white' is true (as spoken by a speaker S at time t) iff the object demonstrated by S at t is green.

Cf. Davidson 1967c, 34.

But (i) is clearly false.

If sentences depend for their meaning on their structure, and we understand the meaning of each item in the structure only as an abstraction from the totality of sentences in which it features, then we can give the meaning of any sentence (or word) only by giving the meaning of every sentence (and word) in the language. Frege said that only in the context of a sentence does a word have meaning; in the same vein he might have added that only in the context of the language does a sentence (and therefore a word) have meaning (Davidson 1967c, 22).

More precisely, the semantic holism Davidson endorses is of the following form:

(SH)   The meanings of expressions in a language L are determined *together*, by a *totality* of relations between expressions in L.[26],[27]

26. Cf. Pagin 1997, 13. It might then seem that (SH) actually conflicts with the principle of compositionality. There are two ways to deal with this apparent conflict. First, the notion of *determination* used in these principles can be interpreted purely mathematically: A determination relation that runs both ways, so to speak, simply is some kind of equivalence, or one-one, relation. On this reading, the conflict is merely apparent. Real conflict, however, results if we read determination *metaphysically*. Then, the question is one of metaphysical priority: Do sentences have meanings in virtue of, or because of, their parts having meaning, or the other way around? Metaphysical determination cannot run both ways. Nevertheless, compositionality and holism can be reconciled: It can both be the case that the meanings of complex expressions are (metaphysically) determined by those of their simple parts (and their mode of composition), *and* that the meanings of simple expressions are determined holistically, i.e. for all simple expressions together and by a totality of facts or data (cf. Pagin 1997). Davidson's holism is of precisely this kind.

27. Semantic holism has been heavily criticized by a number of philosophers, among them Dummett (1976) and Fodor (Fodor and Lepore 1991; Fodor and Lepore 1992); a survey is provided in Pagin 2006. A main line of criticism derives from the claim that if semantic holism is true, a change in the meaning of any single expression of a language L amounts to a change of the meanings of all expressions of L. This, however, is not true for all forms of semantic holism (cf. Pagin 1997). It is, for instance, not true of Davidson's holism since the principle of charity is a many-one determination principle.

Nevertheless, it remains a very good question whether T-theories really can be used as semantic theories for natural language. This question has two rather different aspects. The first is this: Can T-theories ever be made to cover the *whole* of English (and any other natural language)?[28] This question I shall call "the natural language question". The other aspect would remain a question even if the answer to the natural language question was clearly yes: It is the question of whether enough restrictions can be placed on acceptable T-theories to single out those that are *interpretive*; those, that is, that actually allow an interpreter to know what the sentences of the object language *mean*. I shall call this "the interpretive question". In the next two sections, we shall take up the natural language question and the interpretive question in turn. For those of you that would first like to have a closer look at the inner workings of a T-theory, a T-theory for a fragment of English is worked out in some formal detail in the Appendix.

2.2.3.2 A T-theory for the Whole of a Natural Language?

Let's start with the natural language question: Can T-theories be extended so as to cover the whole of, for instance, English? The most obvious question for any kind of truth-conditional semantics is how to deal with all those utterances that do not have any truth-values, utterances such as questions or orders. A truth-conditional semantics does not answer the question what it is to

---

28. Strictly speaking, the question should be formulated more carefully: Can a T-theory ever be made to cover a fragment of a natural language large enough to convince us that it captures the workings of meaning in natural language? This is because it might be the case that we always need to exclude at least the truth predicate from our object language.

ask whether snow is white; it does not provide any analysis of what a speaker asking a question or giving an order does.

It is important, however, to notice that a truth-conditional semantics does not answer the question what it is to claim or assert something—to assert that snow is white, for instance, either. Asserting, asking, ordering, and so on are *speech acts*. Speech acts are kinds of action that speakers can perform by means of using meaningful linguistic expressions. A widespread basic idea is that there is a sort of division of labor here: Semantics provides, or accounts for, the meanings, and a theory of speech acts explains what it is to use words with a certain meaning to perform speech acts. Thus, for instance, virtually the same words can be used to assert that someone put cookies in the larder, to ask whether someone put cookies in the larder, or to order someone to put cookies in the larder.

The theory of speech acts is part of what is called *pragmatics*. Other parts of pragmatics are concerned with phenomena such as irony or metaphor. Accounting for such phenomena is not part of the job description of a semantic theory, either. In general, no account of so-called "indirect" communication is—semantics gives what is often called the "literal meaning" of the expressions of a language. Whatever else sentences with, and by means of having, a given literal meaning can, pragmatically, be used to indirectly convey is not part of semantics. Thus, for instance, irony is the use of a sentence literally meaning that *p* to convey the opposite—*not p*. This, the idea is, would not be possible if the sentence did not literally mean *p* in the first place. The same would seem to hold for the different varieties of Gricean *implicatures*; if, to take a classical example, a professor is asked to provide a reference for a student, and confines himself to saying that the student has excellent handwriting, we might all understand him as conveying that the academic achievements of the student are substandard. Nevertheless, the sentence he actually writes does not (literally) mean this.[29]

Semantics would thus seem to be only part of a comprehensive account of linguistic competence, even though the most central and basic part. To complete the account, a systematic theory of pragmatics, including both speech act theory and a theory of indirect speech, would be needed.[30] Davidson himself, however, is notoriously skeptical towards the possibility of such a completion. He holds that only the realm of the literal shows the systematicity necessary for theoretical description. There is, he claims, no such systematicity when it comes to what speakers can use meaningful expressions to do; there simply are no limits, no rules constraining their pragmatic creativity (cf. Davidson 2005, 313). In this sense literal meaning is "autonomous"; it does not depend on any of the ulterior purposes speakers might have in using language:

> It is not an accidental feature of language that the ulterior purpose of an utterance and its literal meaning are independent, in the sense that the latter cannot be derived from the former: it is of the essence of language. I call this feature of language the principle of *the autonomy of meaning* (Davidson 1982a, 274).

In recent years, however, it has become increasingly contested where exactly the semantics-pragmatics distinction is to be drawn. Moreover, there might be significant overlap between the semantic and the pragmatic. There seems to be a growing

---

29. Grice's classical texts are collected in Grice 1989. Survey in Grandy and Warner 2009.

30. Classical arguments for the need of such a completion can be found in Dummett 1974, 1976.

consensus in the literature, for instance, that pragmatic processes often start having an influence on the interpretation of utterances *before* a full, truth-evaluable propositional content has been reached.[31] This would mean that what speakers actually hold true (or false) often is not the same as what a T-theory for the language in question outputs. And that would mean considerable trouble for the Davidsonian project—as we shall see in section 2.3, the *evidence* for Davidsonian T-theories is supposed to consist precisely of data about when, and under what circumstances, speakers hold sentences to be true. Should it be the case that pragmatic processes (sufficiently often) interfere with this, the Davidsonian project could—somewhat ironically—be saved only by combining T-theories with a systematic account of these pragmatic processes.[32]

Even on the assumption that T-theories do delineate the semantic, or literal, core of a language there are a number of serious problems for their construction, however. In order to be able to 'feed' a sentence *s* into a T-theory, *s* first has to be brought into the regimented form that the theory can handle. As we saw in the last section, this means using the language of first-order quantified logic to 'transcribe' the sentence. In a second step, the theory then

---

31. Radical contextualists draw the conclusion that there is no such thing as a 'literal core' in language use, and that systematic semantic theories therefore do not play any role in accounting for linguistic communication. Philosophical examples include Searle 1978 and Travis 1989. Less radical contextualists such as Recanati 2004 and Pagin and Pelletier 2007 argue that even though pragmatic influences on understanding linguistic utterances usually start before a truth-evaluable content is outputted, this neither prevents semantic theories from being indispensable for explaining linguistic communication nor does it prevent an account of such understanding from being systematic. Semantic minimalists, such as Borg 2004 and Cappelen and Lepore 2004, hold that every utterance of a (non-indexical) sentence expresses one and the same semantic content, the "minimal proposition" (according to Cappelen and Lepore, many other propositions might be expressed at the same time, however).

32. Cf. Pagin 2011a. Here, a first shot at such a systematic account is provided.

can be used to derive T-sentences. But this means that T-theories for a natural language L reach precisely as far as the sentences of L have logical forms that can be 'fed into' them. More precisely, a T-theory applies to a sentence s of L if, and only if, s's logical form can be specified in the language of first-order quantified logic (with identity).

Determining the logical form of the sentences of L can be seen as describing L's structure on two levels: On the subsentential level, the "micro-level", we identify a finite number of simple expressions. The list of simple expressions of a language L is called its *lexicon*. It is essential that the lexicon be finite—otherwise, a T-theory using it cannot provide a model for linguistic competence. On the sentential level, the "macro-level", on the other hand we get a description of L as a *logical structure*: By identifying certain of their components as logical constants, for instance, relations of logical entailment between sentences are automatically identified. Thus, a sentence like (4) has the logical form (4′) and, therefore, logically entails (5):

(4)   The sun and the moon are round.
(4′) $Fa \ \& \ Fb$
(5)   The sun is round.[33]

Now, quite significant parts of natural language *can* be handled adequately by assigning logical forms this way, but it is far from clear that everything can. Problems arise, for instance, for conditionals and for intensional contexts like those created by propositional attitude operators such as 'believes that' or modal

---

33. That a T-theory thus describes the structure of a language L not only at the subsentential, but also at the intersentential level will play an important role for its relation to the empirical data providing the evidence for it. Predicting intersentential relations, especially logical entailments, is one of the aspects that makes such a theory empirically testable, according to Davidson. See section 2.3.

operators such as 'it is necessary that'. Problematic are also attributive adjectives ('good', as in 'good actress'), indexicals ('I', 'this'),
mass terms ('snow', 'water'), tense operators, and many more
(cf. Davidson 1967c, 35f). In many of these areas, considerable
progress has been made since the days when Davidson first to use
T-theories as formal semantic theories. Some of these, notably the
possible worlds treatments of alethic modal operators such as 'it
is necessary that' or 'it is possible that', however, require leaving
'pure' truth-theoretic semantics behind and adopting something
stronger, a version of possible-worlds semantics.[34] Attitude contexts, however, continue to vex formal semantics. I shall therefore
use them as my main example here.

Take the sentence (6):

(6)   Hesperus is a planet.

'Hesperus' is another name for the planet Venus. And so is 'Phosphorus': 'Hesperus' and 'Phosphorus' are co-referring singular
terms. In a sentence like (6), substitution of 'Phosphorus' for
'Hesperus' results in a sentence, (7), that has the same truth value
as the original (6). In this case, both are true:

(7)   Phosphorus is a planet.

Sentences of this kind are often called *extensional contexts*:
They provide contexts in which co-extensional expressions can

---

34. The main difference between truth-theoretic and possible worlds semantics is that the
latter assigns *possible worlds truth conditions* to sentences: Here, sentences are evaluated for
truth relative to different possible circumstances, or ⌜worlds⌝. The basic semantic concept
is *truth at a possible world w*, and truth simpliciter, or truth at the ⌜actualworld⌝, is one
particular instance of this. This allows for interpreting the alethic modal operators as follows: ⌜Possibly, s⌝ is true at a world w iff s is true at a world w′ accessible from w, and
⌜Necessarily, s⌝ is true at a world w iff s is true at all worlds w′ accessible from w. For an
introduction, see King 2006. For an attempt at giving a T-theoretic semantics for the alethic
modal operators, see for instance Peacocke 1978.

be substituted *salva veritate*, that is, without change in truth value. One could also say that in such contexts, the only thing that matters for truth is extension.

But on the face of it, not all sentences of natural language are like that. Some at least seem to violate the principle we could call "the principle of substitution":

(S) Co-extensional expressions can be substituted salva veritate.

A prime example of such *intensional contexts* are so-called belief-sentences: Take (8) and (9):

(8) Peter believes that Hesperus is a planet.
(9) Peter believes that Phosphorus is a planet.

Peter might not know that Hesperus in fact is Phosphorus. In such a situation, (8) might be true while (9) is false (or vice versa). The expression 'believes that ...' thus at least seems to create a context in which the principle of substitution fails: Substituting co-extensional expressions in the that-clause might result in a change of truth value.

Frege, who was the first to draw attention to this phenomenon (cf. Frege 1892), proposed an account of intensional contexts according to which the appearance of substitution failure is illusory. According to Frege, expressions such as proper names have both an extension (a referent) and a "sense": A Fregean sense is something like a mode of presentation, or a way of thinking of an object. Thus, the referent of 'Hesperus' is Venus, and the mode of presentation could be specified by means of the following description: the first heavenly body to be visible in the evening sky. In general, a Fregean sense is a mode of presentation that determines an expression's extension. In belief contexts, Frege maintains, expressions change their extensions: In belief contexts, a proper name, for instance, does not refer to its ordinary referent, but to its sense.[35] Thus, the principle of substitution does hold in belief contexts: Expressions occurring in such contexts refer to their senses, and expressions with the same senses *can* be substituted salva veritate.[36]

Davidson finds the Fregean account very counterintuitive. In the following passage, he voices this criticism with respect to indirect discourse (his example is: 'Galileo said that the earth moves'), but it is completely clear from the surrounding text that he thinks the point carries over directly to belief contexts:

> If we could recover our pre-Fregean semantic innocence, I think it would seem to us plainly incredible that the words 'The earth moves', uttered after the words 'Galileo said that' ['Galileo believes that'], mean anything different, or refer to anything else, than is their wont when they come in other environ-

35. This might be the reason why intensional contexts sometimes are called "opaque" or "non-transparent": There is a certain sense in which it is not transparent what the expressions within such contexts refer to.

36. Sometimes, the term 'intension' is used in a wide sense: In this wide sense, it simply denotes whatever is needed (if anything) in addition to extension to provide an adequate account of semantic meaning. In this wide sense of 'intensional', two expressions that have the same Fregean sense (whatever that precisely amounts to) would be co-intensional. The term derives from Carnap 1947, however, who like Frege works with two aspects of meaning, extension and intension, but for whom 'intension' has a more narrow, technical sense: A Carnapian intension is a function from a "state description" to an extension. In the same tradition, possible worlds semantics works with intensions that are functions from possible worlds to extensions. Possible worlds intensions are not sufficient for restoring substitutability to belief-contexts, however: Substituting co-intensional expressions expressions in belief-contexts can still result in truth value change. This is most drastically illustrated by the fact that all logical necessities have the same possible worlds intension. But it certainly is not the case that anyone who believes one logical necessity believes them all (this is often called "the problem of logical omniscience"). Another example might be proper names. According to many people, co-referring proper names have the same possible worlds intension (a constant function from worlds to the referent). If that is true, (possible worlds) co-intensionality does not solve the original Frege cases. For this reason, contexts such as belief-contexts sometimes are called "hyperintensional contexts".

ments.... Language is the instrument it is because the same expression, with semantic features (meaning) unchanged, can serve countless purposes (Davidson 1968, 108).

The principle Davidson is endorsing here has been called "the principle of semantic innocence":

(Innocence)   For all expressions e and linguistic contexts c of a language L: e's semantic value does not change with c.

Many share Davidson's intuition regarding this principle. It is, however, not entirely clear how innocence is to be interpreted. One question regards semantic value: Innocence may be plausible when interpreted as a principle governing things like Fregean senses. But is innocence as plausible for reference or satisfaction?[37]

37. Consider Davidson's own account of the truth conditions for existentially quantified sentences, for instance (cf. the Appendix). While an n-place predicate $F(x_1, \ldots, x_n)$ is satisfied by a sequence s iff $F(s_1, \ldots, s_n)$, $\exists x F(x_1, \ldots, x_n)$ is satisfied iff there is a sequence s' such that $F(s'_1, \ldots, s'_n)$. The shift from s to s' here would seem to qualify as a change of semantic value in the sense Davidson is talking about. Truth conditional semantics, that is, violates innocence as a principle governing reference or satisfaction as soon as it covers quantified sentences. We do not need to go to possible worlds versions of truth conditional semantics for this.

It is, however, not entirely clear how to understand the idea of a change in semantic value in the first place. Here is a toy example: Assume that an expression e can be evaluated in exactly two ways: as referring to o_1 and as referring to o_2. Which one it is depends systematically on the linguistic context it occurs in: It is o_2 in belief-contexts, and o_1 in all others. What should we say about e's semantic value? We could, for instance, say that it consists of the ordered pair (o_1, o_2). Then, e's semantic value does not change from context to context. Nevertheless, the result of semantically evaluating e changes depending on the context in which it occurs. Is this a violation of innocence or not?

I don't think there is any determinate answer to this question, but nothing much hangs on that. What this shows is rather that innocence ultimately is not very important when it comes to natural language semantics. What *is* important are other properties of a semantics such as compositionality and computability. Recently, semantics have been developed that incorporate systematic evaluation switches triggered by intensional operators; so far, they

But whether we strive for innocence or not, it should be clear that it won't be easy to get a T-theory to handle belief-contexts. The theory must have a finite lexicon.[38] This requires subsentential semantic structure. Subsentential semantic structure, however, comes in a package deal with intersentential logical structure. The logical or inferential connections induced by the structure a T-theory imposes on simple sentences such as (6) and (7), however, is such that the principle of substitution holds: (7) follows from (6) and

(10)   Hesperus is Phosphorus.

Now, the problem is that (6) seems to be a constituent part of (8). Its subsentential semantic structure seems to be the same whether it occurs embedded under 'believes that' or not. But if we analyze its subsentential structure in the same way in both cases, we also get the logical consequences. Thus, (9) would follow from (8) and (10). But it does not seem to do so. Here is how Davidson summarizes the problem:

> So the paradox is this: on the one hand, intuition suggests, and theory demands, that we discover semantically significant structure in the 'content sentences' of indirect discourse [belief contexts] (as I shall call sentences following 'said that' ['believes that']). On the other hand, the failure of consequence-relations invites us to treat contained

cover both modal and quotation contexts (cf. Glüer and Pagin 2006; Glüer and Pagin 2008; Glüer and Pagin 2011; Pagin and Westerståhl 2010c). These semantics, while not compositional in the traditional or basic sense, have the property of generalized compositionality, a closely related property that ensures all the traditional virtues (basic) compositionality was supposed to confer (cf. Pagin and Westerståhl 2010b).

38. Violating this condition is the maybe most serious problem with the Fregean account: Since 'believes that' can be iterated, as for instance in 'Paul believes that Peter believes that p', we need a compositional account of what happens here. Frege's account instead seems to lead to an infinite hierarchy of senses. Cf. Davidson 1968, 99. For a very recent discussion, cf. Kripke 2008.

sentences as semantically inert. Yet logical form and consequence relations cannot be divorced this way (Davidson 1968, 96).

What to do? With respect to an example involving a singular term like our (8), Davidson writes: "Only two lines of explanation, then, are open: we are wrong about the logical form, or we are wrong about the reference of the singular term" (Davidson 1968, 94). And since he finds it unacceptable that the singular term in a belief context refers to anything but its ordinary referent, he goes for the logical form: According to Davidson, the logical form of belief contexts is not quite what one might expect given their surface form.

The basic idea is the following: Since it is the apparent embedding of a simple sentence into a complex one that causes trouble with the logical consequences of the simple sentence, we should analyze away the complexity. Davidson therefore suggests that belief sentences have the logical form of two whole sentences uttered in sequence. Therefore, the suggestion is known as the "paratactic analysis".[39] It analyzes (8) as:

(6)   Hesperus is a planet.
(6a)   Peter believes that.

Where the 'that' in (6a) is a *demonstrative*. This demonstrative refers to the preceding *utterance* of (6).[40] "What follows", Davidson explains, "gives the content of the subject's [believing], but

---

39. The main source for the paratactic analysis is Davidson 1968. There, the analysis is worked out with respect to indirect discourse, but it is clear that it is supposed to also be used for belief- and other attitude contexts. It is explicitly applied to belief-contexts in Davidson 1975, 165f. Cf. also Davidson 1976b, 176ff.

40. According to Davidson, the order does not matter. You might as well utter (6a) first, so that the demonstrative refers to the subsequent utterance of (6). Cf. Davidson 1968, 105.

has no logical or semantic connection with the original attribution of [believing]" (Davidson 1968, 106). This lack of semantic or logical connection explains why (9) does not follow from (8) and (10).

The *truth* of (6a), however, now depends on the holding of a certain relation between the sentence the utterance of which is demonstrated by 'that' and Peter's belief: These must have the *same content*.[41] We cannot discuss the paratactic analysis any further here.[42]

One thing that should have become perfectly clear, however, is the following: The semantic contents a T-theory assigns to simple sentences such as (6) and (7) are supposed to be such that they can serve the purposes of belief ascription. In other words: Davidsonian T-theories are supposed to make precisely as fine-grained

---

41. In Davidson 1968, 104, Davidson informally glosses this relation as one of "same-saying", which is more appropriate for the treatment of indirect discourse that is the main topic of that paper than it is for belief contexts (where there need not be any utterance (maybe not even any potential utterance) by the believer providing the second relatum of same-saying). The paratactic analysis of indirect discourse analyzes a sentence like 'Galileo said that the earth moves' into 'Galileo said that. The earth moves', where 'that' refers to the utterance of 'The earth moves' and 'Galileo said that' is true iff the attributee's utterance of 'the earth moves' and Galileo's original utterance are synonymous, or translations of one another (cf. Davidson 1976b, 176ff).

The worry, voiced for instance by Soames 2008, p. 13, that such an informal paraphrase of the predicate 'said that' uses semantic concepts like synonymy or translation and thereby makes not only the accounts of belief sentences and indirect discourse, but the whole Davidsonian account of meaning circular, is misplaced (cf. Davidson 1976b, 178; Davidson 1968, 104, fn. 14): T-theories do not provide, or make use of, any analyses of individual expressions (cf. Davidson 1967c, 30f). A T-theory will thus treat 'said that' as a semantic primitive and deliver something like (i):

(i) 'Galileo said that the earth moves' is true in English iff Galileo said that the earth moves.

And what provides an account of meaning, according to Davidson, is the T-theory as a whole, *together* with the fact that it fulfills certain formal and empirical constraints. In short: "radical interpretation, if it succeeds, provides us with an adequate concept of synonymy as between utterances" (Davidson 1968, 104, fn. 14).

42. For discussion, see a.o. Burge 1986; Schiffer 1987, 122-38; Lepore and Loewer 1989b; Rumfitt 1993.

semantic differences between the sentences of a language as are needed to keep track of sameness and difference of belief content. Even though T-theories themselves have to be formulated in wholly extensional terms, it is therefore a serious misunderstanding to characterize the Davidsonian program as a form of *extensionalism*: Davidson quite clearly does not subscribe to the doctrine that all that ever matters for semantics is extension.[43]

These considerations not only bring us back to the second aspect of the question whether a T-theory can be used as a formal semantic theory for a natural language: To the question I called "the interpretive question" earlier. They also allow us to see more clearly just what interpretiveness amounts to: Adequate T-theories are supposed to deliver contents sufficiently fine-grained for belief attributions. But is it possible to place enough restrictions on T-theories to allow us to use them for capturing the meanings of object language sentences this finely? We shall look at the interpretive question in the next section.

2.2.3.3 T-Theories and Meaning

Davidson thought there was no alternative to using T-theories as formal semantic theories, and he therefore took "an optimistic and programmatic view of the possibilities for a formal characterization of a truth predicate for a natural language"

---

43. As we saw earlier Davidson does think that *meaning entities* are redundant in the theory of meaning. Fans of such entities usually think of them as propositions or intensions, but the need for meaning entities in the theory of meaning and the question of extensionalism are nevertheless two independent matters. Davidson's main objection to such entities is that we can do without them. That, he claims, holds in full generality, that is, for any kind of entity we might want to use as meanings, be it intensions, extensions, or sets of tin cans. Davidson also shares Quine's doubts as to the possibility of a coherent interpretation of the vocabulary of the alethic modalities, but that, too, is a matter independent of the question of extensionalism—especially as he clearly does *not* share Quine's doubts as to the possibility of a respectable account of the vocabulary of the propositional attitudes.

(Davidson 1967c, 35). Hence the expression "the Davidsonian programme" that is sometimes used in the literature: The Davidsonian programme aims at 'taming' all important areas of natural language for handling by T-theories. In other words, it aims at showing that the natural language question can be answered in the affirmative.

Now, we are going to have a quick look at the second aspect of the question whether T-theories can be used as formal semantic theories for natural language: the interpretive question. Can we place enough restrictions on T-theories to single out the interpretive ones? Restrictions, that is, that guarantee that acceptable T-theories capture meanings with sufficient fineness of grain? I shall also call this "the restriction problem".

Davidson claimed that the restriction problem can be solved. More precisely, he claimed that a certain combination of formal and empirical requirements would do the trick. As we saw in section 2.2.3.1, the first formal requirement on a T-theory is that its theorems are *true*. To see what further restrictions are needed, we can ask again: What reason is there to expect true T-sentences to be interpretive, to capture meanings? As Davidson himself points out, a T-sentence such as

(3)   "Snow is white" is true iff grass is green,

while true, certainly does not specify the meaning of 'snow is white' in English. As we already saw, Davidson argues that T-theories implying T-sentences like (3) can be excluded for holistic reasons: A T-theory is correct for a language L only if it entails a true T-sentence for *every* sentence of L. And it is very unlikely that a (sufficiently simple) T-theory that entails (3) will also entail a true T-sentence for 'That is white'.

The restriction problem is more serious than that, however: Intuitively, there are numerous non-interpretive T-sentences the truth of which depends on nothing but the co-extensionality of non-synonymous predicates. (11) is an example:

(11)   'Pigs are renate' is true iff pigs are cordate.

In response, Davidson stressed the empirical nature of semantic theories. It is an empirical question whether a T-theory is correct for a particular natural language or not. That means, Davidson argues, that its theorems are *law-like statements*: They formulate natural laws, and therefore must not only be true, but also counterfactual supporting. Thus, for instance, (11) would have to be true even under counterfactual circumstances where it is not the case that all creatures with a liver also possess kidneys. This, he argues, goes at least some way towards distinguishing between non-synonymous, but co-extensional expressions (cf. Davidson 2005, 54). Still, it is far from clear that sufficiently fine-grained distinctions in meaning can be achieved this way; necessarily co-extensional, but arguably non-synonymous predicates such as 'triangular' and 'trilateral', for instance, cannot be distinguished this way.[44]

Problematic are also all those non-interpretive true T-sentences the right hand side of which is necessarily equivalent with the right hand side of an interpretive T-sentence, as illustrated by the following pair:

(12)   'Snow is white' is true iff snow is white.

(12a)   'Snow is white' is true iff snow is white and two plus two equals four.

For any such pair of T-sentences, in a sense both are entailed by exactly the same T-theories. That is, even if the inference rules

---

44. This is not a problem, however, that is easily solved by any truth conditional formal semantics: Possible worlds semantics, for instance, does not by itself capture differences between necessarily equivalent predicates, either.

that are part of a T-theory do not license derivation of (12a), it is nevertheless entailed by that theory in the sense of following from one of its theorems, (12), by elementary logic. Against this, Davidson invokes the idea of a *canonical proof*: Only T-sentences derived by means of a canonical proof are interpretive, he claims; that is, only T-sentences that can be directly derived from the relevant axioms alone (cf. Davidson 1973b, 138).[45]

But formal restrictions alone cannot solve the restriction problem, Davidson held. He had another leg to stand on, however. As emphasized before, T-theories for natural languages are *empirical theories*. They are justified by empirical evidence, or data. According to Davidson, there are therefore not only *formal* constraints on acceptable T-theories, but also *empirical* ones. Moreover, Davidson construes meaning as an evidence-constituted property—the correctness or truth of a meaning assignment for a particular language thus is wholly a matter of the empirical data supporting it. Because of the public nature of meaning, there are meaning determining principles leading from the data to the correct assignment. If T-theories can be used as formal semantic theories for natural language, they must be such that they can be construed by an adequately informed interpreter on the basis of data available to him. Which, in turn, means that the relevant data, together with the principles determining meaning, place further substantive restrictions on the acceptable T-theories.

In the next section, we shall look at the scenario of *radical interpretation*. Here, a "radical interpreter" faces the task of construing a T-theory for a radically alien language *L*. The radical interpreter

---

45. Segal 1999 suggests that T-sentences like (12a) can be ruled out by simplicity considerations. Instead of invoking canonical derivations, Larson and Segal 1995, 34ff, suggest restricting the inference rules of a T-theory: The inference rules actually implemented in the "semantic module", they argue, are designed to permit only the derivation of interpretive T-sentences. See also Lepore and Ludwig 2005, 109ff, for further discussion.

has no prior knowledge about L; therefore, the thought is, the data available to him are the "ultimate evidence" (Davidson 1973b, 128) by which all meaning is determined. Therefore, radical interpretation is the paradigm scenario in which the empirical constraints on T-theories will become manifest.

Before we turn to radical interpretation, one more general remark on the restriction problem, however. Solving the restriction problem amounts to restricting the acceptable T-theories for a language L to those entailing T-sentences that specify, or "give", the meanings of all sentences of L. Once the restriction problem is solved, that is, we can go one step further and from each T-sentence derive a sentence explicitly stating what object language sentences mean. We could thus go from (12) to (13):

(12)   'Snow is white' is true iff snow is white.
(13)   'Snow is white' means that snow is white.

That this is possible is a trivial consequence of the (assumed) fact that we have solved the restriction problem; that is, that the T-theory in question in fact is interpretive.[46] This does *not* mean that any meaning theoretical questions have been begged; it does not have any consequences for the Davidsonian idea that by determining the form a formal semantic theory should take we have made a contribution to understanding the nature of meaning. All the explanatory work is done by the inner workings of the T-theory together with the formal and empirical restrictions placed

---

46. Kölbel argues that we even could incorporate this step into our formal semantic theory (cf. Kölbel 2001, 618ff). That is mistaken. Incorporating inference rules that would license the derivation of "meaning theorems" like (13) into the T-theory is possible only on the assumption that the restriction problem has been solved *by formal restrictions alone* (Kölbel in fact seems to assume that T-sentences are interpretive iff they can be canonically derived). But Davidson is very clear that both formal and empirical restrictions are required for solving the restriction problem. The mistake is repeated in Speaks 2006.

on it. And if the project succeeds, not only will the acceptable T-theories be such that their T-sentences specify meanings—we will also have gained a workable understanding or explanation of meaning and synonymy. As Davidson himself once remarked: "It is ... worth observing that radical interpretation, if it succeeds, yields an adequate concept of synonymy as between utterances" (Davidson 1968, 104, fn. 14).[47] And it is to radical interpretation that we now turn.

2.3 Radical Interpretation

2.3.1 The Field Linguist

The idea of sending a field linguist into a ficticious jungle to figure out the essentials of meaning is Quine's. In chapter 2 of *Word and Object* (Quine 1960), a field linguist sets out to investigate a radically alien language. This language Quine sometimes calls "Jungle". The data available to the field linguist consist of nothing but the linguistic and nonlinguistic behavior of the speakers in its

47. Kölbel, however, not only argues that T-theories could incorporate inference rules allowing the derivation of "meaning theorems" like (13), but further suggests that this shows that Davidson is mistaken in taking himself to explain meaning in terms of truth. According to Kölbel, this is just a "dogma of Davidsonian semantics" (cf. Kölbel 2001, 614): In fact, Kölbel claims, the T-predicate used in the T-sentences of an interpretive T-theory does not need to be interpreted at all. According to Kölbel, interpreting the T-predicate would be required only for *testing* the T-theory in radical interpretation, but, he claims, once we have derived explicit meaning theorems, we can test it by means of those.

As pointed out above (fn. 46), however, the empirical constraints provided by radical interpretation are an essential part of the Davidsonian account of meaning: Radical interpretation is precisely what provides the required empirical restrictions on interpretive T-theories. Explicit meaning theorems can only be derived from T-theories on the assumption that the theories actually meet these empirical restrictions. On a Davidsonian account of meaning, the idea of testing T-theories by means of explicit meaning theorems therefore does not make much sense: It would simply be redundant.

Kölbel's attack on the Davidsonian "dogma" is partly motivated by disquotationalism about truth. A somewhat similar line of argument is presented in Williams 1999. Williams, however, argues that radical interpretation itself, as construed by Davidson, does not involve any substantive notion of truth. For more discussion relevant to this claim, see section 5.1.2.

observable circumstances. And his task is to construct a translation manual.

Quine's field linguist uses a two-step method. First, he identifies a certain kind of behavior: that of assenting to, and dissenting from, uttered sentences. Then, he collects data concerning particular sentences of Jungle and the assent- and dissent-behavior of its speakers. These data allow him to correlate sentences of Jungle with sentences of his own language, sentences that he would assent to, or dissent from, under similar circumstances, thus providing the crucial wedge into the alien language.

Despite differences about the details of both the field linguist's method and his main objective, Quine and Davidson share the basic perspective from which such a scenario derives its significance. For both, meaning is completely determined by observable behavior in observable circumstances.[48] Such behavior thus plays a characteristic epistemico-metaphysical double role for them: It metaphysically determines meaning, but at the same time, it provides the data, or evidence, for both the ordinary speaker's and the field linguist's knowledge of those meanings. The field linguist, then, is supposed to be able to determine—in the sense of: work out, or find out about—meanings on the basis of precisely those data that metaphysically determine them. Thus the immense significance of Davidson's radical interpreter: "What a fully informed interpreter could learn about what a speaker means is all there is to learn" (Davidson 1983, 148).

Even though their basic outlook on meaning is very similar, there are important differences between Quine and Davidson

---

48. In contrast to Davidson's, Quine's semantic behaviorism is of a reductive nature, however. Here are the programmatic opening lines of *Word and Object*: "Language is a social art. In acquiring it we have to depend entirely on intersubjective cues as to what to say and when. Hence there is no justification for collating linguistic meanings, unless in terms of men's dispositions to respond overtly to socially observable stimulations" (Quine 1960, ix).

here, too. Because of the more strictly reductionist nature of his semantic behaviorism, Quine is also more skeptical towards any traditional or pre-theoretical notion of meaning. Davidson, as we saw, is skeptical towards the semantic usefulness of entities assigned as meanings to expressions, but he does not object to talk about meaning—as long as meaning is thought of in terms of (contributions to) truth conditions.

This difference is reflected in their respective construals of the main objective for the field linguist in the radical situation: Quine's field linguist is supposed to construct a translation manual, a manual that sets up relations between two sets of linguistic expressions, those of Jungle and those of his own. The objective of this exercise is to "consider how much of language can be made sense of in terms of its stimulus conditions, and what scope this leaves for empirically unconditioned variation in one's conceptual scheme" (Quine 1960, 26). Quine's ultimate concerns are thus epistemological; language is part and and parcel of a naturalized epistemology, an epistemology that most fundamentally consists of reflection, "in a general way, on how surface irritations generate, through language, one's knowledge of the world" (Quine 1960, 26). Davidson's concerns, on the other hand, are semantic and meaning theoretical. He does not doubt that a respectable account of the notion of meaning can be given. Thus, his radical interpreter is supposed to construct a formal semantics, a T-theory for the alien language. And radical interpretation itself is supposed to be a crucial part of the Davidsonian account of meaning.

This is not merely a matter of more or less naturalistic reductionism, however; Davidson argues that, strictly speaking, a translation manual cannot do what he wants a T-theory to do: model linguistic competence. One reason is that it is possible to know that one sentence is the translation of another—without knowing what either means (cf. Davidson 1973b, 129). For instance, you might know that "Meine Schwester, erinnerst du den Berg, die hohe Eiche und die Ladore?" is the (German) translation of (the Russian) "Sestra moya, tï pomnish" goru, i dub vïsokiy, i Ladoru?" But you might still not know what these sentences mean.[49,50]

When it comes to the data the radical interpreter is allowed to use, Davidson agrees with Quine that ultimately, these consist solely of data about the speakers' behavior in its observable circumstances. Moreover, this behavior must be described not only in non-semantic, but more generally in *non-intentional* vocabulary. For Quine, this restriction on the description of the data is motivated by his strict naturalism with its orientation towards the latest relevant science (in his days, behaviorist psychology) and its implicit skepticism towards things of such questionable scientific standing as beliefs, desires, and other objects of intentional psychology.

But again, Davidson does not share this skepticism. His objection to describing the radical interpreter's data in terms of beliefs, desires, and intentions is the same as his objection to describing them in semantic vocabulary: Such description would make the account of meaning circular. Allowing the radical

---

49. The English translation is: "My sister, do you remember the mountain, the tall oak, and the Ladore?" From Vladimir Nabokov's *Ada, or Ardor. A Family Chronicle*, New York 1969, p. 138. English translation provided in his *Notes to Ada by Vivian Darkbloom*, ibid. p. 596.

50. The difference between translation manuals and T-theories must be greater than that, however. Otherwise, a translation manual into a *known* language would be as good as a semantic theory. As Davidson himself points out in a slightly different context, the difference is in fact greater (cf. Davidson 1967c, 21.) Take belief sentences. If we have a translation manual taking, say, Swahili into English, we can translate Swahili belief sentences into English belief sentences. We can even use the manual to form Swahili belief sentences ourselves. But we still have no idea how the meaning of a belief sentence is determined by its parts and its mode of composition. As Davidson points out in the passage referred to, the problem remains if we add a recursive syntax to a translation manual or dictionary: "Recursive syntax with dictionary added is not necessarily recursive semantics" (ibid.).

interpreter any access to the beliefs, desires, and intentions of his speakers—allowing him access, that is, to the *contents* of their mental states, or thoughts—will limit the extent to which any insight is gained into the nature of meaning. For what can be the content of a thought, and what the meaning of an utterance, is, if not the same, at least very intimately related. Moreover, thoughts of a little more sophistication can only be ascribed to a subject by interpreting her linguistic utterances (cf. Davidson 1973b, 134; Davidson 1974a, 144). All in all, Davidson claims, the interpretation of a speaker's utterances and the attribution of intentional contents to her mental states "rest on much the same evidence" (Davidson 1973b, 134). It is thus not only meaning, but *meaning and mental content* that is evidence-constituted, according to Davidson.

That, however, makes the life of the radical interpreter ever so much harder. In fact, the radical interpreter now seems confronted by a dilemma before he can even get started. The origin of the dilemma Davidson calls the "interdependence of belief and meaning" (Davidson 1973b, 134). In principle, this interdependence is supposed to hold between meanings and all of the propositional attitudes, all mental states, that is, the contents of which can be specified by that-clauses. It finds its most dramatic illustration if we take belief as our example, however:

> A central source of trouble is the way beliefs and meanings conspire
> to account for utterances. A speaker who holds a sentence to be true
> on an occasion does so in part because of what he means, or would
> mean, by an utterance of that sentence, and in part because of what
> he believes. If all we have to go on is the fact of honest utterance,
> we cannot infer the belief without knowing the meaning, and have
> no chance of inferring the meaning without the belief (Davidson
> 1973b, 142).

In order to interpret utterances of the alien language, the radical interpreter has to break into this interdependence. He has to succeed in determining both the beliefs of his speaker (or speakers) and the meaning of their utterances simultaneously. But how?

According to Davidson, the key is provided by a special kind of attitude the radical interpreter can detect on the basis of his data: the attitude of *holding a sentence true (at a time)* (cf. Davidson 1973b, 135; Davidson 1974a, 144). This attitude is, as Davidson is the first to emphasize, a kind of belief. But it is a special kind of belief that "an interpreter may plausibly be taken to be able to identify before he can interpret" (Davidson 1973b, 135). The interpreter, that is, does not need to know what a sentence means to detect that, and when, a speaker holds it true. He "may know that a person intends to express a truth in uttering a sentence without having any idea *what* truth" (Davidson 1973b, 135). The attitude of holding a sentence true (at a time) is thus an attitude directed at *uninterpreted* sentences. It is what Davidson calls a "nonindividuative" (Davidson 1991, 211) attitude—that is, a propositional attitude that does not individuate the state in question by means of its propositional content. If detecting this attitude is possible on the basis of his data, the radical interpreter can use it as a basis for constructing his T-theory without begging any meaning theoretical questions.[51]

---

51. Davidson never provides much discussion of, or argument for, the assumption that attitudes of holding true are detectable by the radical interpreter. Here's one of the few relevant passages:

> I hope it will be granted that it is plausible to say we can tell when a speaker holds a sentence to be true without knowing what he means by the sentence, or what beliefs he holds about its unknown subject matter, or what detailed intentions do or might prompt him to utter it. It is often argued that we must assume that most of a speaker's utterances are of sentences he holds true: if this is right, the independent

Just like Quinean radical translation, Davidsonian radical interpretation thus proceeds by way of a middle step: Where Quine has the field linguist determine assent and dissent on the basis of observable behavior in general, Davidson has the radical interpreter determine attitudes of holding true (relativized to times). But while Quinean assent and dissent still is supposed to be purely behavioral, attitudes of holding true, even though directed at uninterpreted sentences, are mental in nature. What is most important for both, though, is the second step: Getting from assent and dissent to translation, and from holding true to interpretation or meaning.

In radical interpretation, the evidential base on which the radical interpreter is to determine meanings consists of data about speakers holding sentences true—and about when and under what circumstances they do so. This is data of a very limited kind. But the interpreter is allowed unlimited amounts of it: "We may as well suppose," Davidson writes, that "we have available all that could be known of such attitudes, past, present, future" (Davidson 1974a, 144).

The radical interpreter then sets to work by forming hypotheses about which sentences speakers hold true under what circumstances. It is two kinds of sentences that play a key role in this process: sentences held true under all circumstances, and sentences where holding true is systematically correlated with certain circumstances of utterance.

The second kind of sentence, called "occasion sentences" by Quine, allows the radical interpreter to construct hypothetical T-sentences. The interpreter collects data like the following:

availability of the evidential base is assured. But weaker assumptions will do, since even the compulsive liar and the perennial kidder may be found out (Davidson 1974a, 144f).

(E)   Kurt belongs to the German speech community and Kurt holds true "Es regnet" on Saturday at noon and it is raining near Kurt on Saturday at noon (Davidson 1973a, 135).

Such an observation, Davidson suggests, should be considered evidence for the following T-sentence:

(T_R) 'Es regnet' is true-in-German when spoken by x at time t if and only if it is raining near x at t.[52]

Testing the hypothesis that (T_R) is an interpretive T-sentence for German first involves gathering further evidence for the following, intermediate claim:

(GE) $\forall x, \forall t$ (if x belongs to the German speech community then (x holds true 'Es regnet' if and only if it is raining near x at t)).

The basic idea is that the conditions under which speakers hold sentences true allow the radical interpreter to determine the truth conditions of those sentences. Of course, the idea cannot be to simply equate the former with the latter—speakers may be wrong even about such mundane observational matters as whether it is raining near them. Therefore, Davidson says, data such as (E) should not be taken to provide conclusive evidence for either (T_R) or (GE). Nor should we expect (GE) to be "more than generally true. The method is rather one of getting a best fit" (cf. Davidson 1973a, 136).

---

52. There has been a lot of recent discussion about the logical form and truth conditions of sentences like the "meteorological sentence" ('It's raining'). Cf. for instance Recanati 2007. Davidson in effect suggests that time and place are not represented in the logical form of this sentence, but are so-called "unarticulated constituents" (the term is Perry's, cf. Perry 1993). Pagin 2005 works out such a semantics in more detail.

Just like any empirical researcher, the Davidsonian radical interpreter collects a vast number of observations like (E). Mostly, they'll consist of speakers holding 'Es regnet' true while it is raining near them, but not in bright sunshine, dense fog or while it is snowing. But then, there will be the occasional speaker making a mistake. For instance the guy who holds 'Es regnet' true while looking out of his window and seeing water pouring down outside—where this, in fact, is a result of the neighbor's kid messing with their sprinkler. Or he who wakes up and thinks it's raining because it sounds as if drops were falling on the roof—where the sound comes from, say, the TV in the living room. And so on. So, the interpreter ends up with a vast collection of such data for lots and lots of sentences, data that show a correlation between each sentence and a certain condition, but not a perfect one. Just like any empirical researcher, the radical interpreter will search for the theory that achieves a best overall fit with his data. This is the theory that is best supported by his evidence.

That evidential support thus is a holistic affair, was vividly brought out by Quine in *Two Dogmas* (Quine 1951). There, he used the now classical metaphor of a web of belief: Beliefs form highly interconnected, weblike systems linked with experience or observation only at the edges. Confirmation, or disconfirmation, always spreads through the whole system, or at least a significant part of it such as a whole theory of some particular phenomenon. Confirmation is thus always a matter of the relation between a totality of data and the whole of a theory. Such epistemological or "confirmation holism" is widely accepted today. Davidson simply applies it to the relation between a formal semantic theory for a natural language and the empirical data supporting it.

From these considerations, an answer to the question of what *empirical* constraints there are on interpretive T-theories is beginning to emerge. What the *method of best fit* provides is a ranking of theories according to the support they receive from the totality of the relevant empirical data. Such a ranking can then be used to limit the acceptable theories—for instance by saying that only the best is, or are, acceptable.

First, however, we need to understand what "fit" exactly amounts to here. Let's consider the following question: Why should we think that (E) is a datum that supports (T_R)? Why does (E) speak for (T_R) rather than for (T_S)—or any other T-sentence for 'Es regnet'?

(T_S) 'Es regnet' is true-in-German when spoken by x at time t if and only if it is snowing near x at t.

Consider what would happen if a T-theory from which we can derive (T_S) instead of (T_R) was used to interpret Kurt's utterance. Here is Kurt, it is raining heavily all around him, he utters 'Es regnet'. The radical interpreter knows that Kurt holds this sentence true, and therefore interprets him as expressing his belief that it is snowing. That belief is clearly false under the circumstances. Now assume further that there is no reason to expect that Kurt would make such an elementary mistake. For instance, there does not seem to be anything wrong with Kurt's eyes, he doesn't seem unusually absent minded or otherwise disturbed in any way. Under these circumstances, the suggested interpretation certainly seems implausible; it is simply not likely that Kurt would make such a seemingly inexplicable mistake. As Quine once put it: "Assertions startingly false on the face of them are likely to turn on hidden differences of language. ... One's interlocutor's silliness, beyond a certain point, is less likely than bad translation—or, in the domestic case, linguistic divergence" (Quine 1960, 59).

Unlikely or not, you might insist that it is certainly *possible* that Kurt believes that it is snowing. He might, after all, hold all sorts of weird beliefs about snow and water. Or about how things appear, or how they appear to him as opposed to other people. Or he might be subject to sudden, unpredictable changes in his beliefs. What seems clear is only the following: As long as the radical interpreter can ascribe to Kurt any beliefs whatsoever, be they ever so absurd, unlikely, or even incoherent, data like (E) do not provide any evidence for (T_R) as opposed to (T_S). In other words, as long as he can ascribe any beliefs he likes, the proposed data are no data at all. They are equally compatible with any T-theory whatsoever.[53] For Davidson, this is just another way of illustrating the interdependence of belief and meaning.

But matters can be turned around: What we have seen is that in order for observations like (E) to provide data for T-theories, belief ascription needs to be restricted in plausible ways. We already saw that it is at least rather unlikely that Kurt actually believes that it is snowing. The by far most plausible hypothesis is that he believes that it is raining. Most probably that is the belief that fits best with other beliefs that it is plausible to ascribe to him. We do not, and we cannot, justifiedly charge people with having very odd or even absurd theories or views, or with changing their beliefs all the time just because that fits some weird way of understanding their words that we have cooked up. Of course, we do disagree with people, and we do think that people hold false beliefs. But, Davidson argues, "disagreement and agreement alike are intelligible only against a background of massive agreement" (Davidson 1973a, 137). If we did not agree with Kurt on at least some very basic things about rain and snow, for instance, about their color or aggregate state, we could not be sure that Kurt is talking about rain, or snow, at all. "Too much mistake," and especially

---

53. For more on this, cf. Glüer 2006a.

mistakes about very basic things, Davidson writes, "simply blurs the focus" (Davidson 1975, 168).

Therefore, radical interpretation must proceed according to the following principle:

(PC)   Assign truth conditions to alien sentences that make native speakers right when plausibly possible (Davidson 1973b, 137).

This principle is known as the "principle of charity".[54] It provides a method for solving the problem of the interdependence of belief and meaning "by holding belief constant as far as possible while solving for meaning. This is accomplished by assigning truth conditions to alien sentences that make native speakers right when plausibly possible, according, of course, to our own view of what is right" (Davidson 1973a, 137). The radical interpreter, that is, tries to hold belief constant both between himself and the alien speaker, but also for the alien speaker over time.

Now, we can see why Davidson proposes to "take the fact that speakers of a language hold a sentence to be true (under observed circumstances) as prima facie evidence that the sentence is true under those circumstances" (Davidson 1974a, 152). If beliefs, and belief ascription, are restricted by the principle of charity, as Davidson argues they are, then a sentence's being held true under certain circumstances does provide evidence that it is true under those circumstances.

The evidence is *prima facie* only, however. That is, it can be overridden by other, stronger evidence. People do make mistakes,

---

54. The name was introduced in Wilson 1959 as a name for a principle for the determination of the referents of proper names: "We select as designatum that individual which will make the largest possible number of...statements true" (532). In *Word and Object*, Quine argues that the translation of the logical constants must obey a charity principle (cf. Quine 1960, 56ff).

after all, and some of the vast number of data that the radical interpreter collects will have to be considered as overridden by others. But which? Davidson: "The basic methodological precept is...that a good theory of interpretation maximizes agreement. Or,...a better word might be *optimize*" (Davidson 1975, 169). Here, we come back to the idea of overall best fit: Given that belief is restricted by the principle of charity, a T-theory fits the data the better the more it makes the speaker(s) come out right. Since this will be right by the lights of the interpreter, Davidson puts it in terms of agreement maximization or optimization. On a first, rough understanding, we can therefore say that the less error a T-theory ascribes to a speaker (or group of speakers) the better it fits the data. Which data are to be overridden, and which utterances to be interpreted as false, is therefore a matter of which T-theory achieves best overall fit with the data.

However, "some disagreements are more destructive of understanding than others" (Davidson 1975, 169). In general, being wrong on simple observational matters such as whether it rains around one is more destructive than disagreement on highly theoretical matters. Being wrong about one's own mental states or about how things look to one is worse than being wrong about other's mental states or about how things are. And so on (cf. Davidson 1975, 169). Thus, even if it were possible to simply compare T-theories by counting the number of mistakes they ascribe—which might not be possible given that the number of sentences is infinite—it would not give quite the right result. Rather, agreement must be optimized, and that involves weighting mistakes according to how destructive they are for understanding. In general, the idea is that a mistake is the more weighty the more epistemologically basic it is, the more basic, that is, to the totality of our knowledge: "The methodology of interpretation is, in this respect, nothing but epistemology seen in the mirror of meaning" (Davidson 1975, 169).

It is not only truth and falsity that is important here, however. Mistakes can also come in the form of incoherence, in the form of drawing the wrong inferences from what one believes. Assume that the interpreter has good reasons to ascribe a certain false belief to a speaker *S*, for instance the belief that Fido is a dog. (In fact, Fido is a car.) Now, from Fido's being a dog, it follows that Fido is an animal. In this situation, it would not be a good idea to maximize truth by ascribing both the belief that Fido is a dog and the belief that Fido is an artifact to *S*. Beliefs, Davidson maintains, come in coherent clusters, if they come at all (cf. Davidson 1977b, 200). While it can be very plausible to think that *S* makes the first mistake, it is much less plausible to think that *S* at the same time fails to draw an obvious inference from it. The maxim to make the speaker right when plausibly possible encompasses both these elements: To make the speaker right when plausibly possible is to optimize the beliefs ascribed in such a way that they are, at least in basic cases, mostly true and coherent. Charitably interpreted speakers therefore always come out as persons of a certain, basic *rationality*. In later writings, Davidson sometimes explicitly separates the two components of charity—truth and coherence:

> The process of separating meaning and opinion invokes two key principles which must be applicable if a speaker is interpretable: the Principle of Coherence and the Principle of Correspondence. The Principle of Coherence prompts the interpreter to discover a degree of logical consistency in the thought of the speaker; the Principle of Correspondence prompts the interpreter to take the speaker to be responding to the same features of the world that he (the interpreter) would be responding to under similar

circumstances. Both principles can be (and have been) called principles of charity: one principle endows the speaker with a modicum
of logic, the other endows him with a degree of what the interpreter
takes to be true belief about the world. Successful interpretation
necessarily invests the person interpreted with basic rationality.
It follows from the nature of correct interpretation that an interpersonal standard of consistency and correspondence to the facts
applies to both the speaker and the speaker's interpreter, to their
utterances and to their beliefs (Davidson 1991, 211).

Because of its central importance for Davidson's philosophy of
language, we shall investigate the principle of charity and its justification in more detail in the next chapter, chapter 3.

Two more observations are in order already now, however.
Both are brought out by the passage just quoted. The first concerns the role causality plays in interpreting observational occasion sentences, sentences like 'It's raining' in English or 'Es regnet'
in German. In the radical interpretation papers, the interpreter is
described as simply seeking correlations between observable circumstances and attitudes of holding true. Later, however, Davidson emphasizes that this amounts to hypotheses about cause and
effect: The interpreter takes the speaker to be reacting to these
circumstances, that is, he takes the speaker's beliefs to be caused
by events or objects in the speakers environment. Moreover, he
takes the speaker to be reacting to the same objects or events
that he himself reacts to in a given situation. More precisely, he
takes the speaker to be reacting to those objects or events that he
himself would react to if he were 'in the speaker's shoes'—that is,
had precisely the speaker's perspective on the given situation.

Observational sentences like 'It's raining' are thus of crucial
importance for interpretation because they provide theoretical
access to basic relations between language and the world. Accord-

ing to Davidson, these relations are causal in nature and form the basis for all understanding: "The causal relations between the world and our beliefs are crucial to meaning...because they are often apparent to others and so form the basis for communication" (Davidson 1990b, 59). Or, more catchy: "Communication begins where causes converge: your utterance means what mine does if belief in its truth is systematically caused by the same events and objects" (Davidson 1983, 151).

The second observation about charity concerns its status. As Davidson makes amply clear, charity is not one principle amongst other equally possible principles of interpretation. Charity is not optional, or a matter of choice. Rather, charity is *the* principle of correct interpretation. Meaning and belief are essentially such that charitable interpretation will be correct interpretation. This brings us back to the epistemico-metaphysical double nature of the radical interpreter's data: These data are his data for figuring out what utterances in the alien language mean, and at the same time these data are the metaphysical base determining meaning. But as we saw, attitudes of holding true towards uninterpreted sentences do not provide any evidence for T-theories just by themselves. We also need a principle restricting acceptable belief attributions. According to Davidson, this principle is the principle of charity. It thus is the principle that metaphysically determines meaning—and belief content. This is why he says, as quoted above: "It follows from the nature of correct interpretation that an interpersonal standard of consistency and correspondence to the facts applies to both the speaker and the speaker's interpreter, to their utterances and to their beliefs" (Davidson 1991, 211).

With all this in place, we can get back to the restriction problem: We can now see how the principle of charity imposes powerful empirical restrictions on T-theories. It does so by serving two basic functions. First, it establishes an evidence relation between attitudes of holding true towards uninterpreted sentences and T-sentences. And second, it effects a ranking of candidate T-theories according to how well they fit the totality of the available data, a ranking such that the best theory—or theories, for there might be more than one—is the correct one. Because of its epistemico-metaphyisical double nature, charity takes the interpreter this last step, too: It does not just establish which theory is best in relation to the available data, it establishes which theory is correct. There is no further matter of fact about meaning, no further question of truth that is left open. This is the full significance of the slogan we already quoted above: "What a fully informed interpreter could learn about what a speaker means is all there is to learn; the same goes for what the speaker believes" (Davidson 1983, 148).

The further details of the radical interpretation of an alien language are of lesser interest here. The philosophically most interesting questions can be raised as soon as we have seen how the radical interpreter forces his way into the alien language by means of occasion sentences; their interpretation establishes the connection between observation and meaning, language and world. And once we have reached a basic understanding of the alien language, the ascription of specific beliefs follows suit. Specific beliefs automatically fall out of the assignment of meanings to sentences held true according to the formula "sentence held true plus interpretation equals belief" (Davidson 1980a, 155f). Davidson himself does not devote much space to describing the procedure of radical interpretation in any detail as it proceeds from the observational to more theoretical sentences. According to a rough sketch in the classical paper *Radical Interpretation* (Davidson 1973b, 136f), the construction of a T-theory for a radically alien language L proceeds in three steps:

1. The radical interpreter starts with logic. On the basis of data about "classes of sentences always held true or always held false by almost everyone almost all of the time" (Davidson 1973b, 136), candidates for logical truths are identified. Data about sentences always held true when certain other sentences are held true allow for the identification of patterns of inference. On this basis, the structure of first-order quantified logic (plus identity) is fitted onto L "in one fell swoop" (ibid.). Predicates, singular terms, quantifiers, connectives, and the identity sign are identified. Thus, the interpreter reads 'his' logic into L. This might prima facie appear to be an act of willfulness on the interpreter's part, but according to Davidson, that is an illusion. If meaning is truth conditional, and if T-theories can be used as formal semantic theories for natural languages, natural language is such that its sentences can be 'transcribed' into the language of first-order quantified logic. This is no imposition, just a way of making certain properties conspicuous that these sentences have anyway. Given that the principle of charity holds, the amount of logic ascribed to speakers in this first step is constitutive of having any beliefs at all. As an end result of this first step, the logical constants are interpreted and, in principle, the logical form of the sentences of L has been determined. But predicates and singular terms remain uninterpreted.

2. Predicates are interpreted in the second step. Here, the interpreter concentrates on sentences with indexicals, especially those for which holding true and false varies with observable changes in the environment.

3. In the last step, all remaining sentences are interpreted. Once the interpreter deals with more theoretical terms and abstract objects and relations, he cannot test his hypothet-

ical T-sentences directly against observations like (E) anymore. He has to rely on observable patterns of inferences,
on the logical form and semantic structure of sentences,
and on those sub-sentential expressions that have already
been interpreted when occurring in observational contexts.

These steps, however, are not supposed to provide a static structure where the first step needs to be completed, and its results
cannot be changed anymore, before the second even begins.
Rather, radical interpretation is a holistic process, and all hypotheses remain hypotheses throughout. Results at any stage can call
for reinterpretation of already interpreted expressions of *L*—if by
such reinterpretation a better overall fit can be obtained.

The Davidsonian solution to the restriction problem, then,
consists of a set of both formal and empirical constraints on
acceptable T-theories. T-theories are interpretive, and do capture
meaning, Davidson submits, if they not only fulfill the formal constraints but on top of that stand in the relation of best fit induced
by the principle of charity towards the relevant speakers' attitudes
of holding true. It remains a matter of debate to this date whether
these constraints in fact are sufficiently restrictive.[55] Davidson
himself does not expect these constraints to limit the number of
acceptable T-theories to one. Rather, he thinks that we cannot
exclude the possibility of more than one T-theory fitting the data
equally well (and better than the rest). He contends, however, that
each such theory can be used to interpret the alien language. That
is, despite a certain *indeterminacy of interpretation,* he claims to
have solved the restriction problem. We shall have a look at the
indeterminacy thesis in the next section.

---

55. For both some classical skeptical voices and defenses, cf. Soames 1992; Soames 2008;
Higginbotham 1992. Cf. also Lepore and Ludwig 2005, part II.

2.3.2 Indeterminacies

Since Quine introduced the scenario of radical translation in order to determine the nature—and the limits—of meaning, this scenario has been connected with the thesis of the *indeterminacy of translation*.[56] This famous claim is often misunderstood, however; Quine does hold that translation is indeterminate, but Quinean indeterminacy does, for instance, not amount to complete nihilism about meaning.[57] So, what does it consist in?

Imagine two field linguists independently of one another setting out to construct translation manuals for the same radically alien language, the Quinean Jungle. According to the later Quine, there is "little reason to expect that two radical translators, working independently on Jungle, would come out with interchangeable manuals" (Quine 1992a, 47). More precisely, there might be two manuals for Jungle such that each of them is equally compatible with the behavior of the Jungle speakers "and yet the two translation relations might not be usable in alternation, from sentence to sentence, without issuing in incoherent sequences" (Quine 1992a, 48). It is, however, not completely clear what the idea of sequential incoherence amounts to; does it demand that a speaker would come out as outrightly contradicting himself? Or is some weaker form of incoherence sufficient? And how do we distinguish between being incoherent and changing one's mind? In *Word and Object*, Quine formulated the indeterminacy claim in a different way. He writes:

---

56. A survey and discussion of the relevant literature on indeterminacy is provided by Weir 2006.

57. Another common misunderstanding has it that Quinean indeterminacy is a result of rejecting the analytic-synthetic distinction; for more on this, cf. Pagin 2008.

Sense can be made of the point by recasting it as follows: the infinite totality of sentences of any given speaker's language can be so permuted, or mapped onto itself, that (a) the totality of the speaker's disposition to verbal behavior remains invariant, and yet (b) the mapping is no mere correlation of sentences with equivalent sentences, in any plausible sense of equivalence however loose (Quine 1960, 27).

Here, it is clear that the indeterminacy claim is not supposed to depend on differences between two field linguists, or between speakers, or even differences between field linguist and speaker. Rather, the idea is to keep the data completely fixed and then look at what can be done with respect to the translation of one and the same sentence *s* of the object language. So, assume we have constructed a translation manual such that it fits the speaker's dispositions to verbal behavior very well. Now, all we do is exchange the object language expressions in this manual for one another in a certain way. Quine claims that this can be done in such a way that (a) the result fits equally well with the speaker's disposition to verbal behavior, but (b) there is at least one sentence *s* such that the original manual M_1 translates *s* into the meta-language sentence s_1, the permuted manual M_2 translates *s* into s_2, and s_1 and s_2 are not equivalent in any plausible sense, not even a loose one. *s*, that is, could be given extremely different translations, translations with meanings that are intuitively completely different, by the two manuals.

Indeterminacy, then, is the claim that there is no fact of the matter as to which is the correct manual: M_1 or M_2. Quine, just like Davidson following him, construes meaning as fully determined by observable behavior. What cannot be determined by the radical translator *is* indeterminate, there is no fact of the matter. Those aspects of the pre-theoretical 'concept' of meaning that cannot be captured, or reconstructed, in radical translation are therefore simply to be abandoned. These aspects are beyond any rigorous understanding, beyond any theoretical reconstruction that is up to scientific standards.

And according to Quine, there are significant aspects of meaning and translation that are indeterminate. This is, of course, an extremely interesting and very radical claim. But we must be careful not to misconstrue it. Most importantly, it would be very misleading to say that, according to Quine, there is no fact of the matter as to what any given sentence of a language means, or that any sentence s could be translated into any sentence of another language. For one thing, the translation of each and every sentence remains severely restricted by that of all the other sentences of L; indeterminacy is a claim about *empirically equivalent whole translation manuals*. There is a certain structure that each acceptable translation manual captures; the choice of manual is thus very far from arbitrary. "Save the structure and you save all," Quine once wrote in a related context (Quine 1992b, 8)—all that is worth saving, that is.

For another thing, that the translation of a given sentence s is indeterminate does by no means mean that s could be translated into any sentence s_i whatsoever. All it means is that there is at least one alternative, non-equivalent translation. Yet more importantly, the indeterminacy claim is *not* that the translation of *all*, or even *most*, sentences of a language is indeterminate. Strictly speaking, it suffices that there is one such sentence. And, most importantly, even according to the Quine of *Word and Object* himself significant parts of language are perfectly determinate. Observation sentences, for instance, have determinate translations. They have what Quine calls "stimulus meanings" (cf. Quine 1960, 30ff), and the translation of an observation sentences is correct if and only if it is translated into an observation sentence with the same stimulus meaning.[58]

But even when correctly understood, Quinean indeterminacy is a radical claim—too radical to accept for many. For many, it remains at least an open question whether Quinean indeterminacy teaches us something important about meaning or in fact constitutes a reductio ad absurdum of the kind of behaviorism he espouses.[59] And the same holds for Davidsonian indeterminacy and Davidsonian behaviorism.

For Davidson, the claim is one of the indeterminacy of *interpretation*. More precisely, the claim is that even the totality of the radical interpreter's data leaves open the possibility that there is more than one T-theory fitting the data best. Even with the principle of charity in place, that is, there is no guarantee that the number of acceptable T-theories can be reduced to exactly one. It remains possible that there are two, or more, T-theories fitting the data equally well, and better than any others. Because of the equal fit, such T-theories are empirically equivalent, according to Davidson. And, he submits, interpretation is indeterminate between such T-theories; such T-theories are equally correct, and they are equally interpretive. And, just as in Quine, this indeterminacy is not due to any lack of knowledge or ability on the part of the interpreter. Quite the contrary; indeterminacy remains even on the assumption that the interpreter has the totality of the data, and thus knows all that is metaphysically relevant. If indeterminacy obtains, it obtains as a matter of objective fact.

---

58. Stimulus meanings, according to *Word and Object*, are ordered pairs of affirmative and negative stimulus meanings, where the affirmative [/negative] stimulus meaning of a sentence for a speaker, to a first approximation, is "the class of all the stimulations ... that would prompt his assent [/dissent]" (Quine 1960, 31). For a critical survey of the development of the Quinean notion of stimulus meaning, see Tersman 1998.

59. For further reading on Quine's indeterminacy thesis, see Føllesdal 1973; Føllesdal 1990; Pagin 2000.

When Davidson talks of indeterminacy, he subsumes three different kinds of indeterminacy under this heading (cf. Davidson 1979, 228):

1. Indeterminacy of truth. Two empirically equivalent T-theories for a language L might be such that one of them makes a certain sentence s of L true while the other makes s false. Davidson argues that, due to the across-the-board application of the principle of charity in radical interpretation, this form of indeterminacy is significantly less for him than for Quine. Nevertheless, it cannot be reduced to zero: "When all the evidence is in, there will remain ... the trade-offs between the beliefs we attribute to the speaker and the interpretations we give his words. But the resulting indeterminacy cannot be so great but that any theory that passes the tests will serve to yield interpretations" (Davidson 1973a, 139).

2. Indeterminacy of logical form. Empirically equivalent T-theories might, for instance, differ in what they count as predicates, singular terms, or quantifiers. According to Davidson, this form of indeterminacy is much more limited for him than for Quine. The task of the radical interpreter is to construe a T-theory, and that forces him to 'impose' quantificational structure onto his object language (cf. Davidson 1973a, 136, footnote 16).

3. Indeterminacy of reference. This is also called "inscrutability of reference" and sometimes distinguished from indeterminacy proper. One idea here is that for any acceptable T-theory, it is possible to so permute the referents assigned to singular terms and the extensions assigned to predicates that sentences remain truth-conditionally equivalent. Here is a simple example Davidson uses to illustrate this

possibility (cf. Davidson 1979, 229f): Suppose that every object has exactly one shadow. Then, we can easily transform a T-theory t_1 into a second t_2 by taking the referents assigned by t_2 to be the shadows of those assigned by t_1. Thus, if 'Wilt' refers to Wilt according to t_1, it refers to the shadow of Wilt according to t_2. And if 'is tall' is satisfied by tall things according to t_1, it is satisfied by shadows of tall things according to t_2.[60]

But you might well wonder: How can two T-theories be equally correct if according to one a sentence s is true, and according to the other s is false? After all, s can hardly be both at once.[61] This apparent mystery can be solved, Davidson suggests, if we stop thinking of utterances as belonging to a single language and no other. Another way of thinking about indeterminacy thus is the following: Let's say that each and every possible T-theory *is* a language. Indeterminacy then is the claim that there always is some indeterminacy as to which language a speaker speaks. And if s is true as belonging to language L_1, but false as belonging to language L_2, there is no mystery about how it can be true in the first case, and false in the second.

Reference, satisfaction, and meaning, as I said above, are theoretical terms for Davidson. And the analogy with physics that Davidson uses to illustrate this idea actually occurs in the context of a discussion of referential indeterminacy. To see the special significance it takes on in this context, I'll quote the relevant passage again:

60. As Davidson himself points out, the example only works on the assumption that everything is, as well as has, a shadow (Davidson 1979, 230, footnote 3). Quine calls the kind of function applied to generate t_2 from t_1 a "proxy function." A classical objection is found in Evans 1975, and disarmed in Weir 2006.

61. This kind of worry is voiced, for instance, by Hacking 1975, 154f.

Within the theory, the conditions of truth of a sentence are specified by adverting to postulated structure and semantic concepts like
that of satisfaction or reference. But when it comes to interpreting
the theory as a whole, it is the notion of truth, as applied to whole
sentences, which must be connected with human ends and activities. The analogy with physics is obvious: we explain macroscopic
phenomena by postulating an unobserved fine structure. But the
theory is tested at the macroscopic level. Sometimes, to be sure, we
are lucky enough to find additional, or more direct, evidence for
the originally postulated structure; but this is not essential to the
enterprise. I suggest that words, meanings of words, reference, and
satisfaction are posits we need to implement a theory of truth. They
serve this purpose without needing independent confirmation or
empirical basis (Davidson 1977a, 222).

What we see now is that according to Davidson, the theories
that the notions of words, meanings, reference, and satisfaction
are part of describe a reality that is, in a sense, less fine-grained
than the acceptable theories: For any given natural language, there
is more than one acceptable 'fine structure'. And in *contrast* to
empirically equivalent physical theories empirically equivalent
T-theories are equally correct according to Davidson. Thus, the
notion of a 'fixed' reference has no place in Davidson's philosophy
of language. Nor can such a notion be meaning-theoretically basic
for him.

Nevertheless, there *is* structure to the reality described by all
acceptable T-theories: This is the 'macrostructure' of Davidson's
analogy with physical reality. It obtains at the level of sentences,
and is formed by the logical and evidential relations obtain-
ing between them. Each sentence has a unique location in the
pattern of these relations. And what remains invariant between
empirically equivalent T-theories is precisely the location of each

sentence within the overall pattern of sentences. Therefore, Davidson claims

> that what is invariant as between acceptable theories of truth is meaning. The meaning (interpretation) of each sentence is given by assigning the sentence a semantic location in the pattern of sentences that comprise the language. Different theories may assign different truth conditions to the same sentence ..., while the theories are (nearly enough) in agreement on the roles of the sentences in the language (Davidson 1977a, 225).

Once we thus identify the meaning of a sentence with its location in the pattern of sentences that comprise the language, indeterminacy can instructively be seen along the lines of another analogy with physics: There are different scales for measuring physical dimensions such as temperature or weight. Temperature can be measured in degrees Celsius or Fahrenheit, but this does not mean that anything essential is lost between these scales (cf. Davidson 1977a, 224f). Rather, they each capture precisely what is essential to temperature. Thus, Davidson writes, the "indeterminacy of interpretation is not on this account any more significant or troublesome than the fact that weight may be measured in grams or in ounces" (Davidson 1980a, 156).[62] According to Davidson, assigning interpretations to sentences is like assigning numbers to physical dimensions to keep track of certain relations between physical objects. But, as Davidson observes, "only some of the properties of numbers are used to capture the empirically justified pattern" (Davidson 1974a, 147). Using the Celsius scale to assign the numbers 10 and 20 to the temperature of the air in

---

62. For more on the measurement analogy, see Lepore and Ludwig 2005, 243ff; Rawling 2001. Matthews 2007 develops a general measurement-theoretic account of propositional attitudes and the sentences by which we attribute them.

the morning and at noon some fine summer day does as well as using Fahrenheit and assigning the numbers 50 and 68. Nevertheless, each assignment "makes sense of comparisons of differences, but not of comparisons of absolute magnitude" (Davidson 1974a, 147): The Celsius assignment might suggest that it is somehow twice as warm at noon than it was in the morning, but 68 is not twice as much as 50. It might thus seem that the Celsius assignment ascribes different temperature properties than the Fahrenheit assignment, but that would be a mistake. These are properties of the numbers that are not used in capturing temperature relations; these are, thus, not properties of temperature at all.

Nevertheless, we need to be careful with this analogy. For it suggests that interpretations indeed do have properties that are not used when keeping track of sentence meanings. Which in turn might suggest that there are these objects, these interpretations or meanings, that somehow are available as sentence meanings but just not quite reached by the means Davidson provides. This, Davidson warns against. We do have a good grasp of the properties of numbers, and also of which of their properties are relevant for the measurement of temperature, but the situation is not like that when it comes to meanings, he argues. As is his wont, he puts the point in terms of propositions:

> In the interpretation of speech, introducing such supposed entities as propositions to be meanings of sentences or objects of belief may mislead us into thinking the evidence justifies, or should justify, a kind of uniqueness that it does not.... Propositions being much vaguer than numbers, it is not clear to what extent they are overdesigned for their job (Davidson 1974a, 147).

Nevertheless, to the extent that we can make the idea precise that propositions indeed are overdesigned for their job—that is, do have properties that are not used in capturing those logical and evidential relations between sentences that according to Davidson are determinate, that is invariant between all acceptable, empirically equivalent T-theories—to that extent we also have reason to suspect that the Davidsonian account of meaning and content determination is at least incomplete, that it fails to capture a kind of uniqueness that is in fact there. And to that extent we would also have to conclude that Davidson ultimately failed to solve the restriction problem. To arrive at a justified verdict on this matter, however, would require a much more sustained investigation than I can provide here. I shall therefore leave the matter open.

2.4 Against Convention

I shall round off this chapter by following Davidson down one of the many roads of thought originating with radical interpretation. As we saw, Davidson considers not only the notions of reference and satisfaction, but even those of meaning and particular languages as entirely theoretical notions: "The notion of meaning depends entirely upon successful cases of communication" (Davidson and Glüer 1995, 81). All these notions derive what content they have from their ability to contribute to an explanation of successful linguistic communication:

> The concept of a language is of a sort with, and depends on, concepts like name, predicate, sentence, reference, meaning.... These are all theoretical concepts... The main point of the concept of a language, then,... is to enable us to give a coherent description of the behavior of speakers, and of what speakers and their interpreters know that allows them to communicate (Davidson 1992, 108f).

In the previous section we saw that the notion of meaning might, so to speak, have less content than we would be pre-theoretically inclined to think: According to Davidson, it is subject to a possibly undramatic, but certainly surprising and substantive indeterminacy. Another set of consequences Davidson draws might strike the reader as almost equally radical: According to Davidson, meaning is an essentially individualistic affair. Despite its public nature, meaning is first and foremost a property of idiolects, that is, of languages as spoken by individual speakers—as opposed to sociolects, that is languages shared by whole speech communities.[63]

Linguistic communication, Davidson claims, does not require a shared language. Moreover, he claims, meaningful speech does not even require regularity of use over time. The meaningful use of linguistic expressions therefore is not essentially conventional or rule-governed. This goes head-on against a tradition in the philosophy of language going at least back to Aristotle. According to this tradition meaning is essentially a matter of shared rules or conventions. David Lewis once wrote that "it is a platitude—something only a philosopher would dream of denying—that there are conventions of language" (Lewis 1975, 7). Now, as we shall soon see, Davidson does not deny that there *are* conventions of language, what he denies is that these are essential to communication and thereby to meaning. It seems fair to say, however, that even the modal form of Lewis's platitude—the claim that there have to be conventions of language, that these are necessary, or essential to meaning—has

---

63. Strictly speaking, this much individualism was present already in the radical interpretation papers. As early as in *Radical Interpretation*, Davidson writes: "The appeal to a speech community cuts a corner but begs no question: speakers belong to the same speech community if the same theories of interpretation work for them" (Davidson 1973a, 135).

dominated foundational thought in the philosophy of language.[64]

Davidson's line of thought culminates in what has been perceived by many as an outright, possibly suicidal attack on language itself. In 1986, he published a famous paper with the apt title *A Nice Derangement of Epitaphs*. In this paper, he argues that the frequency, pervasiveness, and easy interpretability of idiosyncratic language use—use involving such things as malapropism, spoonerism, or sheer neologism—in a certain sense threaten the very idea that speaking a language is necessary for linguistic communication. Here is the original formulation of what I shall call the "no-language claim":

(NL) "There is no such thing as a language, not if a language is anything like what many philosophers and linguists have supposed" (Davidson 1986, 107).

Maybe unsurprisingly, this is a claim for which Davidson got a lot of fire, most notably from Michael Dummett.[65] And there certainly is something funny about a philosopher of language

64. That meaning is essentially rule-governed is one version of the wider claim that meaning is normative. This claim has been very influential in the philosophy of language since the publication of Kripke's *Wittgenstein on Rules and Private Language* (Kripke 1982). For a survey and discussion of the literature, see Glüer and Wikforss 2009b.

65. Cf. Dummett 1986. Among other things, Dummett interprets Davidson as claiming that each and every case of successful linguistic understanding requires interpretation of the uttered expressions, and argues that such an account of understanding would lead into an infinite regress of interpretations, a regress familiar from Wittgenstein's so-called rule-following considerations and clearly vicious in nature. Davidson counters that the supposed regress ensues only if the notions of interpretation is read in the particular way in which Wittgenstein explicitly employs it in those passages (where 'interpretation' means replacing one linguistic expression by another linguistic expression), a notion completely at odds with Davidson's notion of interpretation (cf. Davidson 1994, 112). For other discussions of the no-language and related claims, cf. a.o. George 1990; Bar-On and Risjord 1992; Pietroski 1994; Reimer 2004; Hornsby 2008.

claiming that there is no such thing as a language. But to evaluate its philosophical merits, we have to see the no-language claim in its wider context, and we have to take seriously the proviso it contains—"if a language is anything like what many philosophers and linguists have supposed".

The no-language claim can instructively be seen as resulting from a certain switch in perspective in Davidson's meaning theoretical writings: While the radical interpretation papers are concerned with the publicness of meaning *from the interpreter's perspective*, another cluster of papers, papers that we might call the "anti-conventional papers", bring the speaker back into the picture.[66] In particular, they remind us of the extent to which the speaker is a free and creative agent. These papers focus on actual instances of linguistic communication as an interplay between a particular speaker and his hearer.

Take any particular utterance. The speaker of this utterance intends to mean something—p—by the words she utters: She has, as Davidson puts it, a "semantic intention". This intention is directed at the hearer; according to Davidson, it is an intention to be interpreted a certain way—to be interpreted as meaning p by the words uttered. Moreover, Davidson claims, the speaker also intends the hearer to interpret the utterance as meaning p because he recognizes that the speaker intends him to do so, a feature familiar from Paul Grice's writings on meaning.[67] Looking at it in this way, a particular utterance is a case of success-

---

66. The most important anti-conventional papers are: Davidson 1982a; Davidson 1986; Davidson 1994; Davidson 1989.

67. Cf. Davidson 1986, 91ff; Davidson 1993a, 170ff. For Grice's original suggestion for defining what he calls "non-natural meaning" in terms of intentions to effect certain beliefs in the hearer, and to achieve this effect via the hearer's recognition of the intention, see Grice 1957. Because of the interdependence of belief and meaning, Davidson is skeptical towards the Gricean project insofar as it aims at analyzing meaning in terms of other propositional attitudes. Cf. Davidson 1974a, 143f.

ful linguistic communication iff the speaker's semantic intention is fulfilled. The speaker's semantic intention is fulfilled iff the hearer interprets him the intended way (and by the right Gricean mechanism). Linguistic ability or competence, then, is to be characterized as the ability to engage in successful linguistic communication. All this might seem a bit trivial. Davidson himself comments: "This characterization of linguistic ability is so nearly circular that it cannot be wrong: it comes to saying that the ability to communicate by speech consists in the ability to make oneself understood, and to understand" (Davidson 1986, 106). But, so far at least, the notion of a language is completely absent from this characterization.

A natural idea at this point is that the notion of a language is needed to spell out why cases of successful communication as characterized in terms of the speaker's intentions should be counted as cases of *linguistic* communication. After all, there is a difference between communicating by means of language and communicating by means of extra-linguistic gestures or signs, for instance. Communication by language involves the use of linguistic expressions, signs that have *linguistic* meaning. So, what is required for communicating linguistic meanings? According to Davidson, "the usual answer would ... be that in the case of language the hearer shares a complex system or theory with the speaker, a system which makes possible the articulation of logical relations between utterances, and explains the ability to interpret novel utterances in an organized way" (Davidson 1986, 93). But, Davidson argues, this answer is mistaken: Language *in this sense* is inessential for linguistic communication.

So, what exactly is language *in this sense*? What is the notion of language that Davidson is attacking, a notion he claims had been employed by many philosophers and linguists—including himself? In retrospect, he characterized this notion as follows:

It was this: in learning a language, a person acquires the ability to operate in accord with a precise and specifiable set of syntactic and semantic rules; verbal communication depends on speaker and hearer sharing such such an ability, and it requires no more than this (Davidson 1994, 110).

What is under attack here is not so much a certain notion of a language than a certain notion of a language *together* with a set of ideas about its relation to linguistic competence and the use of linguistic expressions. It is therefore quite consistent with the no language claim that Davidson himself even after *Nice Derangement* gives the following explanation of what a language is: "A language may be viewed as a complex abstract object, defined by giving a finite list of expressions (words), rules for constructing meaningful concatenations of expressions (sentences), and a semantic interpretation of the meaningful expressions based on the semantic features of individual words" (Davidson 1992, 107). The no-language claim does not dispute that there are languages in this sense. What it disputes is that an utterance u is a case of successful linguistic communication if, and only if, there is a language in this technical, abstract sense that both models the speaker's and the hearer's linguistic competence in advance of u and assigns the correct interpretation to u.[68]

---

68. It is, however, not very clear in what sense a speaker is "operating in accord" with the semantic rules of a language in the technical sense. According to Davidson, these are specified by a T-theory. But how can the speaker's production of an utterance be modeled as the product of following the rules of a T-theory? The speaker wants to express a certain meaning, and the theory modeling his ability to do so would presumably tell him how to find the expressions to use. One might think that the speaker could use the T-theory 'the other way around'—as going from T-sentences to expressions, that is. But the number of T-sentences is infinite, and we can hardly model a speaker's ability to find expressions for his thoughts as a capacity to go through an infinite list of T-sentences until an expression with the required meaning is found. For more on this and on the idea of "inverse compositionality" that might provide an answer to this problem, see Pagin 2003.

An important feature of the no-language claim thus is its *modal nature*: It is a claim about what is necessary and/or sufficient for linguistic communication, a claim about what is essential to successful linguistic communication. When Davidson argues that there is no such thing as a language, what he means is that it is not essential to communication that there is a pre-established, shared language.

Equally important is what Davidson does *not* deny: He does not deny that people in fact both speak in very similar ways and use their words regularly over time. Nor does he deny that linguistic communication would be much more difficult if they did not. Consequently, the idea of there being conventions governing the use of linguistic expressions could play a certain explanatory role when it comes to communicative success: It could explain why people speak alike, and why they speak regularly over time, and, consequently, why communicative success is easy to achieve and quite widespread. "But," Davidson comments, "in indicating this element of the conventional, or of the conditioning process that makes speakers rough linguistic facsimiles of their friends and parents, we explain no more than the convergence; we throw no light on the essential nature of the skills that are thus made to converge" (Davidson 1982a, 278). According to Davidson, regularities of use, be they conventional or just "conditioned", are no more than a "practical crutch to interpretation" (Davidson 1982a, 279): Regularities of use are inessential to successful communication.

In *A Nice Derangement*, Davidson further spells out this idea. Focusing on the semantic rules of a language, as specified by a T-theory, he now suggests distinguishing between what he calls "prior theory" and "passing theory":

> For the hearer, the prior theory expresses how he is prepared in advance to interpret an utterance of the speaker, while the passing

theory is how he does interpret the utterance. For the speaker, the prior theory is what he believes the interpreter's prior theory to be, while his passing theory is the theory he intends the interpreter to use (Davidson 1986, 101).[69]

All of these theories are T-theories. So, the question is how these four T-theories relate to one another in cases of successful communication.

As we saw above, Davidson conceives of an utterance u as a case of successful linguistic communication iff the hearer of u interprets it as the speaker intended it to be interpreted. This translates into the terms of the prior and passing T-theories as follows: Communication succeeds iff both S's and H's passing theories assign the same interpretation to u. Prior theories, whether shared or not, are irrelevant to the question of success. In a way, we can therefore reformulate the no-language claim like this:

(NL′)   For an utterance u by a speaker S to a hearer H to be a case of successful communication, it is neither necessary nor sufficient

     i)   that S's prior theory is the same as S's passing theory for u,

     ii)   that H's prior theory is the same as H's passing theory for u, or

     iii) that S's prior theory is the same as H's prior theory.[70]

Put thus, the no-language claim might appear incontrovertible—but the result of a merely terminological trick. Sure, you might say,

---

69. Again, this is not supposed to be taken as implying claims "about the propositional knowledge of an interpreter, nor are they claims about the details of the inner workings of some part of the brain" (Davidson 1986, 96). And the same holds for the speaker.

70. Of course, i)-iii) are *jointly* sufficient for successful communication.

we can *call* these theories "prior" and "passing", and then insist that only the latter need to be shared—but that does nothing to show that prior and passing theory actually *can be significantly different*. And even if they strictly speaking can be different, it does nothing to show that such differences in fact occur frequently and pervasively enough to motivate a change in our characterization of linguistic competence.

Prima facie, it might indeed seem doubtful that ordinary hearers can understand utterances that require brand new passing theories, or that such abilities would count as linguistic. Take Lewis Carroll's Alice. When Humpty Dumpty says to her: "There's glory for you", Alice has no clue what he means. Nor is there any reason why she should be able to interpret him as meaning that there is a nice, knockdown argument for her. Even if this interpretation by sheer coincidence occurred to her, this 'success' would not be generated by her linguistic competence. But it might seem as if Davidson was defending such a "Humpty Dumpty theory of meaning"—as if he was claiming, that is, that what a speaker can mean by her words is completely up to her and free from all social constraint.[71]

But in fact, Davidson is not defending a Humpty Dumpty theory. More precisely, such a theory holds that intending to be interpreted as meaning *p* is necessary and sufficient for meaning *p*. And even though Davidson thinks that intending to be interpreted as meaning *p* is necessary for meaning *p*, he certainly does not think such an intention is sufficient for meaning *p*.[72]

"Humpty Dumpty is out of it," Davidson writes: "He cannot mean what he says he means because he knows that 'There's glory for you' cannot be interpreted by Alice as meaning 'There's a nice

71. For such a charge, see Dummett 1986.

72. Cf. Davidson and Glüer 1995, 80.

knockdown argument for you.' We know he knows this because Alice says 'I don't know what you mean by 'glory'', and Humpty Dumpty retorts, 'Of course you don't—til I tell you' " (Davidson 1986, 98). Stressing the role of the speaker and his intentions thus is not in any way meant to renegotiate on the social and public nature of meaning. Successful communication plays the pivotal role it does for Davidson precisely because cases of successful communication are cases in which meaning is public: Success in communication is necessarily a social affair. After all, communication is successful only if the hearer gets it, so to speak. And this must not be mere coincidence: For the utterance to have the intended meaning, it must at least be possible for the hearer to get it, according to Davidson. And from the speaker's perspective, the expectation that the hearer get it must be sufficiently justified (cf. Davidson and Glüer 1995, 81).[73]

What Davidson needs to make his case is therefore not the interpretability of each and every use of a linguistic expression—be it as wild and idiosyncratic as may be. Rather, he needs to convince us that a substantial amount of successful communication indeed is such that the intended interpretation is both idiosyncratic and can reasonably be expected to be understood. And as we saw above, that is precisely what Davidson claims to be the case: People regularly speak and interpret in idiosyncratic ways, and specific uses of expressions can be extremely short-lived. Moreover,

> there is no word or construction that cannot be converted to a new use by an ingenious or ignorant speaker. And such conversion, while easier to explain because it involves mere substitution, is not the only kind. Sheer invention is equally possible, and we can be

73. For more discussion of the Humpty Dumpty example, cf. Talmage 1996.

as good at interpreting it (say in Joyce or Lewis Carroll) as we
are at interpreting the errors or twists of substitution (Davidson
1986, 100).

To illustrate his point, Davidson provides an amusing
array of malapropisms, cases where a speaker intentionally or
inadvertently produces a different, but often similar sounding
word—as when Archie Bunker says "We need a few laughs to
break up the monogamy" or Mrs. Malaprop speaks of "a nice
derangement of epitaphs" or "the allegories on the bank of the
Nile". World literature contains a number of characters more than
usually prone to this kind of 'mistake'; besides Sheridan's Mrs.
Malaprop there is Frau Stöhr in Thomas Mann's *Magic Mountain*
and the captain of the *Patna* in Joseph Conrad's *Lord Jim*—and,
of course, Dogberry in *Much Ado About Nothing*. But it happens
to every one of us, and, as Davidson stresses, it can happen to
any word or construction. It often happens unintentionally, but
we can do it intentionally—some people are masters at that.
In all these cases, the resulting utterances are very often easily
interpretable. Such utterances, when successful, therefore show
that passing theories can be significantly different from what
can plausibly be assumed to be our prior theories. According
to Davidson, the examples also make it plausible that each
particular element of these theories can be different. Moreover,
they illustrate how frequent and widespread a phenomenon we
are talking about. According to Davidson, the phenomenon is
so ubiquitous that the ability to understand idiosyncratic speech
clearly is part of our normal linguistic competence.

All these cases are such that interpretability is secured by
the presence of further clues. The expectation to be interpreted
as intended thus seems reasonable—whether the speaker is
aware of the idiosyncratic nature of the utterance or not. Many

malapropisms, for instance, are easily interpreted because the sub-stituted expressions are very similar in sound. Often the "absur-dity or inappropriateness of what the speaker would have meant had his words been taken in the 'standard' way" (Davidson 1986, 90) provides an initial clue prompting a more charitable interpre-tation. And often, the surrounding context helps determine this interpretation further. But no specific kind of clue is necessary to secure uptake; the relevant word does not even have to exist before the utterance—it might be a neologism. And what can be done with a new word, or what new use an old word can be put to on occasion depends on that occasion. Moreover, basically any feature of the situation in which the word is uttered can be utilized for providing the relevant clue. Therefore, Davidson maintains, it is not possible to provide a systematic theory of this kind of capacity, a capacity of a truly creative nature both on the speaker's and on the hearer's part. Davidson concludes that it is not possible to provide a systematic theory of (at least an essential part of) our linguistic competence:

> We may say that linguistic ability is the ability to converge on a passing theory from time to time—this is what I have suggested, and I have no better proposal. But if we do say this, then we should realize that we have abandoned not only the ordinary notion of a language, but we have erased the boundary between knowing a language and knowing our way around in the world generally. For there are no rules for arriving at passing theories, no rules in any strict sense, as opposed to rough maxims and methodological gen-eralities. A passing theory really is like a theory at least in this, that it is derived by wit, luck, and wisdom from a private vocabulary and grammar, knowledge of the ways people get their point across, and rules of thumb for figuring out what deviations from the dictionary are most likely (Davidson 1986, 107).

The no-language claim has been attacked from different angles. The maybe first question to ask we have already touched upon above: Why should the meanings that idiosyncratically used expressions have in these cases count as *linguistic* meanings at all? Aren't these uses of words more like spontaneous gestures or the use of non-linguistic objects to signal something than like typical uses of linguistic expressions? The question can also be put like this: Why use whole T-theories for capturing occasional idiosyncratic uses?

"The answer is," Davidson writes, "that when a word or phrase temporally or locally takes over the role of some other word or phrase (as treated in a prior theory, perhaps), the entire burden of that role, with all its implications for logical relations to other words, phrases, and sentences, must be carried along by the passing theory" (Davidson 1986, 103). Potentially, that is, the speaker could go on to speak the language specified by the passing T-theory. For an expression to have a meaning is to (potentially) contribute to the meanings of all the possible complex expressions it could be part of.

A related, second question that Davidson himself is even more concerned about can be put like this: Even if those fleeting, ephemeral interpretations that speaker and hearer bestow upon a malapropism are linguistic meanings, why should we think of them as *literal* meanings? Why not just say that this is some variety of *speaker meaning*, and stick to the idea of conventional, communal, or otherwise standard literal meanings? This would allow us to count malapropisms and other idiosyncrasies as *linguistic mistakes*. And linguistic mistakes, as such, need not be covered by our semantic theories. According to Davidson,

> error or mistake of this kind, with its associated notion of correct usage, is not philosophically interesting. We want a deeper notion

of what words, when spoken in context, mean; and like the shallow notion of correct usage, we want the deep concept to distinguish between what a speaker, on a given occasion, means, and what his words mean (Davidson 1986, 91).

To be philosophically interesting from a Davidsonian perspective, notions like that of standard meaning, and the corresponding notion of a linguistic mistake, would have to be necessary to accounting for successful linguistic communication. They cannot, from this perspective, be used to determine what should count as successful communication, however. What is to be explained, or accounted for, needs to be pre-theoretically available—otherwise, the suggested 'account' simply begs the question it was supposed to answer. The claim, for instance, that literal meaning is essentially conventional is a substantive philosophical claim that needs to be justified by the role it plays in accounting for successful communication. Using it to disqualify cases of seemingly successful communication such as malapropisms from what needs to be explained would thus be question-begging.

But if Davidson does not want to draw the distinction between speaker meaning and literal meaning by means of conventional, regular, or otherwise standard use, how does he propose to draw it? Davidson follows Grice in thinking of speaker meaning as something derived from, and dependent upon, literal meaning. Take irony. Here, the speaker meaning roughly is the opposite of the literal meaning. The speaker literally says one thing, but wants the hearer to understand the opposite. More precisely, the speaker wants the hearer to interpret him as saying one thing but 'meaning' the opposite. The ironic interpretation thus is construed as dependent on a first, literal interpretation. Thus, Davidson suggests, we should think of what is commonly called literal meaning as "first meaning", where "first meaning comes first in the order of interpretation" (Davidson 1986, 91).[74]

Another question that could be asked is the following: Is it really inessential to *linguistic* communication that success usually is very swift and frequent? Davidson emphasizes the ease and swiftness with which idiosyncrasies often are interpreted. According to him, this is sufficient motivation for construing the underlying ability as linguistic. But *standard* language use is understood easily and swiftly, too, and presumably with an even higher success rate than idiosyncratic use. If regular use of linguistic expressions is necessary for this feature of successful communication, it is hard to see why this should be philosophically uninteresting. It would, after all, throw light on the nature of linguistic capacities that we actually use every day. This is not to say that Davidson is wrong when he claims that regular use is not necessary for success, or that the linguistic capacities that we actually use everyday are not exhausted by such a description. It is only to say that our linguistic capacities are essentially such that they allow for effortless, reliable, and predictable success.

Note, however, that even if regularity of use is essential to the kind of success our linguistic endeavors very often meet, this does not imply that conventionality is in any way essential to meaning. Conventionality requires more than regularity; it is for instance intuitively very plausible to think that conventional action needs to be, in some way, *motivated* by the convention.[75] According to

74. More precisely, this order of interpretation can be spelled out by ordering the speakers intentions by the relation of means to ends. If we express this relation in terms of 'in order to', first, or literal, meaning is given by the first of these intentions that is 'Gricean', i.e. accompanied by the intention to achieve the intended end by means of the hearer's recognition of the first intention (cf. Davidson 1986, 92f and note 67 above). For more on this, cf. Talmage 1994.

75. The same would seem to hold for rule-following or norm-guidedness, at least on any intuitive notion of rule following and norm-guidedness. See Glüer 2001 for a discussion

Davidson, this element is redundant when it comes to meaning. In discussion with Dummett, who argues that speakers need to have a "prescriptive attitude" towards the common language (cf. Dummett 1991, 85), he puts the point as follows:

> Suppose that someone learns to talk as others do, but feels no obligation whatever to do so. For this speaker obligation doesn't enter into it. We ask why she talks as others do. "I don't do it because I think I should," she replies, "I just do talk that way. I don't think I have an obligation to walk upright, it just comes naturally." If what she says is true, would she not be speaking a language, or would she cease to be intelligible? In other words, what magic ingredient does holding oneself responsible to the usual way of speaking add to the usual way of speaking? (Davidson 1994, 117.)[76]

Last, but not least, we can ask how the dynamic, fleeting picture of meaning that the no-language claim seems to induce fares with respect to the possibility of radical interpretation. After all, a speaker who does not use his words with a certain regularity would not seem to be radically interpretable. Even though this is certainly true, it would be wrong to think that there consequently is some deep tension between Davidson's earlier and later work. This would be wrong because it again misconstrues the character of Davidson's individualism.[77] For even though Davidson holds

of Davidson's anti-conventionalism in relation to the currently popular idea that meaning is normative, Wittgenstein's game analogy or his rule-following considerations.

76. Lepore and Ludwig (2007b) argue that there is no deep controversy between Davidson and Dummett when it comes to the role of convention in communication, but this would seem to be one clear bone of contention between them.

77. For a rather different way of reconciling the no-language picture, interpreted as an essentially dynamic view of meaning and language, with radical interpretation, cf. Ramberg 1989, 98ff.

that the notion of an idiolect has priority over that of a sociolect when it comes to accounting for meaning (cf. Davidson 1994, 111), this does not mean that there are no social constraints on what an individual speaker can mean by his words. Linguistic meaning, according to Davidson, is essentially public—he never departs one iota from this basic doctrine.

To see why he therefore does not expect the no-language picture to cause any tension with radical interpretation, we need to look at that scenario from the speaker's perspective, too. The most pertinent question then is: What, if anything, can the radical speaker intend the radical interpreter to interpret him as meaning? An important, and intuitively plausible principle Davidson uses here is the following: You cannot intend what you know to be impossible (cf. Davidson 1989, 147). Thus, Humpty Dumpty cannot (intend to) mean *a nice knockdown argument* by 'glory', because he knows that Alice will not be able to understand him. Prima facie, it might seem to follow that the radical speaker cannot (intend to) mean anything by any of his utterances, for he knows that, initially at least, the radical interpreter will not be able to understand him. But there is a crucial difference: The radical speaker can use his words in such a way that they are interpretable, in such a way, that is, that the radical interpreter will eventually be able to figure out what the speaker means: "The best the speaker can do is to be *interpretable*, that is, to use a finite supply of distinguishable sounds applied consistently to objects and situations he believes are apparent to his hearer" (cf. Davidson 1984a, 13). Radical interpretation thus appears as a limiting case on the no-language picture: The case where all other ways of being interpretable are blocked, and the only chance at communicating lies in the regular application of one's words.

Chapter 3

The Principle of Charity

Despite its central role in Davidson's philosophy of language, the literature on the principle of charity is rather sparse.[1] Moreover, the principle is often polemicized against on the basis of simple misunderstandings—as when, for instance, Hacking early on characterized the principle as a "rule of thumb to suppress our romantic inclinations" and ultimately denounces it as an expression of linguistic imperialism.[2] Quite possibly, the worry that charity—with its 'imposition' of a basic logic and shared beliefs—might be 'imperialistic' in some sense is not felt as forcefully today as it seems to have been in the 1970s. In any case, the worry is unfounded. According to Davidson, "charity is not

1. For discussion, see among others Lepore and Ludwig 2005, II.12; II.13; Jackman 2003; Ramberg 1989, 64-82; Malpas 1988; McGinn 1977. I would also like to draw attention to the similarity between the principle of charity and certain principles of philosophical hermeneutics, for instance Gadamer's "Vorgriff der Vollkommenheit". For more on this, cf. Künne 1981; Künne 1990; Ramberg 2003.

2. Hacking 1975, 147ff.

an option.... Charity is forced on us; whether we like it or not, if we want to understand others, we must count them right in most matters" (Davidson 1974b, 197).

The 'force' of charity derives from the very nature of belief. According to Davidson, it is essential to belief that beliefs come in coherent, largely true clusters. Therefore, it holds that:

> If we cannot find a way to interpret the utterances and other behaviour of a creature as revealing a set of beliefs largely consistent and true by our own standards, we have no reason to count that creature as rational, as having beliefs, or as saying anything (Davidson, 1973b, 137).

If Davidson is right about the nature of belief, there simply is no belief 'outside' of charity, and thus nothing to be subjected to imperialism, no beliefs to oppress or colonize by forcing charity onto them.

Despite its central role in his philosophy of language, even Davidson himself does not pay the principle of charity all that much systematic attention. There is no canonical formulation of the principle, for instance. Rather, we find numerous more or less similar formulations and glosses, spread out over a large number of papers. These papers, moreover, were written at quite different times, and over the years, subtle shifts in emphasis took place—not only regarding the formulation of charity, but also its justification. In the next section, we shall therefore look at the most important of these passages—both to get a better grip on what the principle of charity does and does not say, and to trace at least the most important of those shifts in emphasis.

3.1 Correspondence, Coherence, and Rationality

From the very start, there are two components to the principle of charity. In *Truth and Meaning*, Davidson writes:

> The linguist...will attempt to construct a characterization of truth-for-the-alien which yields, so far as possible, a mapping of sentences held true (or false) by the alien on to sentence held true (or false) by the linguist.... Charity in interpreting the words and thoughts of others is unavoidable in another direction as well: just as we must maximize agreement, or risk not making sense of what the alien is talking about, so we must maximize the self-consistency we attribute to him, on pain of not understanding *him* (Davidson 1967c, 27).

Here, maximizing *agreement* is set off against maximizing self-consistency or internal *coherence*. In *Radical Interpretation*, we then find the already quoted, classical formulation of charity connecting agreement with *truth* or what is right (according to our own, or the interpreter's, view of what is true or right):

> The method is intended to solve the problem of the interdependence of belief and meaning by holding belief constant as far as possible while solving for meaning. This is accomplished by assigning truth conditions to alien sentences that make native speakers right when plausibly possible, according, of course, to our own view of what is right (Davidson 1973b, 137).

Even later, Davidson coins separate names for the two aspects of charity: "principle of coherence" and "principle of correspondence." The latter, with its clear evocation of the correspondence theory of truth, shifts the emphasis even more clearly from agreement to truth:

> The process of separating meaning and opinion invokes two key principles which must be applicable if a speaker is interpretable: the Principle of Coherence and the Principle of Correspondence. The Principle of Coherence prompts the interpreter to discover a degree of logical consistency in the thought of the speaker; the Principle of Correspondence prompts the interpreter to take the speaker to be responding to the same features of the world that he (the interpreter) would be responding to under similar circumstances. Both principles can be (and have been) called principles of charity: one principle endows the speaker with a modicum of logic, the other endows him with a degree of what the interpreter takes to be true belief about the world (Davidson 1991, 211).

Moreover, we now have an explicitly causal element in the picture, an element that is missing from the radical interpretation papers.

3.1.1 Coherence and Rationality

When it comes to what we shall with Davidson call the "coherence" aspect of charity, the picture more or less remains the same through the years. From the very start, alien speakers are, to the extent that that is plausible, supposed to be interpreted as internally coherent, and in this sense as *rational* believers. Interpretation that is charitable in this sense is good interpretation, according to Davidson, because beliefs essentially form largely true and coherent clusters:

> Beliefs are identified and described only within a dense pattern of beliefs. I can believe a cloud is passing before the sun, but only because I believe there is a sun, that clouds are made of water vapour, that water can exist in liquid and gaseous form; and so on, without end. No particular list of further beliefs is required to give substance to my belief that a cloud is passing before the sun; *but some appropriate set of related beliefs must be there.* If I suppose that you believe a cloud is passing before the sun, I suppose you have the right sort of pattern of beliefs to support that one belief, and these beliefs I assume you to have must, to do their supporting work, be enough like my beliefs to justify the description of your belief as a belief that a cloud is passing before the sun (Davidson 1977b, 200, emphasis added).

Davidson sometimes refers to the claim that beliefs essentially come in clusters in terms of "the holistic character" of belief, or "the holism of the mental" in general (cf. for instance Davidson 1982b, 183f, and especially Davidson 1995c, 13ff.) This is a bit misleading, however, since the holism of the mental is of quite a different kind than the semantic holism we saw Davidson subscribing to in the previous chapter (cf. p. 48f). Regarding semantics, Davidson holds that meanings, or semantic contents, are determined holistically, by the principle of charity, on the basis of the holding-true attitudes of speakers. And since this determination automatically also solves for belief, the same holds for belief contents. But that is not what he has in mind in the passage just quoted; here, we are not concerned with holistic content determination, but rather with the claim that there cannot be such a thing as what Fodor has called a "punctate mind" (Fodor 1987), a mind containing only a single belief. More precisely, according to Davidson, it is impossible to have just one belief about any subject matter whatsoever.

This is a controversial claim, not the least because Davidson (in)famously thinks that the density of belief required for any single belief is so high that all nonlinguistic creatures are excluded from the realm of the believers (cf. Davidson 1982c; Davidson 1995c). That claim is too extreme for many philosophers. At the same time, many agree that ascriptions of belief to nonlinguistic creatures are true, or justified, only if there are sufficiently complex patterns of behavior and interaction, patterns that require the kind of explanation—reasons explanation—that only the ascription of contentful mental states affords.

Clusters of beliefs are held together by relations of a certain sort. Davidson often calls these relations "logical relations" (see, for instance, Davidson 1983, 143). What he has in mind includes, but is not limited to relations of logical consequence. Rather, the relevant relations are *rational or reasons relations* in a wide sense. Davidson most often writes as if beliefs themselves were reasons for beliefs, but that is a bit misleading. *That I believe that p* hardly ever is a (good) reason for believing q. Rather, reasons relations hold between beliefs because *what one believes*—that is, the *content* of a belief—is a reason for further belief. A reasons relation might thus hold between the belief that p and the belief that q, if p is a reason for believing q.

According to Davidson, reasons relations between beliefs are relations of *evidential support* (cf. Davidson 1980a, 157). There must, in other words, be a valid inference of some sort, be it logical or 'material', from p to q. For instance, believing that there is smoke coming from the neighbor's garden provides a pretty good 'material' reason for believing that there is a fire in the neighbor's garden. In this sense, Davidsonian reasons are *objective* reasons.

But *p does not have to be true* in order to be a reason for someone. Thus, you have a reason for believing that there is a fire in the neighbor's garden even if your belief that there is smoke coming from it is, in fact, false. Nor do Davidsonian reasons have to be *good* reasons; reasons can be overridden by other reasons, and you might over- or underestimate the degree of evidential support *p* in fact provides for *q*. In these senses, Davidsonian reasons are *subjective* reasons.

Framing the coherence aspect of charity thus in terms of clusters of beliefs held together by reasons relations, it is easy to understand why Davidson so closely connects the principle of charity with rationality: "Successful interpretation necessarily invests the person interpreted with basic rationality. It follows from the nature of correct interpretation that an interpersonal standard of consistency ... applies to both the speaker and the speaker's interpreter, to their utterances and to their beliefs" (Davidson 1991, 211). Interpretable creatures essentially are *rational animals*, according to Davidson. The rationality in question is subjective in character in that Davidsonian reasons are designed to capture the subject's perspective on things, but in order to be a perspective, this perspective needs to be recognizable as a perspective by other subjects, according to Davidson.

The claim that a basic rationality is essential to belief, too, has struck many as at least unrealistic; not even humans, it is often claimed, are rational enough for the principle of charity to be true of them.[3] Charity is not meant to exclude the possibility of irrationality, of course. Coherence, and rationality, are to be achieved in interpretation *where plausibly possible*.[4] Moreover, the rationality required is, as Davidson repeatedly stresses, of a

3. Cf. for instance Goldman 1989.

4. For more on irrationality, especially practical irrationality, see chapter 4, section 4.3.

very basic and partly subjective nature: Coherence requires only a "modicum of logic" and relations recognizable as reasons relations between a subject's beliefs. That a certain amount of very basic rational thinking would be required for belief does seem quite plausible: If someone seems to violate basic logical laws all the time, for instance seems to permanently contradict himself, we very soon have no idea anymore what the person believes at all. And the same holds for someone whose beliefs do not seem to at all cohere in more 'material' ways. If we cannot at all make out why believing one thing would seem to speak in favor of believing another, it becomes unclear what it really is a person believes in the first place. Requiring a basic rationality thus not so much limits irrationality as delineates the realm of the rational—not as opposed to the irrational, but as opposed to the *non*-rational.

Now, suppose Davidson is right. Suppose, that is, that belief essentially comes in coherent clusters. Then, the idea that correct belief ascription requires large-scale *agreement* comes along almost automatically. For each and every belief an interpreter ascribes to another person, it holds that:

> If I am right in attributing the belief to you, then you must have a pattern of beliefs much like mine. No wonder, then, I can interpret your words correctly only by interpreting so as to put us largely in agreement (Davidson 1977b, 200).

In these early papers, there is thus a very close connection between the two aspects of charity, between coherence and agreement. Moreover, the main *motivation* for charity here derives precisely from the claim that beliefs essentially form coherent clusters.

3.1.2 Correspondence

When it comes to agreement and truth, or as Davidson later has it, "correspondence", this from the start can be seen as a sort of anchor for these holistic patterns, or systems, of beliefs. More precisely, it is the interpretation of observation sentences that ties such systems 'down to earth' and secures their empirical content.

It is also because of the special role observation sentences play in interpretation, that agreement or correspondence can be distinguished from coherence as an independent parameter of charity at all. As Davidson notes early on, these two aspects can pull in different directions, however. Gains in agreement, or observational truth might have to be weighed against gains in internal coherence: "No single principle of optimum charity emerges" (Davidson 1967c, 27).

As we saw in the previous chapter, Davidson proposes that "we take the fact that speakers of a language hold a sentence to be true (under observed circumstances) as prima facie evidence that the sentence is true under those circumstances" (Davidson 1974a, 152). Following the maxim to assign truth conditions to sentences such that they are (mostly) held true when they are in fact true not only results (largely) in agreement, or *shared belief*, between speaker and interpreter, it also essentially ties the content of such sentences (and of the beliefs thereby ascribed) to the *observable conditions* under which they are (held) true.

Nevertheless, what agreement, or correspondence, results in is *truth-by-the-interpreter's-lights*. For even if the charitable interpreter aims at assigning truth conditions to sentences such that the speaker's beliefs are mostly true, he can do so only according to what he himself takes to be true in a given situation. Thus, in interpreting observation sentences, he assigns contents to the speaker's beliefs that are such that he himself believes them under the given conditions. Or, more precisely, he assigns contents such that he himself would believe them were he in precisely the same situation as the speaker. He will, for instance, not interpret the speaker as having a perceptual belief that there is a rabbit behind a certain tree if he knows that the speaker cannot see that rabbit (even though he, the interpreter can see it or knows by some other means that it is there).[5] And ascribing beliefs to me that you yourself have is, of course, ascribing beliefs to me that are true by your lights. But that we both hold *p* true does of course not imply that *p is* true.

As far as the radical interpretation papers are concerned, this is where Davidson leaves matters. But in later writings, he becomes increasingly interested in the further question of how to get from agreement to truth. And in the light of this interest, the focus of the passages concerning charity changes in the way hinted at earlier.

Davidson now is concerned not only with meaning theory, but also with its epistemological consequences. He argues that beliefs not only form largely coherent clusters of mostly shared beliefs, but that they in fact form clusters that are largely coherent and *true*. In particular, Davidson launches a fundamental campaign against the most radical forms of epistemological *skepticism*, first and foremost skepticism about our knowledge of the external world.[6] His conclusion: "Massive error about the world is simply unintelligible" (Davidson 1977b, 201). Why? In a nutshell,

---

5. See also Lewis 1974, 336f; Føllesdal 1975.

6. In a similar vein, he also attacks radical skepticism about other minds and about one's own mind; cf. esp. Davidson 1991, but also Davidson 1984a; Davidson 1987b; Davidson 1990a.

the answer comes from the nature of belief again: "Belief is in its nature veridical" (Davidson 1982a, 146).[7]

What we are interested in right now is not Davidson's anti-skepticism as such.[8] Rather, we want to hear more about the connection between agreement and truth. It is in his anti-skeptical considerations, however, that the role causality plays in this context comes into focus: According to Davidson, belief is in its nature veridical because of the way the content of belief is determined. Belief content, he argues, is determined in such a way as to ensure that our epistemically most fundamental beliefs are (mostly) true.

In order to see the shift in emphasis here, compare the following two passages concerning the determination of belief content. The first is from *Thought and Talk* (1975):

> A belief is identified by its location in a pattern of beliefs; it is this pattern that determines the subject matter of the belief, what the belief is about. Before some object in, or aspect of, the world can become part of the subject matter a belief (true or false) there must be endless true beliefs about the subject matter (Davidson 1975, 168).

But eight years later, Davidson writes in *A Coherence Theory of Truth and Knowledge*:

> What stands in the way of global skepticism of the senses is, in my view, the fact that we must, in the plainest and methodologically

---

7. By "veridical", Davidson means something like *mostly true*. Or, as he himself explains: "A somewhat better way to put the point is to say there is a presumption in favor of the truth of a belief that coheres with a significant mass of belief" (Davidson 1982a, 139).

8. For more on skepticism, see chapter 5, section 5.3. See also B. Stroud 2002a.

most basic cases, take the objects of a belief to be the causes of that belief (Davidson 1983, 151).

Between these passages, the focus has shifted from the idea that the content of a belief, what it is about, is determined by its location in a pattern, to the idea that it is determined by its causal links with objects and events in the believer's environment.

These two ideas about belief content do not necessarily exclude one another, of course. Davidson, for one, is happy to combine them. The resulting picture is one on which beliefs form coherent patterns 'tied down to earth'—that is, construed as being 'about' certain objects or events in the believer's environment—by the causal relations between the believer and these objects or events. Thus, Davidson describes what he now calls "the principle of correspondence" as prompting "the interpreter to take the speaker to be responding to the same features of the world that he (the interpreter) would be responding to under similar circumstances" (Davidson 1991, 211). And he cashes out the notion of responding to features of the world in terms of *systematic and shared* causation: "Communication begins where causes converge: your utterance means what mine does if belief in its truth is systematically caused by the same events and objects" (Davidson 1983, 151).

This is a form of *externalism* about belief content: Belief content is determined by factors that are, in some relevant sense, 'external' to the subject. Davidson qualifies his externalism as both perceptual and social (cf. Davidson 1990a; Davidson 2001b).[9]

---

9. Davidson's externalism, besides being perceptual and social, also encompasses an *historical* element: To have a certain meaning or content, expressions or concepts need to have the right kind of acquisition history. To illustrate this point, Davidson at one point asked us to imagine the "swampman": A perfect Davidson-replica, created the very moment and very

Perceptual, because it first and foremost concerns the determination of content for observational belief according to the principle: "If anything is systematically causing certain experiences (or verbal responses), that is what the thoughts or utterances are about" (Davidson 1990a, 201). And *social* because systematicity is not enough: For any belief, there are many systematic causes, or many aspects of any systematic cause. To determine objects, or contents, for beliefs, we need causes that are both systematic and *common, or shared.* In his later writings, Davidson often explains this point in terms of very elementary learning situations, situations in which someone learns how to talk (and think) about ordinary things from someone else:

> Success at the first level is achieved to the extent that the learner responds with sounds the teacher finds similar to situations the teacher finds similar. The teacher is responding to two things: the external situation and the responses of the learner. The learner is responding to two things: the external situation and the responses of the teacher. All these relations are causal. Thus the essential triangle is formed which makes communication about shared objects and events possible. But it is also this triangle that determines the

close to the place in a swamp where Davidson himself is struck by lightning and completely pulverized. The swampman (who consists of molecules different from those Davidson was composed of) then walks out of the swamp, moves into Davidson's house, and writes articles on radical interpretation. Not even Davidson's wife can tell the difference. Nevertheless, Davidson claims, intuition has it that the swampman (at least initially) does not mean anything by his words. Nor does he have any beliefs or thoughts (cf. Davidson 1987b, 443f). This intuition is disputed, however. Nor is it clear that this historical element in Davidson's externalism is not in tension with his semantic behaviorism. After all, on the assumption that Davidson is radically interpretable, the swampman is, too. Thus, if what Davidson means and believes is determined, by charity, on the basis of his behavior in its observable circumstances, so is the what the swampman means and believes. (In Davidson 1973c, 245ff Davidson himself seems to argue this very claim with respect to another fictitious creature: the artificial Art. See also Glüer 2007). In conversation, Davidson later expressed regret over ever having invented the swampman, but he held on to the historical element in his externalism.

content of the learner's words and thoughts when these become complex enough to deserve the term. The role of the teacher in determining the content of the learner's attitude is not just the 'determine' of causality. For in addition to being a cause of those thoughts, *what makes the particular aspect of the cause of the learner's responses the aspect that gives them the content they have is the fact that this aspect of the cause is shared by the teacher and the learner* (Davidson 1990a, 203, emphasis added).

The idea of this "essential triangle", its role in content determination, and the philosophical consequences thereof, came to take center stage in Davidson's late writings. We shall come back to triangulation and its consequences later (see chapter 5, section 5.3). What is important here is that Davidson construes perceptual beliefs as being about their systematic and common, or shared, causes. This is why, as we saw above, Davidson came to describe the principle of correspondence as prompting "the interpreter to take the speaker to be responding to the same features of the world that he (the interpreter) would be responding to under similar circumstances" (Davidson 1991, 211).

Summing up his arguments for charity in later years, he brings the two ideas—the idea that beliefs come in coherent clusters and that perceptual beliefs are about their systematic, shared causes—together. While earlier most weight rested on the first idea, Davidson now stresses that the argument actually has two parts, one corresponding to each of the parts of charity itself:

The first part has to do with coherence. Thoughts with a propositional content have logical properties; they entail and are entailed by other thoughts. Our actual reasonings or fixed attitudes don't always reflect these logical relations. But since it is the logical relations of a thought that partly identify it as the thought it is, thoughts can't be totally incoherent.... The principle of charity expresses this by saying: unless there is some coherence in a mind, there are no thoughts.... The second part of the argument has to do with the empirical content of perceptions, and of the observation sentences that express them. We learn how to apply our earliest observation sentences from others in the conspicuous (to us) presence of mutually sensed objects, events, and features of the world. It is this that anchors language and belief to the world, and guarantees that what we mean in using these sentences is usually true.... The principle of charity recognizes the way in which we must learn perceptual sentences (Davidson 1999a, 343).

Again, whether Davidson's anti-skeptical arguments are ultimately successful is not our concern right now. For the radical interpreter striving to obey charity, striving for truth always amounts to striving for truth by his own lights, anyway. How else could anyone strive for truth? The point, however, is that in the light of the anti-skeptical considerations, the maxim for the radical interpreter subtly changes. In the radical interpretation papers, we find the general maxim "to choose truth conditions that do as well as possible in making speakers hold sentences true when (according to the theory and theory builder's view of the facts) those sentences are true" (Davidson 1974a, 152). What is added in the later papers is how this is more precisely to be done for a certain class of sentences and beliefs: the observational or perceptual ones. Here, the ascription of true beliefs is to be achieved by means of interpreting speakers, where plausibly possible, as responding to the systematic and shared causes of their beliefs.

This later stress on shared causes also illustrates that, when it comes to agreement, or correspondence, not everything is equal: There are sentences, and subject matters or contents, that are more central, more important, than others. Observational matters are one example, but there are others. This brings us to the question of what it more precisely means to "do as well as possible" in making speakers right. We shall look at that in the next section.

3.1.3 Maximizing and Optimizing

As quoted above, one of the earliest, most classical formulations of charity is found in *Radical Interpretation*: According to this version, the interpreter is to assign "truth conditions to alien sentences that make native speakers right when plausibly possible, according, of course, to our own view of what is right" (Davidson 1973b, 137). Our question now is: What does it mean, a little more precisely, to *make a speaker right when plausibly possible*?

The "when plausibly possible" qualification obviously makes some room for the possibility of mistake. Moreover, it indicates the kind of situation, or consideration, that not only allows for ascribing mistakes, but actually calls for it. For instance, an interpreter might know that a speaker has been misinformed about a certain matter. In such a situation, coherence will call for ascribing further mistaken beliefs, beliefs that the speaker because of his misinformation has reasons for holding. Other examples are provided by perceptual illusions. For instance, in a situation where the interpreter knows, but the speaker has no reason to suspect, that she is subject to an illusion, it is plausible to ascribe false perceptual beliefs to her. More examples can be derived from the perspectival nature of certain facts, for instance perceptual ones. If the interpreter, from his vantage point, can see that there is a rabbit behind the tree, but the speaker cannot, it is implausible to ascribe the true belief that there is a rabbit behind the tree to the speaker. Given some further information, for instance that the speaker believes that there are no rabbits around here, it would even be plausible to ascribe the (false) belief that there is no rabbit behind the tree.

Examples such as these illustrate how correspondence and coherence interact and thus bring out the nature of the relevant plausibility considerations: These are considerations to do with rational belief formation and maintenance, considerations about what is a reason for what. Such considerations help *locate* mistakes once it is clear that a mistake needs to be ascribed somewhere. Such considerations do not yet amount to an explanation of the main objective of "doing as well as possible" in making speakers right, however.

As we saw in the previous chapter, the principle of charity has two functions in radical interpretation: It is the principle that makes the data available to the radical interpreter, data about sentences held true under observable circumstances, into evidence for a T-theory. And it ranks T-theories such that the best are correct. The best T-theories are those that achieve the best overall fit with the data, and a T-theory fits the data the better the more charitable it is. Doing as well as possible in making speakers right accordingly is to be assessed holistically: It is a property that whole T-theories have vis-a-vis the totality of the evidence for them. Thus, Davidson writes in *Radical Interpretation*: "We want a theory ... that *maximizes agreement*, in the sense of making [the speaker(s)] right, as far as we can tell, as often as possible" (Davidson 1973b, 136, emphasis added).

A couple of lines later, however, Davidson glosses charity as "the methodological advice to interpret in a way that *optimizes* agreement" (emphasis added). In the preface to *Inquiries into Truth and Interpretation*, he explains why:

> Maximizing agreement is a confused ideal. The aim of interpretation is not agreement but understanding. My point has always been that understanding can be secured only by interpreting in a way that makes for the right sort of agreement. The 'right sort', however, is no easier to specify than to say what constitutes a good reason for holding a particular belief (Davidson 1984b, xvii).

One difficulty with maximizing agreement concerns the possibility of counting a person's beliefs. What exactly does it mean to say that on one way of interpreting a subject S, S has *more* true beliefs than on another? If S, for instance, believes that snow is white and grass is green, does that count as one belief? Or two? Or three? According to Davidson, "there is no useful way of counting beliefs, and so no clear meaning to the idea that most of a person's beliefs are true" (Davidson 1983, 138). The same, of course, then holds for the idea that on some interpretation, S has more true beliefs than on another.[10]

Moreover, even if there was a clear way of counting beliefs, it seems intuitively wrong that, all else being equal, a T-theory interpreting a speaker as making an outright perceptual mistake is as good, or plausible, as one interpreting a speaker as making a mistake concerning some highly theoretical matter such as the color

10. A similar point is sometimes put in terms of *infinity*. For instance, Davidson writes:

The basic methodological precept is … that a good theory of interpretation maximizes agreement. Or, given that sentences are infinite in number …, a better word might be *optimize* (Davidson 1975, 169).

or spin of some quark. Here, plausibility considerations kick in again: It is often much more plausible to ascribe the latter kind of mistake than the former. Moreover, ascribing an outright perceptual mistake—that is, a perceptual mistake that is not explained by rationality considerations like those above—almost immediately casts doubt on the assumption that the subject understands his own words in the way she is interpreted. If someone without any reason whatsoever seems to claim that an object in plain sight and bright daylight is blue when it in fact is bright yellow, this immediately provides some reason to doubt that she means *blue* by whatever expression she used, for instance 'blue'. Not so for the subject that makes a mistake about quarks—unless she is a particle physicist.

Optimizing agreement thus is based on the idea that not all mistakes are equally destructive when it comes to understanding someone else. Davidson here uses the metaphor of "epistemology seen in the mirror of meaning" (Davidson 1975, 169); epistemologically more basic mistakes, such as mistakes about one's own states of mind or mistakes about what things look like, for instance, are more destructive for understanding than mistakes about particle physics or other people's states of mind. Optimizing agreement thus involves the idea of assigning different weights to different kinds of mistakes and preferring interpretations that, on the whole, assign mistakes of lesser weight to those that assign mistakes of greater weight. When Davidson speaks of the "right sort of agreement", this is what he means: Not every agreement counts as much as any other.

The maxim to optimize agreement could easily be made more precise if, for every concept such as *red*, or *cloud*, or *quark*, there was a definite list of things any subject needs to believe in order to have, or be able to express, that concept. But according to Davidson, there are no such lists. The existence of such lists would amount to a clear distinction between the conceptual truths and the non-conceptual truths, and, applied to the sentences expressing them, to a clear analytic-synthetic distinction. On these matters, Davidson is "Quine's faithful student" (Davidson 1983, 144); while there are truths that are more conceptual than others, and sentences that are more analytic than others, these are matters of degree. There is no clear distinction, and, on top of that, there are no truths, or sentences, occupying the conceptual or analytic endpoints on these scales. In general, there is no belief about a subject matter, no belief about clouds, for instance, that is such that if a subject S does not have that belief then S has no beliefs about clouds at all. Another way of putting this point is the following: There is no belief such that having it is 'constitutive' of having the concept of cloud or of meaning *cloud*.[11]

That does not mean that certain mistakes are not more destructive of understanding than others, or that too many basic mistakes cannot make an interpretation utterly implausible. What it means, however, is that

> it is hard to be precise about the rules for deciding where agreement most needs to be taken for granted. General principles are relatively easy to state: agreement on laws and regularities usually matters more than agreement on cases; agreement on what is openly and publicly observable is more to be favored than agreement on what is hidden, inferred, or ill observed; evidential relations should be preserved the more they verge on being constitutive of meaning (Davidson 1980a, 157).

11. For more on this, and a comparison with Wittgenstein's ideas about agreement in judgment, cf. Glüer 2000. For Quine's classical attack on the analytic-synthetic distinction, see Quine 1951. An influential recent defense of a relevant notion of analyticity against Quine is Boghossian 1996. For more discussion, see Glüer 2003a, Boghossian 2003, and Williamson 2006.

And Davidson concludes: "It is uncertain to what extent these principles can be made definite—it is the problem of rationalizing and codifying our epistemology" (Davidson 1980a, 157).

3.2 Meaning Determination and the Interpreter

Now that we have gained a more detailed understanding of the aspects of charity itself, we can take a step back and consider the overall role that it according to Davidson plays in the theory of meaning.

Earlier, we already saw that the principle of charity has two essential functions vis-a-vis the data available to the radical interpreter: By constraining belief, it first of all enables observations about sentences held true to play the role of data, or evidence, for T-theories at all. And second, it ranks candidate T-theories according to which achieves the best fit towards the totality of these data (see chapter 2, section 2.3.1). In this way, it allows the radical interpreter to determine meanings for the expressions of the alien language.

Looked at in this way, the principle of charity is an epistemic principle, a principle governing not only the pursuit of knowledge about meaning by the radical interpreter but, crucially, the *justification* of beliefs about meaning in general. However, according to Davidson, there is more to charity than just determining the *best* interpretation we could hope to achieve: "What a fully informed interpreter could learn about what a speaker means is all there is to learn; the same goes for what the speaker believes" (Davidson 1983, 148). The most charitable interpretation, or T-theory, is not just the best one, it is the *correct* one. Charity not only determines what *can be known* about meaning, it determines *meaning*.

This absolutely basic idea of Davidsonian theory of meaning has, time and again, been criticized as being a form of *verificationism*. Here is one recent voice:

> Davidson's application of the methodology of radical interpretation to the philosophy of language embodies a kind of ideal verificationism, on which agents have just the intentional states that a good interpreter with unlimited access to non-intentional data would ascribe to them (Williamson 2004, 137).

The verificationism in question is not, of course, of the meaning theoretical kind; what we are concerned with here is not the claim that meaning is to be understood in terms of verification conditions, rather than in terms of truth-conditions. Rather, what is called "verificationism" here is simply a certain claim of *knowability*: the claim that a certain range of facts is such that it can, in principle, be known.

For Davidson, this range of facts is, first and foremost, that of facts about the meanings of linguistic expressions. Meanings, he submits, are essentially public. And for him, that amounts to the claim that meanings can, in principle, be known by an interpreter with access to all the relevant data. Another way of putting the same claim is this: According to Davidson, natural language is radically interpretable. Thus, he writes: "The requirement that the evidence be publicly accessible is not due to an atavistic yearning for behavioristic or verificationist foundations, but to the fact that what is to be explained is a social phenomenon. Mental phenomena in general may or may not be private," Davidson writes, "but the correct interpretation of one person's speech by another must *in principle* be possible" (Davidson 2005, 56).

Now, intuitively, there certainly are areas of reality where the truth might well be such that it, even in principle, outruns, or transcends, what we can know. But claims of in principle knowability are nevertheless not objectionable just by themselves. For even if we thought that most domains of facts are such that we might be radically mistaken about them, no matter how much evidence we had, it is by no means obvious that the whole of reality is like that. In particular, we must ask: Is it intuitively true that no matter how much of the relevant evidence we have, it might remain unknowable what a given linguistic expression means? We might not agree with Davidson about what that evidence precisely is, or what principle governs its relations to our semantic theories. But if we abstract from such matters of detail for a moment, it seems to me that on the most basic issue, intuition is with Davidson: Linguistic meaning is essentially public.

What about beliefs (and the other propositional attitudes)? Intuitions here are probably more divided. For Davidson, belief and meaning are interdependent; the radical interpreter determines both belief contents and meanings simultaneously. Assignments of belief automatically fall out of assignments of meanings to sentences held true. Therefore, beliefs are as public as meanings are. Whether Davidson is right about this or not, the matter is at least not obvious either way. Claiming in principle knowability for both belief and meaning is not an obviously false position.[12]

That there appears to be something objectionable here might be due to another common misunderstanding. This misunderstanding concerns the role the (radical) interpreter plays in the Davidsonian account of meaning determination. For instance, it is often thought that, on the Davidsonian picture, expressions have

---

12. Child 1996, ch. 1, argues that both meaning and belief are necessarily interpretable, where "interpretable" means in principle accessible via "interpretation," i.e. our practice of ascribing intentional states on the basis of what is said and done. For an opposing, merely epistemological view on charity, see McGinn 1986.

their meanings *because*, or in virtue of, being the meanings that the radical interpreter would assign. Views of this kind are sometimes called "interpretationism", or "interpretivism."[13] On such a view, interpretation takes explanatory, or metaphysical, priority over meaning. And such a view might well be rather suspect. I think such an interpretationism gets things exactly the wrong way around: According to Davidson, it is the way meaning is determined that explains interpretability. Metaphysically speaking, that is, it is not the radical interpreter that is responsible for meaning. Metaphysically, meaning is determined in a way that makes natural language radically interpretable, but the determining is done by something else.

As I have stressed in the previous chapter, the Davidsonian account of meaning determination *is both epistemological and metaphysical*. On the one hand, we have the data on the basis of which the radical interpreter constructs his T-theory: Facts about which sentences speakers hold true under which observable circumstances. Epistemologically, these provide the evidence justifying, or empirically supporting, a T-theory: its evidential base. But at the same time, these facts also provide *the metaphysical determination base* for meaning: The T-theory (or theories) best supported by the evidence is the correct one. And the relation of best support (or best fit) between what is both the evidential and the determination base and the T-theory is established by the principle of charity. Because of its holistic character, the relation is of a many-one character: There is more than one possible

---

13. Both Davidson and Daniel Dennett (Dennett 1990) are seen as among the main proponents of interpretationism. See, for instance, Child 1996, who distinguishes a number of different versions of interpretationism; the version under consideration here he calls "constitutive interpretationism." See also Goldman 1989 who speaks of the "interpretion strategy," an strategy he attributes, among others, to Davidson. According to this strategy, we can learn everything essential to the propositional attitudes from reflection on our actual practices of ascribing them.

evidential base that one and the same T-theory would fit best, and, consequently, there is more than one metaphysical determination base that would determine the same meanings for the expressions of the language in question. Such determination relations are often called relations of "supervenience": For every change in supervenient fact, some subvenient fact must change. But not vice versa.[14]

Metaphysically speaking, that is, the radical interpreter is out of it. Expressions do not have the meanings they have because he would assign them. Quite the contrary: It is because, or in virtue of the fact that meanings are determined by the principle of charity that natural languages are radically interpretable. Radical interpretation is precisely what Davids Lewis said it is: "a way of dramatizing our problem [of meaning determination]—safe enough, so long as we can take it or leave it alone" (Lewis 1974, 334). As documented in Davidson's reply to Lewis's paper (Davidson 1974d), they disagree on a number of things when it comes to meaning determination.[15] But there is no disagreement on the use of the radical interpretation scenario as a merely dramatic device.

Most importantly, Lewis and Davidson disagree on what is in the determination base. According to Lewis, it's the totality of physical facts, widely construed, and this, Davidson has reservations about (cf. Davidson 1974d, 345). Despite their crucially non-individuative nature, his determination base contains hold-

14. Cf. Davidson 1974d, 345. The term 'supervenience' comes from moral philosophy and is probably first used in this sense in Hare 1952. See also Davidson 1993b, 4.

15. Lewis and Davidson disagree, to a certain extent, about the principles governing the determination, and the order of determination. For Lewis, the determination of propositional attitude content is prior to the determination of meaning, while Davidson maintains that meaning and intentional content are interdependent.

ing true attitudes—that is, characteristically mental, or intentional, facts. There is thus one important function the radical interpreter does have for Davidson in this context. He is to dramatize the determination of a property in principle knowable by ordinary speakers on the basis of evidence *available to such speakers*. The function of the radical interpreter thus is to *limit, or motivate, the choice of determination base*. The question here is: What kind of fact that could play the role of meaning determination base is accessible to an interpreter just like us? And, as we have seen, the Davidsonian answer to this is: attitudes of holding true towards uninterpreted sentences.

Attitudes of holding true thus form the base on which the principle of charity metaphysically determines meanings—and belief contents. This determination base is, according to Davidson, sufficiently non-semantic to make sure that no meaning-theoretical questions are begged. At the same time, it is sufficiently mental to make sure that no topics are switched. The relation the principle of charity establishes is one of supervenience: On the Davidsonian picture, linguistic meanings (and belief contents) are determined by non-semantic facts. But the relation is one of supervenience only; according to Davidson, there is no chance of any reduction of the semantic to the non-semantic, or the intentional to the non-intentional. His is a *non-reductive naturalism*.

The main reason Davidson advances against the possibility of reduction is the nature of the principle of charity. As determined by the principle of charity, beliefs and the meanings of a person's words are individuated by means of standards of rationality and coherence. Therefore, the principle of individuation for mental states such as belief is radically different from the principles involved in individuating physical states, such as length or mass. Consequently, Davidson submits, it is more than unlikely that types of mental states in general can be reduced to types of physical states.[16]

Lately, many commentators have counted Davidson among those who argue that meaning, or the intentional in general, cannot be reduced to the physical because of its essential *normativity*.[17] This may be based on the idea that the principle of charity is a *maxim* for the radical interpreter, that is, some sort of *prescription* he is supposed to follow. As we have seen, however, the radical interpreter is merely a dramatic device when it comes to meaning determination. To be sure, if Davidson is right, then meaning is determined in such a way that a radical interpreter *can* use the principle of charity as a maxim guiding the construction of his T-theory, a maxim such as:

(PC$_P$) Assign truth conditions to alien sentences that make native speakers right when plausibly possible.

But that this works is due to the fact that meaning is determined by the principle of charity. There is nothing essentially normative about the derivability of certain methods—maxims, or imperatives, of how to do certain things—from independently given facts. Assume that all and only MacIntosh apples are red. Then, you can pick out the MacIntosh apples from a large basket of mixed apples by following the maxim "Take the red ones!" That does not show that there is anything essentially normative about being a MacIntosh apple.

16. Cf. Davidson 1970b; Davidson 2005, 56f. For more on this, see chapter 6.

17. The master template for such arguments is to be found in Kripke 1982. For an overview and discussion, cf. Glüer and Wikforss 2009b.

The principle of charity does involve notions such as truth, rationality and coherence, however. And many have taken these to be essentially normative notions. There is some textual evidence that Davidson himself thinks of these notions as normative in some sense, for instance when he writes about the task of the radical interpreter: "What makes the task practicable at all is the structure that the normative character of thought, desire, speech, and action imposes on correct attributions of attitudes to others, and hence on interpretations of their speech" (Davidson 2005, 74). It never becomes clear precisely what he meant by "normative" in passages like this, however. There are other places where Davidson makes it completely clear that he does not think that truth is a norm (cf. Davidson 1999d), and that the standards of rationality are normative only in the sense of, somehow and in some sense, being "ours" (cf. Davidson 2001a, 297). What should be clear is that Davidson cannot, and does not, hold that the standards of rationality are *made by us*. Nor can he hold that they are *to be followed in order to be an intentional creature*, a creature who has beliefs and means something by their words. According to Davidson, a creature whose states do not already instantiate a minimal rationality does not have any beliefs, and does not mean anything by their 'utterances'. In this sense, the standards of rationality are constitutive of having beliefs and meaning something. Following rules, maxims, or prescriptions, as well as making something, are intentional actions; being able to do these things presupposes that you have beliefs, desires, and intentions. You cannot do them if you don't already have beliefs, that is, and it makes no sense to follow rules in order to have beliefs if you already have beliefs.[18]

---

18. Cf. Glüer 2001; Schroeder 2003; Glüer and Wikforss 2009a.

The upshot of these considerations is this: According to Davidson, the claim that

(PC$_M$)   Meaning is determined by the principle of charity

is a descriptive metaphysical claim or truth. But what kind of truth is this supposed to be? In the next section, we shall investigate this question. More precisely, we shall look into both the epistemic and the metaphysical status of charity.

3.3 The Status of Charity

According to Davidson, meaning is determined by the principle of charity. How do we know this? Or better: What kind of *justification* is there for believing this? According to a long philosophical tradition often associated with Kant, but with roots reaching back at least to Aristotle, not all truths are empirical truths. There are some that can be known *a priori*. For such truths, there is justification that *cannot be defeated by empirical evidence*. Is charity a priori? Can we know a priori that meaning is determined by charity?

There are numerous passages indicating that Davidson thought that this in fact is the correct answer to the question of the epistemic status of charity. Here are just two, rather early ones:

> Crediting people with a large degree of consistency cannot be counted mere charity: It is *unavoidable* if we are to be in a position to accuse them meaningfully of error and some degree of irrationality. Global confusion, like universal mistake, is *unthinkable* ... (Davidson 1970b, 221, emphasis added).

What makes interpretation possible, then, is the fact that we can dismiss *a priori* the chance of massive error (Davidson 1975, 168f, emphasis added).

But this is somewhat surprising. As we saw above, Davidson is with Quine on the analytic-synthetic distinction (see, for instance, Davidson 1983, 144). That is, just like Quine 1951, Davidson holds that the only sensible understanding of the notion of analyticity is one according to which analytic sentences are immune to revision in the light of empirical evidence. On this understanding, analyticity and apriority not only coincide, they might well be the same thing. Moreover, just like Quine, Davidson officially holds that even though there are degrees of openness to revision in the light of experience, there are no statements (or beliefs) that are completely immune to it. Officially, that is, Davidson holds that there are no a priori truths in the strict, traditional sense.

There is, thus, some tension here. On the one hand, Davidson subscribes to a Quinean epistemology that recognizes degrees of independence from experience, but no strictly a priori truths. On the other hand, he does think that the arguments for charity provide a priori justification for it. One way of dealing with this tension might be to use a less traditional, less strict notion of the a priori. According to such notions, the a priori does not so much distinguish between kinds of truths, as between kinds of justification. On such an understanding, we can allow that there are no truths that are completely immune to revision in the light of experience, but insist that there nevertheless is justification that does not derive from experience.[19] It is not so clear how that

19. For such a proposal, see for instance Casullo 1988. For more references, see Casullo 2002, esp. fn. 6.

would help the claims Davidson wants to make about charity, however. A relative notion of apriority does not really back up the categorical claim that the possibility of massive error can be dismissed a priori, for instance.[20]

Another way out would be to take the passages on charity as showing that Davidson does not fully subscribe to a Quinean epistemology. On such a reading, it is an a priori truth in the full, traditional sense that charity determines meaning. Some commentators, for instance Lepore and Ludwig (cf. Lepore and Ludwig 2005, 166ff), come close to taking this line.[21] They claim that Davidson must provide us with a priori arguments for the claim that the evidence available to the radical interpreter suffices for interpretation. They call the project of providing such an a priori argument "the ambitious project" (Lepore and Ludwig 2005, 168). If Davidson is not pursuing this ambitious project, they argue, "many of his conclusions about the nature of thought, language, meaning, truth, and knowledge will be unattainable" (Lepore and Ludwig 2005, 169). Why? The idea here is that for instance the claim that belief is governed by charity is a claim that derives its justification from the fact that this is something the radical interpreter must assume: "that justification must rest on

---

20. There is textual evidence that Davidson himself did not think in terms of a weaker notion of apriority. In his more careful formulations, he puts the matter in terms of a certain skepticism: There is, he says, reason to be skeptical towards the claim that principles like charity can be defeated by experience: "I am profoundly skeptical about the possibility of significant experimental tests of theories of rationality" (Davidson 1985a, 88). What he weakens, thus, is not the notion of the a priori, but the strength with which he believes that charity is a priori—in the traditional sense. For more on this, see Glüer 2006a.

21. Cf. Lepore and Ludwig 2005, 169, note 139 for some qualifications: "We will...continue to employ the traditional terms 'a priori' and 'a posteriori'. However, for our purposes, these terms could be replaced with *any* pair that captures the kind of grounding involved in establishing truths constitutive of a subject-matter, and in establishing truths which are not."

the assumption that the radical interpreter can correctly interpret a speaker, and that charity is required for this" (Lepore and Ludwig 2005, 171, see also 198ff). As far as I can tell, this gets things backwards. Considerations of radical interpretation do not suffice to motivate charity. Davidson certainly thought it was true that

(1)   If charity is true, radical interpretation is possible,

but that, by itself, does not show that charity is the only principle of meaning determination that would make radical interpretation possible. If the purpose is nothing but making radical interpretation possible, *any* principle determining truth conditions on the basis of holding true attitudes would do.

However, even if the justification for charity does not derive from radical interpretation, it might nevertheless be true that it is a priori. As argued above, I think that Davidson's real argument for charity comes from *the nature of belief*: According to him, belief is essentially such that it comes in true and coherent clusters. And it might well seem that inquiry into the nature, or essence, of belief is a priori.

This appears to have been Davidson's own opinion. When looking back on his own work on interpretation in the Dewey Lectures he gave at Columbia University in 1989, he commented:

> I have been engaged in *a conceptual exercise* aimed at revealing the dependencies among our basic propositional attitudes at a level fundamental enough to avoid the assumption that we can come to grasp them, or intelligibly attribute them to others, one at a time. Performing the exercise has required showing how it is in principle possible to arrive at all of them at once. Showing this amounts to

presenting an informal proof that we have endowed thought, desire, and speech with a structure that makes interpretation possible.[22] Of course, we know this was possible in advance. The philosophical question was, what makes it possible? (Davidson 2005, 73f, emphasis added.)

This suggests that we can, as he says, "dismiss *a priori* the chance of massive error" (Davidson 1975, 168f, emph. added) because it is *a conceptual truth* about belief that it comes in largely true and coherent clusters. At other times, Davidson puts this in terms of constitutivity:

> Just as the satisfaction of the conditions for measuring length or mass may be viewed as constitutive of the range of application of the sciences that employ these measures, so the satisfaction of conditions of consistency and rational coherence may be viewed as *constitutive* of the range of applications of such concepts as those of belief, desire, intention and action (Davidson 1974c, 237, emphasis added).

What all this suggests is that Davidson himself at least tended to think of charity as a conceptual truth. As a conceptual truth charity's epistemic status would be a priori. Moreover, as a conceptual truth charity's modal status would be given, too: Conceptual truths, at least as traditionally conceived, are *necessary truths*. According to Davidson, that is, charity is a conceptual necessity knowable a priori.[23]

---

22. For the motivation of why desire needs to be on this list, and not just belief and meaning (thought and speech), see section 3.4.

23. Does this mean that charity is analytic? Apparently not. Kant famously divided the a priori into the analytic and the synthetic a priori, and Davidson—while never calling charity

This has lead some commentators to suggest that Davidson is best interpreted as thinking of charity as *implicitly defining* notions like that of belief.[24] This idea is due to David Lewis. He thought of *folk psychology*—that is, our everyday practices of attributing, predicting, and explaining our own and other people's mental states such as beliefs, desires, intentions, and their intentional actions in terms of further mental states of these kinds—as a collection of platitudes that together form a (highly implicit) theory. The platitudes making up this theory can be made explicit and treated as implicit definitions of the theoretical terms used in them, theoretical terms such as 'belief', 'desire', and 'intention'.[25] Since these states in effect are defined in terms of their folk-psychological *functional role*, this position has been called "analytic functionalism." Davidson does agree with a lot of what Lewis says when it comes to beliefs, desires, intentions, and their role in action explanation, so this is an interesting line to pursue.

Still, one might feel that construing charity as (part of) an implicit definition along Lewisian lines does not completely fit

"analytic"—does at least suggest a strong analogy between principles in physics that he calls "constitutive (or synthetic a priori)" and charity:

> I suggest that the existence of lawlike statements in physical science depends upon the existence of constitutive (or *synthetic a priori*) laws like those of the measurement of length within the same conceptual domain. Just as we cannot intelligibly assign length to any object unless a comprehensive theory holds of objects of that sort, we cannot intelligibly attribute any propositional attitude to an agent except within the framework of a viable theory of his beliefs, desires intentions, and decisions (Davidson 1970b, 221, emphasis added).

I am not suggesting that there is a readily available conception of the synthetic a priori that would fit easily into a Quinean epistemology; it is just that this passage makes it fairly clear that Davidson, even though thinking of charity as conceptually true, did nevertheless not think of it as analytic.

24. See, for instance, Evnine 1991, 111ff.

25. Cf. Lewis 1972; Lewis 1974.

the Davidsonian way of thinking. Davidson wanted charity to be a conceptual truth, and he repeatedly expressed skepticism as to the possibility of empirically testing theories explicitly spelling out folk-psychological rationality assumptions:

> I am profoundly skeptical about the possibility of significant experimental tests of theories of rationality. This does not mean that such theories, or the considerations that lie behind them, have no empirical application. On the contrary, I think of such theories as attempts to illuminate an essential aspect of the concepts of belief, desire, intention and meaning. One criterion a theory of these concepts must meet is this: it must show how it is possible for one person ('the experimenter') to come to understand another ('the subject') (Davidson 1985a, 88).[26]

Analytic functionalism, on the other hand, treats these theories precisely as empirical theories. It does not secure the (conceptual) truth of the platitudes of folk-psychology. As Lewis himself points out, what holds is rather the following: "If the names of mental states are like theoretical terms, they name nothing unless the theory (the cluster of platitudes) is more or less true. Hence it is analytic that *either* pain, etc., do not exist *or* most of our platitudes about them are true" (Lewis 1972, 257). There is thus no readily available way of dealing with the tension between Davidson's construal of charity as a conceptual necessity and his general acceptance of a Quinean epistemology.

Faced with this tension, most commentators tend towards letting the idea that charity is a conceptual truth trump the Quinean

---

26. Davidson thinks that any 'experiment' seeming to show that a subject's beliefs are not even minimally rational would give us at least as much reason to think that our method of testing was flawed (cf. Davidson 1976a, 272). For critical discussion of this claim as applied to the idea that charity determines meaning, see Glüer 2006a.

epistemology. We might want to try to go the other way, though. After all, a general acceptance of Quinean epistemology is fairly uncontroversial these days. And that rationality is *essential* to belief it is arguably more important to the Davidsonian picture than that this is a conceptual truth. The idea that rationality is essential to belief *can* be integrated into a generally Quinean epistemology—if we give up the claims that charity is a priori and that its necessity is conceptual: The idea would be to interpret the claim that charity determines meaning (and belief content) as an *a posteriori necessity*.[27] Such an interpretation might allow us to stick to a Quinean epistemology—while at the same time understanding Davidson's frequent use of expressions like 'essential' and 'constitutive' as making hard metaphysical claims. Those liking the relative a priori might even argue that charity nevertheless remains a truth as a priori as they come in a Quinean epistemology.

3.4 A Wide Notion of Interpretation

In the passages quoted in the course of the last section, we have often seen the notion of belief in combination not only with that of meaning, but also with notions such as *desire, intention,* and *action.* All of these, Davidson thinks of as forming a very tight conceptual cluster, and for all of them Davidson claims a basic rationality to be essential.

---

27. That there are metaphysical necessities that are a posteriori, i.e. necessary truths knowledge of which requires empirical justification, has been accepted by a vast majority of philosophers in the analytic tradition since Kripke 1972. That charity is a posteriori is also suggested in Gallois and O'Leary-Hawthorne 1996, and the interpretation of Davidson proposed in this paragraph has been worked out in Glüer 2006a.

One reason for construing belief, and its rationality, as very closely related to the whole family of intentional states (including action) is the following: In interpreting the sentences a speaker holds true, contents are automatically assigned to his beliefs. These beliefs, however, must not only be internally coherent and fairly rational—they must also form an adequate background for his *actions* (cf. Davidson 1975, 159f). For beliefs not only provide (theoretical) reasons for further beliefs; together with desires, beliefs provide *practical reasons* for action.[28] If our belief ascriptions end up making the speaker completely irrational in his actions, such *practical* irrationality is as implausible and as much of a problem as when these ascriptions end up making him hold completely unfounded or contradictory beliefs. And this holds not only for the actions the interpreter is primarily concerned with—that is, the linguistic utterances of the speaker—but for all his actions. The rationality involved in belief ascription is thus twofold from the very beginning: It is *both practical and theoretical* in character.

Davidson, however, goes further than this. According to him, it is not only meaning and belief that are fundamentally interdependent—rather, ultimately the interdependence holds between meaning, belief, *and desire*. To see why, we need to once more go back to the procedure of the radical interpreter. As we saw earlier, Davidson provides us with a rather rough sketch of how the radical interpreter proceeds on the basis of the holding true attitudes of his speakers. A first step identifies the logical constants, the second interprets predicates in indexical observation sentences, and the third all the rest. The hitch comes when we

---

28. 'Desire' here is a slightly technical umbrella term for any of the so-called 'conative' states. It encompasses everything from sudden wants and urges to moral and other principles held by a subject. Davidson sometimes uses 'pro-attitude' to signal this. For more on action explanation and practical reasoning, see chapter 4.

think more in detail about sentences and predicates more remote from the observational. To interpret these, we said, the interpreter needs to know about relations of evidential support: He needs to know "to what extent the speaker counts the truth of one sentence in support of the truth of another" (Davidson 1980a, 157). This is were we left matters in the previous chapter.

But Davidson does not think matters can be left here. According to him, counting the truth of one sentence in support of the truth of another is a construct out of more basic attitudes towards sentences. To a first approximation, these can be characterized as *degrees of belief*:

> What is needed for an adequate theory of belief and meaning, then, is not merely knowledge of what causes a speaker to hold a sentence true, but knowledge of the degree of belief in its truth. It would then be possible to detect degrees of evidential support by noting how changes in the degree of credence placed on one sentence were accompanied by changes in the degree of credence placed on other sentences (Davidson 1980a, 157).

The problem with degree of belief, however, is that it is "remote from what can generally be introspected by an agent or diagnosed by an interpreter" (Davidson 1980a, 157), because it in turn is a construction on more elementary attitudes.

At this point, Davidson turns to decision theory. In decision theory, it is assumed that we can determine how likely a subject *S* thinks certain given alternatives—and which he choses if we know how much *S desires or values* any of these alternatives. For *choice* is a function of subjective probability and strength of desire (or value). On the basis of this basic insight, Frank Ramsey devised a method for determining both preferences (desires, values) and degrees of belief on the basis of the choices a subject makes.[29] The only way the radical interpreter could get at degrees of belief thus seems to go via desires or preferences. Desires or preferences, however, are not available to the radical interpreter. Nor can his data be extended to include information about them—desires or preferences are states with propositional or intentional content just as much as belief is. Including them into the radical interpreter's evidence would just as much beg Davidson's basic meaning theoretical questions as the inclusion of beliefs would. If Davidson is right, then, and holding true attitudes by themselves do not provide sufficient evidence for radical interpretation, it is indeed all three—meaning, belief, and desire—that are fundamentally interdependent.

Ramsey's method for disentangling preference and degree of belief is of no direct help to the interpreter, either. For this method presupposes that the experimenter—or interpreter—understands the choices the subjects make. This in turn involves interpreting their speech. For even if we can take someone to express preferences not only by saying so, but also directly by his actions,

> this cannot settle the question of what he has chosen. A man who takes an apple rather than a pear when offered both may be expressing a preference for what is on his left rather than his right, what is red rather than yellow, what is seen first, or judged more expensive. Repeated tests may make some readings of his actions more plausible than others, but the problem will remain how to determine when he judges two objects of choice to be identical. Tests that involve uncertain events—choices between gambles—are even harder to present without using words. The psychologist, sceptical of his ability to be certain how a subject is interpreting his

29. Cf. Ramsey 1931.

instructions, must add a theory of verbal interpretation to the theory to be tested (Davidson 1975, 163).

What is needed, then, is "*a unified theory* that yields degree of belief, desirabilities on an interval scale, and an interpretation of speech" (Davidson 2005, 66). This theory must not assume that beliefs, desires, or meanings have been identified in advance. Much as before, what is needed is a non-individuative propositional attitude that allows the interpreter to solve for his unknowns—now three instead of two—and that he can detect on the basis of observable behavior in observable circumstances alone. Holding uninterpreted sentences true will not do. But, according to Davidson,

> the following attitude will serve: the attitude an agent has toward two of his sentences when he prefers the truth of one to the truth of the other. ... What the interpreter has to go on, then, is information about what episodes and situations in the world cause an agent to prefer that one rather than another sentence be true. Clearly an interpreter can know this without knowing what the sentences mean, what states of affairs the agent values, or what he believes. But the preferring true of one sentence to another by an agent is equally clearly a function of what the agent takes the sentences to mean, the value he sets on various possible or actual states of the world, and the probability he attaches to those states contingent on the truth of the relevant sentences. So it is not absurd to think that all three attitudes of the agent can be abstracted from the pattern of an agent's preferences among sentences (Davidson 2005, 66).

In this way, the radical interpreter ends up interpreting not only the language of his aliens. From the start, that also amounted to constructing a theory of their beliefs. But ultimately, the task is a theory that also ascribes desires or preferences. Meanings, beliefs and desires together, in turn, explain intentional action. Together, they allow the interpreter to understand the intention with which for instance the apple in Davidson's example was chosen: Was it chosen because it was an apple, a red thing, or simply because it was seen first? Determining the intentions on which agents act, the descriptions under which they choose alternatives, thus amounts to interpreting their non-verbal behavior—just as much as ascribing meanings interprets their verbal behavior. For Davidson the interpretation of linguistic utterances and the interpretation of non-verbal behavior thus become part of one and the same project; in a sense, radical interpretation becomes the hermeneutics of intentional action, be it linguistic or not. On the basis of this *wide notion of interpretation*, Davidson's ultimate aim is a unification of the theories of meaning and of action: a unified theory of the interpretation of intentional agents.

Chapter 4

Davidson's Theory of Action

Action theory is of great relevance to a number of traditional philosophical problems. What an action is, where and when it begins and ends, what its consequences are, how to understand the relation between action and intention, and how to describe and explain action in general—these are questions of significance not only for ethics, but also for the mind-body problem and the problem of free will, to name but a few. Of particular interest is also the distinction between reasons and causes and the relation between hermeneutic interpretation, reasons explanation, and scientific explanation. For Davidson, action theoretic question have another dimension of peculiar significance: To understand, or interpret, the actions of a person has become an integral part of the radical interpreter's mission. Even though we will encounter numerous intriguing problems of independent interest in this chapter, the solutions Davidson suggests get their full significance only in the context of that mission.

By the end of the last chapter, the radical interpreter had become an interpreter in the widest sense: He simultaneously tries to understand the totality of the actions, including the linguistic utterances, and propositional attitudes of a person. To fully appreciate this task, we need to know what it exactly means to 'understand' nonverbal action—at first blush, this way of talking appears metaphorical, derived from understanding people's linguistic utterances. In particular, we need to get clearer about the relation between non-verbal action and the propositional attitudes, since it is the propositional attitudes of a person Davidson's radical interpreter hopes to get at through action.

That we can 'read off' a person's beliefs or desires from their actions is intuitively only too plausible. That character traits express themselves in action is part of everyday psychology—and biblical heritage: "By their fruit you will recognize them" (Matthew 7:16). According to Davidson, the relation between the propositional attitudes of a person and their actions is *explanatory*: Beliefs, desires, and other propositional attitudes explain action. There is nothing esoteric about this claim; citing someone's beliefs or desires to explain their behavior is part of common sense and its folk-psychology (cf. Davidson 1975, 158f). We do it all the time. But for Davidson's purposes, a more precise analysis of this explanatory relation is required.

Davidson's classical paper in this context is the extremely influential *Actions, Reasons, and Causes* from 1963. In the debate around reasons and causes, Davidson here takes the side of Aristotle and defends the "ancient—and common sense—position that *rationalization is a species of causal explanation*" (Davidson 1963, 3, emphasis added). The paper marks a turning point in action theory; since then, causal accounts of action explanation have dominated the field.

4.1 Actions, Reasons, and Causes

Davidson's starting point is the plausible and intuitive idea that we can explain actions by citing the *reasons* for which the agent did what he did. Such reasons explanations *rationalize* the action: By giving the agent's reasons, such explanations show that—from the agent's perspective—there was something that 'spoke for' the action, something that made it rational to do what the agent did—from the agent's perspective. The rationality inherent in such explanations is quite weak: That the agent did what he did for a reason does not mean that he did it for a *good* reason. And it is subjective in the sense that the perspective taken in the rationalization is the agent's perspective: What is provided are the agent's reasons, reasons that were reasons *for* the agent. But to provide a genuine explanation, there also needs to be a certain objectivity to these reasons: They must be such that *"anyone who had* [those reasons] would have a reason to act that way" (Davidson 1975, 159, emphasis added). Without this much objectivity, or intersubjective validity, to the reasons given, the perspective of the agent would not be recognizable as a perspective by those the action is explained to.

Aristotle provided a model for the structure of reasons explanations: the *practical syllogism*. The practical syllogism explains an action in terms of a belief and a desire. It is the basic form of what we now call the *belief-desire model* of action explanation. Built into it is a form of Humean view of action motivation: To explain an action we always need both a belief and a desire, a cognitive and a conative component.[1]

1. This is not uncontroversial, of course. On the Humean view, see for instance Smith 1987; Smith 2003. For recent criticism of the belief-desire model, see for instance Velleman 2000.

According to Davidson, one of the main proponents and developers of the belief-desire model in modern analytic philosophy, the practical syllogism promises "to give an analysis of what it is to act with an intention; to illuminate how we explain an action by giving the reasons an agent had in acting; and to provide the beginning of an account of practical reasoning, i.e. reasoning about what to do, reasoning that leads to action" (Davidson 1970a, 31). Davidson is mainly interested in the second promise, in gaining a deeper understanding of reasons explanations. Accordingly, we shall focus on that, too. As we shall see, his investigation of reasons explanations led him to give up on the idea of fully analyzing what it is to act with an intention (see section 4.2). And it made it very clear that the practical syllogism is but a beginning of an account of practical reasoning; more on that in section 4.3.

Nevertheless, the practical syllogism *is* a beginning. Here is an example: Assume that I have a desire to eat something sweet. And I believe that that piece of chocolate over there is sweet. Then, I have a reason to eat that piece of chocolate. And if I eat it (for that reason), my action can be explained by means of my belief and desire. We can bring out the explanatory structure of such an explanation by construing it as a simple deduction. More precisely, we can construe it as a practical syllogism. A syllogism has two premises, a major and a minor one, and a conclusion. In this case, the major premise is general in nature, the minor one particular. The conclusion derived is particular, too. Construing desire as a general "pro-attitude" towards actions of a certain kind, our example looks like this:

(1)   Any act of mine that is an eating of something sweet is desirable.

(2) My eating that piece of chocolate over there is eating something sweet.

(3) My eating that piece of chocolate over there is desirable.

A bit more formalized, such a practical syllogism looks like this:

(1′) $\forall x\,(\psi x \rightarrow Dx)$

(2′) ψa

(3′) Da

where the quantifier ranges over acts of mine, ψ is a type of action, and 'D' stands for 'is desirable'. Like Aristotle, Davidson initially construed the conclusion directly as an action (cf. Davidson 1970a, 31f). Thus, the syllogism explains the action as the logical conclusion of its premises.

To use a syllogistic model of action explanation is *not* to make any claims about the conscious reasoning of the agent. It does not commit us to the implausible idea that any intentional action is preceded by a conscious deliberation in deductive form. Of course, sophisticated agents do, on occasion, consciously deliberate about what to do. But even then, they rarely consciously run through inferences as elementary as those we are mainly concerned with here. Moreover, they don't have to do this in order to act intentionally. The claim is, rather, one of *rational reconstruction*: When an agent acts intentionally, she does have the beliefs and desires the model ascribes to her, and having these beliefs and desires shapes or conditions her decision making in such a way that the process can be rationally reconstructed as being syllogistic in form.

Having the relevant beliefs and desires is only a necessary condition for intentional action, however. According to Davidson, a further (necessary) condition is that these beliefs and desires caused the action. Just like Aristotle, Davidson thus interprets the syllogism in causal terms: If I eat the chocolate *because* I have the belief and desire forming its premises, then my having these reasons is the *cause* of my action.

As Davidson emphasizes, such a causal interpretation of the practical syllogism not only has an ancient tradition, it also is rather intuitive. Nevertheless, at the time *Actions, Reasons, and Causes* was written, there was a broad consensus among philosophers that the deductive nature of the relation between reasons and action necessarily precluded it from being causal. A number of closely related arguments for this anti-Aristotelian take on the syllogism were put forth; these arguments are often subsumed under the label "logical connection argument." Their main idea derives from some remarks by Wittgenstein. In the *Blue Book*, he argues that causal statements are empirical hypotheses. These hypotheses are formed by induction, and they are of nomological character. None of this, he argues, is true for statements someone makes about their own reasons for action: "When I say: 'we can only conjecture the cause but we know the motive' this statement will be seen later on to be grammatical one. The 'can' refers to a *logical* possibility" (Wittgenstein 1958, 15). According to Wittgenstein, the capacity to provide reasons for our own actions—in sharp contrast to the knowledge we might have about causal matters—thus is not part of our empirical knowledge of the world, but belongs with our linguistic ability, our knowledge of our own language.

All logical connection arguments are variations on this basic idea.[2] They argue that the logical, or conceptual, relation between reasons and actions prevents reasons and actions from being dis-

2. For a classical formulation, see Melden 1961. For discussion, see Stoutland 1970.

tinct events. Only numerically distinct events can stand in causal relations. But, the logical connection argument says, to be distinct, these events would have to be such that they could occur independently. Moreover, claims about the relation between causes and effects are empirical in nature, and the relation itself is contingent. According to the logical connection argument, all of this is made impossible by the logical or conceptual nature of the relation between reasons and actions. Reasons explanations and causal explanations are thus mutually exclusive; their explanatory power has completely different, incompatible sources.

According to Davidson, the appearance of incompatibility is misleading. Reasons and action must be related *both logically and causally* for there to be reasons explanations (cf. Davidson 1982b, 173). Thus, the logical connection not only does not prevent the explanation from being causal. Rather, capturing their explanatory power requires construing action explanations as causal explanations. Why? To explain an action, for instance my eating of that piece of chocolate, it is not sufficient to provide *a* reason that I had for eating it. For I might very well have had some particular reason for eating the chocolate, for instance a desire for something sweet, *without having eaten the chocolate for that reason.* I might, for instance, have eaten the chocolate because it was the polite thing to do in the situation. Nor does having *a* reason for eating any particular piece of chocolate necessarily lead to eating it.

What we are interested in when asking why an agent A performed a particular action is *the* reason for which A did it—not *some* reason or other A had for doing it. And this is precisely what a (true) reasons explanation gives us: *The* reason for which the action in question was performed. "Central to the relation between a reason and an action it explains is the idea that the agent performed the action *because* he had the reason," Davidson writes, and we have not fully captured the nature of reasons explanations "until we can account for the force of that 'because' " (Davidson 1963, 9).

But, Davidson argues, there is no better way of accounting for that 'because' than reading it as causal: *The* reason for which an agent *A* did what he did is the reason that *caused* his action. Another way of putting this is the following: Among the various reasons *A* had for his action, the reason for which he actually did it is the one that was causally efficacious in bringing the action about. There simply is no way to distinguish *the* reason from all the other reasons an agent had but for which he did *not* do the action we want explained. Davidson's decisive argument for the claim that "rationalization is a species of causal explanation" (Davidson 1963, 3) thus is an argument to the best explanation: "I would urge that, failing a satisfactory alternative, the best argument for a scheme like Aristotle's is that it alone promises to give an account of the 'mysterious connection' between reasons and actions" (Davidson 1963, 11). What he has to show, therefore, is how reasons explanations *can* be understood as causal explanations—despite the logical or conceptual relation between reasons and actions. More precisely, he needs to show that reasons can be understood as causes without reasons explanations losing any of their specific 'hermeneutic' quality—that is, any of their rationalizing force.

4.2 Reasons are Causes

According to Davidson, two different relations are required to account for the full force of (true) reasons explanations: a logical relation and a causal relation. These relations, however, obtain on different levels or, more precisely, they take different kinds of relata. In general, logical relations hold between propositions or interpreted sentences. The logical relation we are concerned with here—between reasons and actions—thus must be understood as holding between the *propositions* or *contents* that are the agent's reasons and his action *as described, or conceptualized, a certain way.*[3]

Causal relations, on the other hand, Davidson construes as holding directly between events, independently of how these events are described or conceptualized. According to Davidson, such causal relations obtain between the beliefs and desires of an agent and her actions. And there is nothing special about these causal relations; what we are dealing with is 'common and garden' causality between ordinary events in the world. Speaking of reasons, of beliefs, desires, and action is, according to Davidson, simply a particular way of describing certain of these ordinary events. Actions, for instance, are events that can also be described as bodily movements. Categorizing such a movement as, for instance, eating a piece of chocolate amounts to subsuming it under a particular type: a type of action. Correspondingly, beliefs and desires, or rather their formation, can be construed as mental events. The relevant causal relation then is supposed to hold directly between event *tokens*—irrespective of how these events are typed, that is, described or conceptualized. This distinction between 'event tokens' and their descriptions provides the key to the Davidsonian attempt at reconciling the two modes of explanation that otherwise might appear incompatible: reasons explanation and causal explanation. To see that they can be recon-

---

3. Davidson calls beliefs and desires themselves 'reasons'. This is harmless as long as it is not taken to mean that an agent's reason for doing something was *that he desired p* or *that he believed q*. Today, there is fairly widespread consensus that it is the proposition or content believed/desired that is an agent's reason. In order to *have* that reason, however, the agent has to have a propositional attitude towards that proposition or content. This is precisely the sense in which Davidson speaks of beliefs and desires as reasons: They are reasons had or possessed by the agent.

ciled, Davidson submits, we need to understand that one of them holds on the level of description while the other holds between description independent events. In what follows, we shall have a closer look at both levels, starting with the descriptions.

4.2.1 Reasons Explanations

4.2.1.1 Events and Descriptions

One of the two main claims of *Actions, Reasons, and Causes*, is the following: "In order to understand how a reason of any kind rationalizes an action it is necessary and sufficient that we see, at least in essential outline, how to construct a primary reason" (Davidson 1963, 4).[4] All the different ways of giving reasons for actions ultimately derive from a basic form of reason: *primary reasons*. Primary reasons are reasons of the most basic kind—such reasons exist for every action, be it ever so spontaneous, silly, or inconsequential. At the same time, their existence is presupposed in every more elaborate explanation.

According to Davidson, primary reasons consist of belief-desire pairs. Explanations by primary reasons work on the model of the practical syllogism. Imagine that I am sitting quietly on my living room sofa, pouring myself a cup of coffee. Asked why I am doing that, I could for instance provide the following reason: Because I want to drink a cup of coffee. This explanation, perfectly fine in everyday contexts, though a tiny bit pedantic, cites only the desire part. To see that something is missing, or rather that there is more to the explanation than has been made explicit, consider a different situation in which I am on an airplane going through a turbulence. Assume that we both believe that, in the

---

4. The second main claim, of course, is this: "The primary reason for an action is its cause" (Davidson 1963, 4).

current circumstances, pouring coffee into a cup is not a good way of getting to drink any. In these circumstances, the explanation given above would be no good. Explaining an action by a desire thus presupposes that the agent also has a belief of a certain kind, often a belief that the action performed is a good means to the end of satisfying one's desire. This is quite trivial and therefore most often not explicitly stated.

But even if we complete the explanation for my pouring the coffee by the belief that (in my quiet living room) pouring coffee into a cup is a good means for getting to drink it, what we have here is—despite its air of pedantry—not yet a primary reason. There are actions for which not even this much planning, this much means-ends rationality is in place. We do act on sudden urges or impulses without having any idea that such an action would be a means for some further end. Nevertheless, even such things can be intentional actions. If I feel a sudden urge to tap the table with my fingers, and act on it, I am doing it intentionally, even though I might very well not pursue any further end by doing that.

Even for intentionally tapping one's fingers on the table, there is a primary reason, Davidson claims. These most fundamental, most basic of reasons consist of the desire for an action of the relevant type ψ, for instance finger tapping, and the belief that a particular action a is of that type, is a ψing, for instance a finger tapping.[5]

Now, the number of our actions that are so clearly motivated by desires as drinking coffee is probably not that great. In order to cover all kinds of motivations for action, Davidson

---

5. It is sometimes said that according to Davidson all (practical) rationality is means-ends rationality (see, for instance, Wilson's reconstruction of Davidson's original causal account of intentional action, esp. (7*), in Wilson 2009). This strikes many as objectionable. But the objection is misguided. According to Davidson, the most fundamental form of practical rationality is that of having, and acting on, primary reasons. These do not involve any means-ends reasoning. Rather, what happens here is simply type-subsumption.

therefore introduces the quite general term "pro-attitude". Under the pro-attitudes fall "desires, wantings, urges, promptings, and a great variety of moral views, aesthetic principles, economic prejudices, social conventions, and public and private goals and values in so far as these can be interpreted as attitudes of an agent towards actions of a certain kind" (Davidson 1963, 4). Pro-attitudes can be very short-lived, but they can also be lifelong character traits of a person. Common to them all is that they are directed at those properties of actions that make them appear desirable to the agent: The agent has a positive attitude towards actions of that type. If the agent also believes that a particular action belongs to that type, he has a primary reason for performing that very action. We can now see that our earlier practical syllogism about eating chocolate actually was one involving a primary reason. It is primary reasons that have the form specified there:

(PR) (PA) $\forall x(\psi x \to Dx)$
      (Bel) ψa
      (Act) Da

Less basic reasons explanations could be of this form:

(R)   (PA$_1$) $\forall x(\phi x \to Dx)$
     (Bel$_1$) $\forall x(\psi x \rightsquigarrow \phi x)$
     (PA$_2$) $\forall x(\psi x \to Dx)$

where '$\rightsquigarrow$' stands for 'is a means for.' Such explanations do not conclude into actions; their conclusions are further pro-attitudes. If you have a pro-attitude towards an action of a certain type, let's say drinking coffee, and you believe that an action of another type, for instance, pouring coffee into a cup, will result in, or is a means for, your drinking coffee, then you have a reason to have a further pro-attitude towards this second type of action (cf. Davidson 1982b, 174). And now, we can see why primary reasons are both needed to complete the explanation, and why they are able to complete it: No other reasons conclude into, and thus explain, *particular* actions. But that is what needs explanation: particular actions.

Of course, for many actions it would feel rather unsatisfactory to be provided *only* with a primary reason; especially when actions are undertaken as means for further goals we are usually more interested in knowing about those goals than in knowing the primary reason. For instance, if I flip a switch in order to switch on the light in order to scare a burglar, these further goals and aims of my flipping will be far more important than the primary reason. In such cases, further explanations of the form (R) can be provided. If we look at these reasons as a reconstruction of a chain of reasoning on the agent's part, a chain of reasoning the agent of course need not have gone through explicitly or consciously, they can be seen as preceding the primary reason into which they in the end conclude. Primary reasons illustrate the way in which reasons 'rationalize:' They show what at the most basic level speaks for an action in the eyes of the agent. Moreover, they forge the link between the general reasoning, the general explanations an agent can provide, and particular actions. Without them, reasons explanations would 'run empty', so to speak; they would never 'touch the ground' of real action.[6] That is why understanding how

---

6. You might object that actions can be explained by citing character traits such as greed. Davidson counters that we only understand explanations citing character traits because we know which kinds of actions for instance a greedy person in general has pro-attitudes towards. We only understand such explanations, that is, because we know what kind of primary reasons such a person will be motivated by. Cf. Davidson 1963, 7.

to construct primary reasons is necessary for understanding "how a reason of any kind rationalizes an action" (Davidson 1963, 4).[7]

For this to be plausible, Davidson has to defend the claim that there is a primary reason *for each and every action*. Here is an objection we find in several places in the literature: Imagine that Mary kills her father thinking that he is a burglar. Imagine further that she does so by firing a single, deadly shot. We can explain her shooting her father by her falsely believing him to be a burglar. But, or so the objection goes, we cannot claim that Mary had a primary reason to shoot her father: Mary most certainly did not have any pro-attitude towards shooting her father.[8] Doesn't this show that *non-intentional actions* are not done for primary reasons?

But what *are* non-intentional actions? This question leads right into one of the most disputed areas of the theory of action—the question of *the identity of actions*. When are two actions identical? In our example, the question becomes acute because the following substitution goes through:

(4) Mary shot the burglar.
(5) The burglar = Mary's father.
(6) Mary shot her father.

So, how many actions did Mary perform? The proponents of nonintentional actions will have to say: Two. One of them, the

---

7. According to Davidson, understanding primary reasons is not only necessary, but also sufficient for understanding rationalization. This does not mean that there is no rationalization except rationalization by primary reasons. But since the 'logical mechanics' of rationalization are the same regardless of whether the reasons are primary or not, primary reasons are the heart of the matter: Once you have gotten your mind around them, the rest will fall into place.

8. Example from: Lepore and McLaughlin 1985, 10.

shooting of the burglar, was intentional, the other, the shooting of the father, was not. But did Mary shoot twice?

According to Davidson, this consequence is too counterintuitive to accept. He suggests an action theoretic *identity thesis* instead. Mary shoots just once, and Oedipus—to take a more classical example—marries just once: His mother and Iocasta. The difference, Davidson submits, is in the *description*. (4) is about the same event token as (6), but the latter provides a different description of that very same event.

Intuitive as this claim may be, it gives rise to a number of difficulties. The maybe most obvious difficulty is that the following substitution does not go through:

(7) Mary intentionally shot the burglar.
(5) The burglar = Mary's father.
(8) Mary intentionally shot her father.

In contrast to (6), (8) is false, even though (7) and (5) are true. It therefore seems false to say that (4) and (6) are about the same object—one and the same action can hardly be intentional and nonintentional at the same time. Moreover, merely observing that the adverb 'intentionally' somehow creates an intensional context does not seem to help. In intensional contexts, substitution of co-referential terms might not preserve truth value. That is what happens when we substitute 'her father' for 'burglar' in (7). But we were not concerned with the identity of the burglar. We were concerned with the identity of the event somehow 'described' by the whole of (4). And it seems as if in (7) and (8), the same property—being intentional—is both ascribed to, and denied of, this event.

In order to defend the identity thesis, Davidson thus first and foremost has to investigate what it even means to speak of an *event under a description* at all.[9] One issue here is that speaking of one and the same thing under different descriptions presupposes that there is such a thing, an object for these descriptions to be about. We have seen that Davidson thinks of this object as an event, but another issue immediately arises: Action sentences like (4) do not look as if they contained any references to events. Prima facie, no singular term referring to, nor any definite description of, any event is to be found in such sentences. Nevertheless, there is the intuitive feeling that these sentences are 'about' actions, or events. Davidson's solution to this puzzle is presented in one of his most controversial articles: *The Logical Form of Action Sentences* from 1967. We shall look at it in some detail in the following section.

4.2.1.2   The Logical Form of Action Sentences and Davidson's Ontology of Events

The basic idea of *The Logical Form of Action Sentences* is simple and intuitive: Actions are events in the spatio-temporal world, and as such one and the same event can satisfy very different predicates, and thus be described in very different terms. Oedipus's wedding is a particular, dated event that satisfies both 'is a marrying of Iocasta' and 'is a marrying of Oedipus's mother'. 'The wedding of Oedipus and Iocasta' and 'the wedding of Oedipus and his mother' thus literally are definite descriptions of one and the same event.

Events have been the focus of lively debate not only among philosophers, but also among linguists and logicians for quite a

---

9. The intuitively very appealing "under a description" formula is taken from Anscombe (cf. Anscombe 1957; 1979). Davidson's use of it is intended to be technical, however (cf. Davidson 1971b, 194).

while now. In the wake of Davidson's *The Logical Form of Action Sentences,*

> it has been generally agreed that a a great many natural lan-
> guage phenomena can be explained if (and—according to some
> authors—only if) we make room for logical forms in which ref-
> erence to or quantification over events is genuinely admitted.
> Nominalization, adverbial modification, tense and aspect, factives,
> anaphora, plurals, naked infinitives, singular causal statements,
> temporal reasoning—all of these (to mention just a few) are
> topics that have led to the formulation of sophisticated event-based
> semantic theories (Varzi and Pianesi 2000, 3f).

Here, we can only look at the Davidsonian beginnings of the rise of events.

In construing events as objects of description and reference Davidson is making an ontological claim: There are events. More-over, construing them as dated particulars that can be described in different terms, but exist independently of their descriptions, is making a whole bunch of metaphysical claims about events. Davidson thus has to defend both his semantics for action sentences and his metaphysics of events—his causal analysis of reasons explanations hinges on both. And both are highly controversial.[10]

---

10. Events have been construed both as particulars and as universals. The main defenders of the universal view are Montague 1969 and Chisholm 1970. Those construing events as particulars can be positioned on a scale of 'thickness' of individuation: On one extreme, there is Quine according to who's four-dimensional perdurantism events, just like mater-ial objects, are individuated solely by their spatio-temporal extension. This collapses the category of events into that of material objects (cf. Quine 1960, 131). Davidson construes events as three-dimensional, enduring entities (cf. Davidson 1985e); his events are some-what 'thinner' than Quine's, but by far not as 'thin' as, for instance, Kim's. Kim 1976, among others, construes events as property exemplifications. This excludes the possibility of dif-ferent descriptions of one and the same event. Kim, however, argues that his metaphysics

Suggestions for extending our ontology, the basic list of the categories of things that there are, are always controversial. Any suggested extension is suspect of violating Ockham's famous "razor": the maxim of ontological parsimony. According to this maxim, the question "What is there?" must be answered such that the number of categories or kinds is as small as possible.[11] And in the empiricist tradition, science is supposed to be the final arbiter of which categories are necessary. Quine, for instance, speaks with great satisfaction of his "well-swept ontology": It does not contain anything but concrete individuals and classes (cf. Quine 1985, 164).[12] According to Quine, these are the only kinds of objects our scientific theories force us to accept. Postulating additional entities thus is highly suspect.

How are existence claims to be justified? Quine's answer is this:

> What clinches matters is rather the quantification $'(\exists x)\,(x = a)'$. ... The bound variable 'x' ranges over the universe, and the existential quantification says that at least one of the objects in the universe satisfies the appended condition—in this case the condition

is compatible with the Davidsonian semantic analysis. For arguments against the independence of the metaphysics and semantics of events, and an excellent general introduction into event semantics and metaphysics, see Varzi and Pianesi 2000. Casati and Varzi 1997 provides a bibliography of the area up to 1997. A recent defense of the Davidsonian semantic analysis is Pietroski 2005.

11. The maxim of ontological parsimony is introduced by William of Ockham as a methodological principle of scientific explanation. It is often quoted as "entia non sunt multiplicanda preater necessitatem" (entities are not to be multiplied without necessity), but this formulation is not found in Ockham himself. Authentic however are the formulations: "pluralitas non est ponenda sine necessitate" (a multiplicity must not be assumed without necessity) and "frustra fix per plura quod fieri potest per pauciora" (it is pointless to do with more what can be achieved with less).

12. See also Quine 1992b, 5-9. In some places, Quine even argues that ultimately only classes are needed; cf. Quine 1976.

of being the object *a*. To show that some given object is required in a theory, what we have to show is no more nor less than that that object is required, for the truth of the theory, to be among the values over which the bound variables range (Quine 1968, 94).

Davidson does not quite agree. For him, the ultimate arbiter is, in a sense, natural language as a whole. What he is interested in is the implicit ontology of natural language, the shared intersubjective reality natural language presupposes. To make this ontology explicit then becomes a question of semantics: Which entities do we have to assume in our theoretical account of the meanings of natural language expressions? For Davidson, that question naturally is answered by investigating what kinds of entities a correct T-theory for a language *L* construes expressions of *L* as referring to and quantifying over.[13]

Determining which entities are referred to and quantified over in a language *L* depends on the logical form assigned to its sentences. This form has to be determined in accordance with two factors: First, the position of the sentence in the logical structure of *L*—that is, its logical or inferential relations to other sentences of *L*—and second, its composition out of less complex components also occurring in other sentences. Both the logical form of a sentence and the semantic interpretation of its components are theoretical constructions testable only on the level of whole sentences. Naturally, the same goes for the resulting ontology: "The logical relations between sentences provide the only real

---

13. These days, many metaphysicians are very skeptical towards semantic considerations as guides to ontology. See, for instance, Williamson 2007. But even though there of course is a difference between our concepts of things and the metaphysical constitution of those things, it is not completely clear that the 'evidence' the metaphysician has to go on, and the data used by semanticists ultimately are very different. Both work on the basis of widely shared intuitions as to the truth values of certain sentences.

test of when our language commits us to the existence of entities" (Davidson 1971b, 203).

Now we can see how Davidson can substantiate his claim about events and action sentences: He has to show that certain sentences can only be handled by T-theories if their logical form is such that it involves *reference to or quantification over events*. To satisfy more metaphysical qualms, however, Davidson also needs to tell us something about what events *are*. We would like to know what exactly distinguishes events from other kinds of entities, in particular from material objects. As we already saw, the question of their identity is also crucial; we need to know their criteria of identity, the conditions under which what might seem like two events really are one and the same—under different descriptions.

Here is the by now classical opening of *The Logical Form of Action Sentences*: "Strange goings on! Jones did it slowly, deliberately, in the bathroom, with a knife, at midnight. What he did was butter a piece of toast" (Davidson 1967b, 105). To facilitate analysis, Davidson starts with the following simpler example:[14]

(9)   Jones buttered a toast in the bathroom with a knife at midnight.

Here we have an action sentence containing multiple adverbial modifications. This plurality of descriptive elements appears to be somehow 'about' a single entity: that specific buttering. What we want to know is the logical form of (9). One very important job for logical forms to perform is to capture intuitive entailment

---

14. 'Deliberately' is left out because of its intensional nature. This is to be dealt with later. 'Slowly' is left out because attributive adjectives do pose a problem for logical form, but not one that is limited to action sentences.

relations. It is, for instance, intuitively extremely plausible to think that both (10) and (11) are entailed by (9):

(10)   Jones buttered the toast in the bathroom.
(11)   Jones buttered the toast.

To capture these entailments, Davidson construes action predicates as containing an additional place for an event, a place not reflected in their surface form: 'butter' thus would be a three-place predicate with places for an agent, an object, and an event. He completes the analysis of simple action sentences like (11) by construing them as existentially quantified (cf. Davidson 1967b, 119).[15] For (11), we thus get:

(11′) $\exists x$ (butters (Jones, the toast, x)).

In English, we could render (11′) along the following, admittedly inelegant lines: There is an event x such that x is a buttering of the toast by Jones.

According to Davidson, simple action sentences thus have the form of existentially quantified predications. They are *not*, and that is important, descriptions of events in the sense of referring, as a whole, to events. And despite being clearly reminiscent of Russell's theory of descriptions, Davidsonian action sentences do not contain any condition of singularity, either.[16] Rather, an action sentence is true iff there is at least one event that satisfies the predicate. But of course, one can form definite descriptions on the

15. As in Davidson himself, the tense of the analyzed sentence is neglected here. For more on this, see Davidson 1967b, 123f.

16. Russell 1905 famously analyzed sentences containing definite descriptions, e.g. sentences like 'The present king of France is bald', as existentially quantified sentences of the following form:

(i) $(\exists x)(Kx \,\&\, ((\forall y)(Ky \to y = x) \,\&\, Bx))$.

basis of such predications, descriptions such as 'the buttering of the toast by Jones'. Definite descriptions might, or might not be singular terms—but one can presumably also name these events and subsequently refer to them by what clearly are singular terms.[17] Davidson thus commits to the existence of events as dated particulars: *non-repeatable entities with definite spatio-temporal location.*

More complex adverbially modified action sentences Davidson construes as existentially quantified conjunctions. (10) then looks like this:

$$(10')\quad \exists x\,(\text{butters}\,(\text{Jones, the toast, } x))\ \&\ \text{in the bathroom}(x)).$$

This is true iff there is at least one event that is a buttering of the toast by Jones and happening in the bathroom. On this analysis, the entailment relation between (10) and (11) is obvious.[18]

There are, however, at least two sorts of adverbs resisting this kind of analysis. For one, the analysis is restricted to those adverbs that can be eliminated from a sentence without changing its truth value. A sentence like (12), however, should better not be treated as a conjunction of the suggested kind:

(12)   He almost hit the target.

17. According to Russell's analysis, definite descriptions are not singular terms. But Russell's analysis remains controversial; many semanticists prefer to think of definite descriptions as singular terms of the form *the F.*

18. By contrast, these entailments would be hard to explain if the predicate was analyzed as a two-place predicate. Other entailments we might be interested in here are, for instance, entailments of the following kind: (11) appears to entail (i):

(i)   Jones did something to the toast.

Such entailments are not captured by the original Davidsonian analysis. Parsons 1990 suggests amending the analysis by dedicating the places of action predicates to different "roles", roles such as that of agent and object. For more on this, as well as for general alternatives to Davidson's Russellian version of event semantics, see Varzi and Pianesi 2000.

And secondly, the analysis cannot be applied to attributive adverbs. As noted above, Davidson in the original example initially passes by the adverb 'slowly'. Other examples are 'tall', 'small', 'good' and 'bad'. One and the same channel crossing can, for instance, be a slow crossing but a fast swimming. Application of the suggested conjunctive analysis would imply that there is an event that is both slow and fast. However, the same problem arises with attributive adjectives—for instance, we can quite felicitously say of a man that he is tall for a man, but short for a basketball player. The problem, in other words, is not one generated by, or restricted to, the suggested analysis of action sentences. In this respect, the introduction of events into our ontology does not result in any problems that we didn't already have for material objects anyway. Since we have to solve this problem for both kinds of entities, Davidson argues, it can hardly be used as an argument against only one of them (cf. Davidson 1967b, 107.)[19]

In a way, Davidson builds the whole of his action theory on the ontology of events and the intuitively very appealing distinction between events and their descriptions. But how safe a foundation is this? *Identity conditions* are an important factor in arguments for and against admitting a category C of objects into our ontology. Only if we know how to distinguish an object o in C from other such objects, and how to reidentify o, do we know what kind of category of objects we are dealing with. Thus the Quinean maxim: "No entity without identity!" (cf. Quine 1958, 23). According to Davidson's take on this maxim, we must not allow a category C unless we can formulate a general criterion for the truth of identity statements about objects of C (cf. Davidson 1969a, 163).

---

19. For more on this, see Davidson 1969a, 180 and Davidson 1985d, 228f. Künne 1991 offers a suggestion for solving this problem, but in contrast to Davidson, he is willing to quantify over properties, too.

What, then, is the identity criterion for events? Davidson's first suggestion was the following:

(IE$_1$)   Events are identical if and only they have exactly the same causes and effects.   (Davidson 1969a, 179.)

(IE$_1$) is an expression of the idea that the causal nexus of events provides a framework in which each event has a unique position—"somewhat the way objects have a unique position in the spatial framework of objects" (Davidson 1969a, 179).

This criterion has been heavily criticized. Quine, for instance, argues that (IE$_1$), even though not formally circular, is nevertheless useless. For (IE$_1$) presupposes that we already know what it is supposed to teach us. Causes and effects of events are themselves events with their own unique place in the causal nexus. (IE$_1$) therefore "purports to individuate events by quantifying over events themselves" (Quine 1985, 166).[20]

In his reply to Quine, Davidson abondons (IE$_1$) and replaces it by the idea that events, like physical objects, are individuated by their space-time coordinates (cf. Davidson 1985e, 175):[21]

(IE$_2$)   Events are identical if and only if they occupy the same places at the same times.

Davidson also revokes the claim that (IE$_2$) forces us to identify events with material objects; events, he argues, may stand in a different relation to the space-time regions identifying them than objects occupying the very same regions do:

20. Cf. also Lepore 1985, 160.

21. This was first proposed by Lemmon 1967, but rejected in Davidson 1969a, 178f.

> Occupying the same portion of space-time, event and object differ. One is an object which remains the same object through changes, the other a change in an object or objects. Spatiotemporal areas do not distinguish them, but our predicates, our basic grammar, our ways of sorting do. Given my interest in the metaphysics implicit in our language, this is a distinction I do not want to give up (Davidson 1985e, 176).

But one might well wonder whether it is really the case that an identity statement '$a = b$', where a and b are events, is true iff a and b happen at the same place at the same time. Davidson himself earlier rejected this suggestion and claimed that two different events could without much problem happen at the same place and the same time. His example was that of a metal ball that gets warmer during a certain short interval of time and simultaneously rotates by 35 degrees (cf. Davidson 1969a, 178). Later, he seems to accept these as descriptions of one and the same event, commenting only that his earlier concern might have been overdone.

There might be more serious trouble, though, once we combine (IE_2) with the Davidsonian analysis of adverbially modified action sentences. Take an example: An astronaut is traveling on her spaceship, singing during the whole trip. She travels to Venus and she sings in F-major. Does this imply that our astronout sings to Venus? And that she travels in F-major?[22] It would also be interesting to investigate the relation between the causal criterion and the space-time criterion in a little more detail. After all, the causal criterion did seem intuitively correct, even though it wasn't suitable for working as a criterion of identity. The worry would be that (IE_2) prima facie seems to deliver identities that are not licensed

22. Cf. Bennett 1985, 200.

by (IE_1). Assume, for instance assume that our singing astronaut runs 10K and sings all the way. Her legs get quite sore from this—from what? Do we have to say that her singing caused the soreness in her legs?[23] If there is no way out of these difficulties, (IE_2) might not be the right criterion for event identity, either.

We will have to leave the final assessment of Davidson's ontology of events open here. We only went into events for the sake of his action theory, and it is high time to get back to that. In what follows, we shall simply assume that the identity problems of Davidsonian events can be solved.

4.2.1.3 Explanation is Redescription

Determining the logical form of action sentences advances Davidson's theory of action a decisive step. Now we can see what it means to speak of one and the same action under different descriptions. But one of our initial problems remains. Remember Mary who accidentally shot her father thinking he was a burglar. Above, we considered the sentence:

(7)   Mary intentionally shot the burglar.

Does (7) have the form of an existentially quantified conjunction? Is (7) true iff there is at least one event that is a shooting of the burglar by Mary *and intentional*? Never mind that it is a bit odd to talk of "intentional events" in ordinary English—construing (7) along the lines of the Davidsonian analysis of adverbially modified action sentences lands us in precisely the unhappy situation the analysis was supposed to get us out of. Since Mary's shooting

---

23. It is assumed here that causality is a relation between events, and statements to the effect that one event caused another are extensional. This is controversial, but clearly endorsed by Davidson himself. For more on this, see chapter 6.

of the burglar is the same event as her shooting her father, we would still have to say that one and the same event is both intentional and non-intentional. So far, all Davidson has gained is an understanding of what it means to speak of events under different descriptions—as long as these descriptions do *not* contain intentional adverbs.

But we still want to say that the shooting was intentional under one description, but not under the other. What does that mean, then? Davidson suggests that being intentional is *not* a property of an event. Rather, being intentional is *a relation between an agent, an event, and a description* (cf. Davidson 1967b, 121f; Davidson 1971b, 195).

This manoeuvre is made possible by a further characteristic of attributions of intent like (7), a characteristic they share with certain other 'mixed' attitudes like knowing, remembering, or perceiving that something is the case. All of these create intensional contexts in the sense that substitutions of co-extensional expressions do not necessarily preserve truth value. But they lack a characteristic that other attitude contexts, most notably belief contexts, possess: For it to be true that Mary believes that there is a winged horse there does not have to be any winged horse. By contrast,

(4)   Mary shot the burglar.

does follow from (7).[24] Thus, we can derive an ordinary action sentence—a sentence like (4)—from an attribution of intention.

---

24. Together with

(5)   The burglar = Mary's father,

(7) also implies that Mary shot her father. For these reasons, Davidson called attributions of intention (or knowledge, memory, perception etc.) "quasi-intensional" (cf. Davidson 1963, 5; Davidson 1985d, 225f).

This sentence in turn can be analyzed as an existential quantification over events, and since an event satisfying the description provided by the sentence is guaranteed to exist, this event is then available as a relatum in the three place relation that Davidson wants to construe being intentional as. Thus, he can analyze an ascription of intention like (7) in terms of a relation between the relevant agent, an ordinary action sentence derived from the original sentence, and the event satisfying the description given in that sentence. In somewhat awkward but plain English, we get for our example: It was intentional of Mary that there was an event that was her shooting the burglar. But it was not intentional of Mary that there was an event identical with her shooting her father. Importantly, this is not the same as an event's having and not having a certain property. Rather, the event, Mary and a certain description have a relation that the same event, Mary, and a different description do not have (cf. Davidson 1971b, 195).[25]

A consequence of this analysis of 'intentional' is that "intentional actions are not a class of actions, or, to put the point a little differently, doing something intentionally is not a manner of doing it" (Davidson 1967b, 121). Rather, if an event is an action at all, then there is at least one description under which it was intentional. Thus, we get the following condition for *agency*:

25. Davidson does not provide a more detailed analysis of the logical form of attributions of intention. What he does provide remains unsatisfactory insofar as it seems to require quantification over descriptions. Descriptions presumably are linguistic items, and just as for beliefs or other propositional attitudes, it is very implausible to construe intentions as dependent on any specific language, or as somehow 'about' sentences. However, what would be needed to complete the analysis seems to be precisely an analysis of propositional attitude contexts. In a footnote, Davidson consequently suggests completing the analysis of attributions of intention along the lines of the paratactic analysis of propositional attitude contexts (cf. Davidson 1971b, 196, fn. 12; see section 2.2.3.2). The third relatum required by ascriptions of intention, besides the agent and the event then would be an utterance, not a sentence. Thus, the third relatum would be a further event.

(A)   A person is the agent of an event iff there is a description of
      what he did that makes true a sentence that says he did it
      intentionally.   (Davidson 1971a, 46.)

Events for which there is no such description, no description characterizing them as the doings of an agent, are not actions at all.
In this sense, then, the Davidsonian claim is that *all actions are
intentional.*

Consequently, 'nonintentional actions' are no counterexample to the claim that all actions have primary reasons. What the
relevant examples show, according to Davidson, is merely that
there can be descriptions under which the agent did not intend
what is nevertheless her action—just as Mary certainly did not
intend to shoot her father:

> The relation that holds between a person and an event, when the
> event is an action performed by the person, holds regardless of how
> the terms are described. Therefore we can without confusion speak
> of the class of events that are actions, which we cannot do with
> intentional actions (Davidson 1971a, 47).

Moreover, we can now see how *redescriptions* at different levels of
intention can contribute to the explanation of one and the same
action. Here is an example:

> *Explaining* an action by giving an intention with which is was done
> provides new descriptions of the action: I am writing my name on a
> piece of paper with the intention of writing a cheque with the inten-
> tion of paying my gambling debt. List all the different descriptions
> of my action. Here are a few for a start: I am writing my name. I am
> writing my name on a piece of paper. I am writing my name on a
> piece of paper with the intention of writing a cheque. I am writing

a cheque. I am paying my gambling debt. It is hard to imagine how we can have a coherent theory of action unless we are allowed to say that each of these sentences is made true by the same action. *Redescription* may supply the motive ('I was getting my revenge'), place the action in the context of a rule ('I am castling'), give the outcome ('I killed him'), or provide evaluation ('I did the right thing') (Davidson 1967b, 110, second emph. added).

At the same time, new difficulties arise: Prima facie, the Davidsonian claim that all these descriptions are about the same event, seems to have counterintuitive consequences.[26] Let's return once more to Mary. She has fired her shot—but the burglar dies only much later. But clearly, Mary has both a) fired a shot at the burglar and b) killed him. According to Davidson, these are descriptions of the same action. But Mary stopped shooting long before the poor guy died. And shouldn't events that occupy different stretches of time be different events?

Davidson's answer is that it is a mistake to think that we are dealing with events occupying different stretches of time here: "The mistake consists in thinking that when the description of an event is made to include reference to a consequence, then the consequence itself is included in the described event" (Davidson 1971a, 58). And he gives an instructive analogue: his paternal great-great-grandfather. When Clarence Herbert Davidson from Inverness was still alive, he could not truly be described as Donald Davidson's paternal great-great-grandfather. Nevertheless, this is the same person (cf. Davidson 1987c, 105).

Actions can thus be described in terms of their causal consequences even if those consequences are temporally quite far away from the event that is the action. In order to kill, Mary does not

---

26. For difficulties of the following type, see in particular the classical Thompson 1971.

have to do anything more than shoot. According to Davidson, this has the following intriguing consequence:

> We must conclude, perhaps with a shock of surprise, that our primitive actions, the ones we do not do by doing something else, mere movements of the body—these are all the actions there are. We never do more than move our bodies: the rest is up to nature (Davidson 1971a, 59).

The redescriptions of an action in terms of its consequences are by no means restricted to so-called "causal verbs" like 'to kill'. These predicates presuppose the 'success' of the relevant action. But what is called the "accordion effect" shows that actions—independently of the kind of predicate used—can be described in terms of their effects no matter how far away these are on the relevant causal chain: "A man moves his finger, let us say intentionally, thus flicking the switch, causing a light to comes on, the room to be illuminated, and a prowler to be alerted" (Davidson 1971a, 53). The chain could be continued. Just like an accordion, the description of the action can be extended to remote consequences of the action; at the same time, just like an accordion, it can be squeezed down to primitive actions such as finger movements.[27]

Where does all this leave us? With the claim that for every action there is a primary reason, Davidson has provided a necessary condition for an event's being an action. An event *x*, that is, is an action by an agent *A* only if *A* has a primary reason for *x*. A primary reason, again, is a belief-desire pair where the desire

---

27. Of course, not every redescription of an action in terms of its consequences will be explanatory: "The difference between explanatory and non-explanatory redescriptions is that the explanatory redescriptions supply a purpose with which which the agent acted, an intention" (cf. Davidson 1987c, 105).

is directed at a type of action ψ and the belief is a belief that a particular action a is of type ψ. But this condition is, of course, not sufficient. As we saw above, A can have any number of suitable primary reasons for a. What we are interested in is *the* reason for which A did a, that is, the reason that *explains* the action. According to Davidson that is the *causally effective reason*. It is to this part of the Davidsonian account of action explanation that we shall turn now.

4.2.2 Rationalization and Causal Explanation

Davidson wants to show that reasons explanation and causal explanation are compatible. More precisely, his claim is that any (true) reasons explanation in fact describes a causal relation between two events. To see how he implements this, we have to have a quick look at the notion of causality.

In the empiricist tradition, Hume is the crown witness when it comes to causal matters. Causal relations, according to Hume, cannot be observed as such. Rather, we speak of cause and effect where certain types of event always occur together; more precisely, when they occur in a way allowing the formulation of *causal laws* about them. Causal laws, then, are understood as universally quantified conditionals. These conditionals are based on induction, confirmed by observation, and they support counterfactuals.

According to this view, a singular causal statement—a statement of the form 'event x caused event y'—can only be understood as an *explanation* of y if there is a corresponding law 'covering it' or 'backing it up'. To say of a particular event x that it caused another particular event y, that is, is saying that x and y each belong to a type of event for which there is a causal law to the effect that

Xs cause Ys. Davidson calls this "the Principle of the Nomological Character of Causality" (Davidson 1970b, 208):

(NCC)   If two events are related as cause and effect, there is a strict law covering the case.   (Davidson 1995b, 266.)

This is the background on which Davidson now brings to bear the distinction between event tokens and their various descriptions. According to him, the logical form of singular causal statements is such that they contain descriptions of two event tokens. (13), for instance, has the logical form (13'):

(13)   The short circuit caused the fire.

(13') $(\imath x)\,(\imath y)\,((x = \text{a short circuit})\ \&\ (y = \text{a fire})\ \&\ (x \text{ caused } y))$

In other words: This x and this y are such that x is a short circuit, y is a fire, and x caused y.

The causal *relation* itself, Davidson claims, obtains between two event tokens—no matter how they are described. Consequently, sentences of the form (13') are extensional: coextensional expressions can be substituted salva veritate. Causal *laws*, by contrast, operate on the level of descriptions; their truth or validity depends on how events are described—that is, how they are *typed*. Moreover, the laws whose existence is entailed by true singular causal statements are *strict* laws: According to Davidson, strict laws do not admit of exceptions, they are not hedged by ceteris paribus clauses, they are supported by their instances and they support counterfactuals.[28]

---

28. For more on strict laws, see chapter 6, section 6.1. According to Davidson, such laws are possible only within a "closed system". Such a system both possesses the conceptual resources to describe every event y causally interacting with any event x within its domain

We thus get the following picture: Whenever two events x and y are causally related, there have to be descriptions under which these events can be subsumed under a strict law. That is, x and y have to be tokens of types for which there is such a law. Let's symbolize these types by 'P_1' and 'P_2'. If we know the law subsuming x and y, we can derive a singular causal statement from it describing x and y as belonging to these types. This statement has the following form:

(14) $(\iota x)\,(\iota y)\,((P_1\ x)\ \&\ (P_2\ y)\ \&\ (x\ \text{caused}\ y))$

But x and y can be described in various other ways. And since a statement of the form (14) is as extensional as any other singular causal statements, any of these descriptions can be substituted into it without changing its truth value. (13) would be precisely an example of a true singular causal statement where the causally related events are subsumed under types prima facie not suited for the formulation of strict laws.

Thus, according to Davidson, there can be any number of singular causal statements about any two causally related events. For these to be true, the events do not have to be described as instances of a causal law. Moreover, we do not even have to have any idea what the relevant law would be. All we need to know is that, if the statement is true, there is a law.[29]

and to subsume the interaction under a law belonging to the system. There are a number of places in which Davidson argues that only an ideal physics could provide such a closed system; outside an ideal physics, there are no strict laws (cf. Davidson 1987c, 113, Davidson 1993b, 8). It is not quite clear how much overall weight he intended to be put on this, though. For critical discussion, see Yalowitz 2005, 5.5.

29. An influential objection to Davidson's construal of singular causal statements is the following: According to Davidson, singular causal statements are extensional. But explanations are *not*. Explanatory force *is* dependent upon the properties the events cited as

Davidson's central action theoretic claim now is: Reasons explanations can be understood *as singular causal statements*. Contrary to the conclusion of the logical connection argument, that is, reasons explanations are statements about distinct events. What was right about these arguments, Davidson contends, is that reasons explanations do not provide an independent description of the cause of an action. But it is precisely the *description* of the cause that is dependent on that of the action, not the cause itself.

But are reasons events? Reasons themselves are not events, but having a reason is a mental event, Davidson maintains. More precisely, there are mental events related to the having of reasons that are suitable for his purposes:

> In many cases it is not difficult at all to find events very closely associated with the primary reason. States and dispositions are not events, but the onslaught of a state or disposition is. A desire to hurt your feelings may spring up at the moment you anger me; I may start wanting to eat a melon just when I see one; and beliefs may begin at the moment we notice, learn, or remember something (Davidson 1963, 12).[30]

cause and effect are described as having. The main underlying idea here is that of a certain counterfactual dependence: Event *a* would not have caused event *b* had *a* lacked property *P*. There is thus a distinction between those properties of *a* that are relevant to its causing another event *b*, and those that are not. That the blue billiard ball went into the hole when hit by the red billiard ball, for instance, does *not* seem to depend on the red ball's color—in contrast to its speed and direction. A singular causal statement, the claim then is, provides a causal explanation only if the causally relevant properties figure in it. For Davidson's reply and a more detailed discussion of both objection and reply, see chapter 6, section 6.2.

30. Davidson is by no means alone in thinking of (the formation of) mental states as events. Not only is this idea quite intuitive and widely shared throughout analytic philosophy, it is also found in the phenomenological tradition from Brentano and Husserl onwards.

Providing reasons explanations is ascribing propositional attitudes: beliefs and desires. By construing ascriptions of propositional attitudes in the context of action explanations as descriptions of independent events, Davidson can thus reconcile reasons explanation and causal explanation: Reasons explanations are singular causal statements. And that, Davidson maintains, suffices to vindicate the second main claim he made in *Actions, Reasons, and Causes*: "A primary reason for an action is its cause" (Davidson 1963, 12).

His analysis of the logical form of action sentences together with that of singular causal statements and his account of causal relations in general thus allows Davidson to account for the full force of the 'because' that is so central to the relation between a reason and the action it explains. He can now spell out "the idea that the agent performed the action *because* he had the reason" (Davidson 1963, 9) by singling out *the* primary reason for which the agent acted as the reason that *caused* the action.[31]

---

31. The view that reasons explanations are causal explanation has been dominant ever since Davidson 1963, and it remains dominant even today. Nevertheless, it is not uncontroversial. Objections have mainly come from two sides. Some philosophers have maintained that action explanations have a *teleological*, goal-directed dimension that is not captured by the idea of being caused by reasons (cf. Wilson 1989; Ginet 1990). More recently, the distinction between "motivating" and "justifying" or "normative" reasons has been used to argue that action explanation has a normative dimension that is not captured by the causal construal. Motivating and normative reasons can come apart, and what makes an action intelligible from his own perspective, the claim is, are an agent's normative reasons. So far, both the existence and the precise nature of "normative reasons" remain very controversial, however. (For a good introduction and overview, cf. Lenman 2010.) An unresolved issue relevant in this context is, for instance, how to account for the influence an agent's normative reasons have on his desires or his practical reasoning. This crucially depends on whether or not the relation between motivating reasons and action is construed as causal, but even if it is, it is not immediately clear how to implement the influence of normative reasons in a Davidsonian belief-desire model. For a suggestion, cf. Smith 2003. For a recent defense of causalism and further references, see Mele 2003.

4.2.3 Neither Laws nor Definitions

Davidson draws two intriguing consequences from the results obtained so far. Both are of a negative character, and both are somewhat surprising. For one, analyzing reasons explanations as singular causal statements does not commit us to the existence of *psychological laws*, Davidson argues. Nor, and that is the other, does it provide us with the materials for a *definition of intentional action*.

Let's look at the laws first. If rationalization is a species of causal explanation, there are strict laws covering the relevant singular causal statements. This is a simple consequence of the Neo-Humean conception of causation Davidson develops. But, and that is Davidson's point, these laws do not have to be formulated in the same terms as the singular causal statements. Applied to any particular reasons explanation, this means that there does not have to be a *psychological* law subsuming having those reasons and acting in that way. There does not have to be any law, that is, that describes the relevant events *as mental events* at all.

Moreover, not only is it the case that there does not have to be any such law—according to Davidson there *cannot be*. The significance of this issue must not be underestimated: What is at stake might well be the possibility of a scientific psychology. Are there any psychological laws worth speaking of? And does Davidson claim that there cannot be? We'll return to these questions soon. First, let's ask why there cannot be strict psychological laws, laws describing events as belonging to mental types such as beliefs and desires.

A strict psychological law would describe causes (propositional attitudes) and effects (actions) in intentional vocabulary. But, Davidson argues, no strict laws can be formulated in this vocabulary. Take my pouring a cup of coffee and its primary reason again. A corresponding law would have to be formulated along the following lines:

(MM) For all agents A: If A has a pro-attitude towards actions of the type pouring-a-cup-of-coffee and believes that a particular action a is of this type then A performs a.

But (MM) is obviously false. In order to make it into some sort of true generalization, (MM) would have to be hedged by as many exception clauses as there are possible reasons for, or even mere causes of, not performing an action for which one has a primary reason. And there are plenty of those: The agent can have other, more weighty reasons against a, or simply desire an action of a different, incompatible type even more, the agent can simply neglect to ever put his belief and desire together, he can be prevented from doing a, or lack the practical knowledge of how to do a, to name but a few. In general, there probably is something like a tendency to perform an action if one has a primary reason for, and no stronger reasons against it. If that is correct, then ascribing a primary reason is ascribing a *disposition*, a disposition to act in a certain way. But there certainly is no strict psychological law backing up reasons explanations: Strict laws do not allow of exceptions—but when it comes to tendencies to act on a primary reasons, "most such tendencies are not realized" (Davidson 1987c, 109).

This claim—that there are no strict psychological laws—is part of the famous Davidsonian doctrine of the *anomalism of the mental*: This is is the claim that there are no strict laws at all on the basis of which we could predict and explain mental events (cf. Davidson 1970b, 208). We shall look at this claim in much more detail when we examine Davidson's metaphysics of the mental in chapter 6. From the extensive debate surrounding it we shall only consider those elements most pertinent to psychological explanation and action theory now.

The claim that there are no strict psychological laws might well appear objectionable enough just by itself. The doctrine might not only threaten the possibility of a scientific psychology, it might moreover ultimately endanger precisely what Davidson most wants to account for—the explanatory force of the intentional, of explanations in terms of beliefs, desires, and reasons in general.

The explanatory force of the intentional might seem to be threatened because reasons explanations—construed the Davidsonian way—do not cite those properties, or types of events, that figure in the strict laws covering them. But surely, one might feel like saying, the properties figuring in the relevant covering laws are the properties that are *causally relevant*.[32] They are the ones doing the explaining, so to speak. Citing some other properties the events we are interested in also happen to have might be completely irrelevant and thus not explain anything.

Consider the following example taken from Dretske (1989): A soprano is singing an aria. Her singing of the aria shatters the glass in a nearby window. Intuitively, it is facts about the acoustic properties of the singing that are relevant to the breaking. The glass did not break because the soprano was singing words, and even less because of the meanings those words had. By contrast, when we explain an action by means of propositional attitudes, what intuitively matters are precisely the *contents* of those attitudes. But how do we account for this contrast if there are no psychological laws? Shouldn't the law covering a causal explanation be formulated precisely in terms of the causally relevant properties?

32. See note 29.

We can develop Davidson's answers to these worries together. Davidson claims that there are no strict psychological laws. The absence of strict laws, however, is not specific to psychology. According to Davidson, it affects not only the social sciences, but all of the special sciences—that is, even natural sciences such as geology, biology, and, of course, meteorology (cf. Davidson 1987c, 113). That mental events cannot be predicted and explained by strict laws is thus something they have in common with a lot of other natural phenomena, including the weather. Psychology as a science thus stands or falls together with all these other sciences. According to Davidson, it stands: "This feature in itself makes psychological theory no less scientific than volcanology, biology, meteorology, or the theory of evolution" (Davidson 1995a, 131).

Most interesting here is, of course, the comparison with the special sciences. These do not make any essential use of intentional vocabulary. But according to Davidson, their explanations nevertheless share a crucial characteristic with reasons explanations: they use notions that are *irreducibly causal* (cf. Davidson 1991, 216). As we saw, Davidson construes beliefs and desires as causal notions, as dispositions to cause certain types of actions. According to Davidson, explanations in the special sciences also contain ineliminable causal elements of this kind. Generalizations or laws formulated in terms of these notions cannot be strict; they will always admit of exceptions and contain so-called ceteris paribus clauses. Moreover, in the absence of strict laws subsuming the event types figuring in such explanations, the use of causal concepts is precisely what provides them with explanatory force:

> Lacking a law of the right kind, it is essential to advert to the causal relation, since the belief and the desire might be present, and the action take place, and yet the belief and the desire not explain the

action. If adequate laws were available, there would be no need to describe the cause in terms of the effects it tends to produce, just as, when sophisticated laws are in hand, we can dispense with reference to such dispositions as being soluble or frangible in explaining why an object dissolved or broke (Davidson 1987c, 109).

To illustrate, Davidson compares using causal notions like those of belief and desire to explain actions with explaining the attraction a piece of iron has on other pieces of iron by its being a magnet.

This very comparison, however, might already raise worries about explanatory force. Davidson dubs the maybe most pressing worry here "the Moliere factor": Isn't using causal dispositions to explain events like 'explaining' the fact that a pill put someone to sleep by its dormitive power? That is, no explanation at all? Davidson counters that it is simply not true that citing the dormitive power of the pill has no explanatory power. We do learn something from that explanation, namely that the pill was not a placebo. Explanatory power, that is, comes with the exclusion of (relevant) possibilities. And when it comes to action explanation, a lot of possibilities are excluded: "Much of the explanatory force of reasons-explanations comes from the fact that they specify which pair, from among the vast number of belief-desire pairs that were suited to cause the action, actually did cause it" (Davidson 1987c, 109).[33]

According to Davidson, it is thus not the case that the absence of strict covering laws necessarily robs singular causal statements of all explanatory force. Not even simple Moliere-style causal explanations are completely without such force—much less so,

---

33. Jacob 1991, 62ff further develops this idea to defend the causal efficacy of the mental in general.

according to Davidson, are reasons explanations. Nevertheless, there is a sense in which explanations in terms of causal concepts "are in some sense low-grade; they explain less than the best explanations in the hard sciences because of their heavy dependence on causal propensities" (Davidson 1987c, 109).

The absence of strict covering laws also does not imply the absence of laws in general. Even if there is no *strict* law covering a singular causal statement there might well be a true generalization or ceteris paribus law that does. Davidson does not deny that there are important and interesting psychological regularities; "indeed," he comments, "much of my writing on action is devoted to spelling out the sort of *general causal connections* that are essential to our ways of understanding, describing, explaining, and predicting actions, what causes them and what they cause" (Davidson 1993b, 14, emphasis added). If you want to call these regularities "laws", Davidson says, that's fine (Davidson 1993b, 9). His point is that these laws aren't strict—and cannot be made into, or reduced to, strict laws, either.[34] But, as we already saw, this is the case for the laws of the special sciences, too. And it would certainly be very implausible to demand more in terms of strictness from the laws of psychology than from those of the special sciences.

---

34. Davidson's idea here is that the strict laws covering intentional explanations are physical laws, laws, that is, formulated in the terminology of a completed, or ideal, physics. We do not have to know these laws in order to know the truth of an intentional explanation. All we need to know is that there is such a law. For more on reduction, and the Davidsonian arguments against the reducibility of the mental to the physical, see chapter 6. Kim 1989a argues that if psychological generalizations cannot be reduced to the laws of physics, there will be two complete, but independent explanations for actions, a physical and a psychological one. This, he argues, violates a "principle of explanatory exclusion": if there are two complete and independent explanations of the same event, one of them must be false. This principle is very controversial, however (for discussion, see Lepore and Loewer 1987; Jacob 1991). Wilson 2009 argues that if explanatory exclusion holds for action explanation construed as causal, this would be a strong reason to search for a workable account of action explanation that construes it as non-causal.

According to Davidson, psychology thus is as much of a science as the special sciences are.[35]

We shall leave the issue of psychological laws for now (but there will be more in chapter 6) and turn to the other, maybe even more surprising claim Davidson makes about construing reasons explanations as causal explanations: This move does *not* provide us with the materials for *a definition of intentional action*. Central to Davidson's argument is a phenomenon called "deviant causal chains": Deviant causal chains provide counterexamples to the idea that an intentional action could be defined as an event caused by a primary reason.

Take the following scenario: a desolate mountain range in the American West. Smith is pursuing Jones with the intention of shooting him. He confronts Jones, aims and fires. The shot misses Jones. But its echo, horribly magnified by the steep slopes of the Sierra Nevada, causes panic amongst a herd of wild boar. In blind fury, they stampede down the mountain side and trample Jones to death (cf. Davidson 1973a, 78).[36]

In this example, Smith clearly doesn't shoot Jones. But the point is that he does not even kill Jones intentionally—even though he has the right kind of primary reason *and* this primary reason is the cause of Jones' death. Davidson comments: "The point is that not just any causal connection between rationalizing attitudes and a wanted effect suffices to guarantee that producing

---

35. Jerry Fodor agrees: "All that anybody could reasonably want for psychology is that its constructs should enjoy whatever sort of explanatory/causal role is proper to the constructs of the special sciences" (Fodor 1989, 63). However, the worry was that psychological properties are causally irrelevant. In order to show that they are not, we need to do more, Fodor argues, than just show that we could use the very same reasons to argue that all the (non-physical) properties mentioned in the theories of the special sciences are causally irrelevant. We also need an account of causal relevance or efficacy. The question then would be what a Davidsonian account of causal efficacy would look like. For more on this, see chapter 6.2.

36. Davidson credits the example to Daniel Bennett.

the wanted effect was intentional. The causal chain must follow *the right sort of route*" (Davidson 1973a, 78, emphasis added).

The right sort of route, however, cannot be further specified, Davidson argues. For even if we could find criteria for excluding deviant *external* causal chains like the one in the example, there always remains the possibility of *internally* deviant chains. Even a primitive bodily movement has to be caused in the right way to be an intentional action. Here is Davidson's example of an internally deviant chain:

> A climber might want to rid himself of the weight and danger of holding another man on a rope, and he might know that by loosening his hold on the rope he could rid himself of the weight and danger. This belief and want might so unnerve him as to cause him to loosen his hold, and yet it might be the case that he never chose to loosen his hold, nor did he do it intentionally (Davidson 1973a, 79).

In this example, the climber loosens his hold, but this bodily movement is not an action at all; it remains a mere event. It is not something he does, but something that happens to him. According to Davidson, it is simply impossible to get rid of the possibility of deviant causal chains (cf. Davidson 1973a, 79): Intentional action cannot be defined, or fully analyzed, in terms of primary reasons and causality.[37]

37. Amongst those who disagree is John Searle. In Searle 1983, he proposes to distinguish between two kinds of intention, "prior intentions" and "intentions in action" (84ff). Acting on a prior intention requires this intention to cause an intention in action (91ff). Since even this allows for deviances (cf. 135ff), however, Searle adds further conditions. One of them is that the causal chain must instantiate some "plannable regularity" (140). What is plannable for an agent, however, depends not only on the way the world is, but also on what she believes about it. Consequently, there seems little chance of completing the analysis along these lines, either.

4.3 Practical Reasoning

According to Davidson, reasons explanations must be understood as causal explanations to account for their explanatory force. For reasons explanations not only tell us that the agent had a certain primary reason, but "they specify which pair, from among the vast number of belief-desire pairs that were suited to cause the action, actually did cause it" (Davidson 1987c, 109). To round off our tour of Davidsonian action theory we now need to get back to the beginnings: to the practical syllogism. For it is as yet completely unclear how the syllogistic model of action explanation can even allow for a plurality of primary reasons, only some of which are acted upon.

In its original, Aristotelian form, a practical syllogism is a simple deduction concluding into an action. It models actions as logical consequences of beliefs and desires. Not acting on a primary reason would thus amount to some sort of irrationality. But not only is it the case that an agent normally has any number of suitable primary reasons for any particular action, it is moreover normally the case that the decision for a particular action at the same time is a decision against any number of other actions that the agent also has (any number of) primary reasons for. In this sense, any decision for a particular action expresses, or is the result of, an evaluative judgment about the relative merits of a plurality of (possible) actions.

The simple syllogistic model of action explanation completely misses this comparative character of the practical reasoning it must aim at providing a rational reconstruction of.[38] If this reasoning were syllogistic, outright contradictions would arise as soon

---

38. These days, 'practical reasoning' is sometimes used to exclusively mean practical deliberation, i.e. explicit, conscious reasoning about one's reasons for action. It is important to remember that this is not at all how Davidson uses the term; see section 4.1, esp. p.157.

as an agent has reasons both for, and against, a particular action. Remember the chocolate I wanted to eat because I craved something sweet? Now, assume that I know that that piece of chocolate is poisoned (and that I do not desire to eat something poisonous). But I still desire to eat something sweet. So, I have both a primary reason to eat that piece of chocolate and a primary reason not to eat it. According to the simple syllogistic model this not only lands me in an outright contradiction—it also has the impossible consequence that I both eat the chocolate and do not eat it.

Thus, processes of practical reasoning cannot adequately be reconstructed by means of the practical syllogism. The relation between primary reason and action is more complex than so far assumed. To deal with this complexity, Davidson develops a revised model of practical reasoning. This model is designed to not only deal with conflicting reasons, but also with two other phenomena the practical syllogism cannot handle: "pure" intentions and weakness of the will.

Pure intentions are intentions an agent forms, but—for some reason or other—does not act on. Their existence requires that practical reasoning concludes into intentions, not directly into actions. There needs to be a mental event 'between' primary reason and action, so to speak.[39] Davidson construes intentions as, or models them by, evaluative judgments.[40] We shall come back

39. Cf. Davidson 1978. In Davidson 1963, Davidson claimed that "the expression 'the intention with which James went to church' has the outward from of a description, but in fact it is syncategorematic and cannot be taken to refer to an entity, state, disposition, or event" (8). At that time, Davidson took the notion of acting with an intention to be basic to action theory (cf. Davidson 1980a, xiii.) Recognizing pure intentions forced him to revise this.

40. Alternative construals of intention include the following: Inspired by Grice 1971, Velleman 1989 identifies an intention with a self-referential belief of the agent to the effect that he is presently, or will in the future be, doing a certain act, and that this act is performed as a consequence of this belief. Castañeda 1975, influenced by Sellars 1966, construed intentions as "practitions", a species of self-command. Bratman 1987 proposes a functionalist account: According to him, intentions can be defined in terms of their functional role.

to pure intentions later; for now, it suffices to say that, just as the practical syllogism, the revised model of practical reasoning concludes with an evaluative judgement, a judgment of desirability, but this now represents an intention, not an action.

Weakness of the will or *akrasia* is a form of practical irrationality: The akratic is someone who judges it best to do one thing—but intentionally does another. Thus, you might judge it best not to have dessert, but nevertheless order mousse au chocolat. Or you might come to the conclusion that, since you are already in bed, it is best not to get up again and brush your teeth. Nevertheless, duty getting the better of you, you jump out of bed and do brush your teeth (cf. Davidson 1970a, 30).[41] Weakness of the will is important here simply because most people think that it not only is possible, but even that it happens all the time. But if the relation between reasons and intentions is deductive, weakness of the will is simply impossible. As long as the conclusion, the intention, follows logically from the premises, there is no room for the akratic.

We thus need a model of practical reasoning that accomplishes three things: It distinguishes between intention and action, it models practical decision making as a process of weighing reasons, and it allows for weakness of the will. To achieve all this, Davidson argues, the first thing we need to do is modify the logical form assigned to desires or pro-attitudes.

All our problems, Davidson observes, result from construing these as universally quantified conditionals. But this is a mistake; surely a desire for eating something sweet cannot be construed as an "unconditional" judgment that any such action of mine is desirable. Rather, such an action is desirable only *insofar as* it is

---

41. Davidson uses this example to show that weakness of the will does not imply breach of duty or acting against what's judged to be morally best.

eating something sweet. In other words, an action that is eating something sweet has a certain desirable characteristic. But the very same action might very well have other, undesirable characteristics. Such a judgement warrants nothing more than a conclusion to the effect that an action is desirable in a certain respect.

Therefore, Davidson suggests construing desires as "conditional" judgements of a certain type. Borrowing from moral philosophy, he calls such judgements "prima facie judgements."[42] So, instead of (1) we want something like

(PFPA)   That an action is eating something sweet prima facie makes it desirable.

Formally, 'prima facie' is construed as a sentential connective. More precisely, 'prima facie' operates on pairs of sentences just like 'if then': "The concept of the prima facie ... relates propositions. In logical grammar, 'prima facie' is not an operator on single sentences, much less on predicates of actions, but on pairs of sentences related as (expressing) ... judgment and ground" (Davidson 1970a, 38). 'Prima facie' is very different from the material conditional, however: It does not allow for detachment. Any conclusion drawn from a prima facie judgement is itself a prima facie judgment: The desirability judgment cannot be detached from the reasons given for it. The conclusion always is a conclusion to the effect that an action is desirable for certain reasons—never a conclusion to the effect that an action simply is desirable.[43]

---

42. Cf. Davidson 1978, 98; Davidson 1970a, 38f; Spitzley 1990.

43. Davidson suggests assigning the following logical form to (15):

(i) $pf(Dx, \psi x)$

The crucial point then is supposed to be the following: The conclusion to be drawn from (i) and

According to Davidson, this is as it should be. Modeling desire as prima facie judgement of desirability allows us to understand how one and the same action can have characteristics that make it both desirable and undesirable—without getting into contradictions. Reasons for and against an action then can be weighed against each other; the result will depend on the strengths of the desires and the likelihood accorded to achieving them. Reasons for and against different, but incompatible actions can also be weighed against one another. These processes can be described by means of the calculus of decision theory and they result in judgements Davidson calls "all things considered judgements" (cf. Davidson 1970a, 39). An all things considered judgement is one an agent has reached by taking into account all relevant reasons known to her. Even an all things considered judgement remains prima facie, however. Such a judgement has the form

(16) $pf(Da, r)$,

where r is all the relevant reasons known to the agent.

(ii) ψa

would be

(iii) $pf(Da, (\text{i}) \text{ and } (\text{ii}))$ (cf. Davidson 1970a, 38.)

But this is odd. As formulated, (i) contains free variables and therefore does not express a proposition. Nevertheless, it is put into argument position in (iii). Presumably, Davidson is suppressing a universal quantifier here (cf. Spitzley 1990, 50, fn. 4). The 'real' logical form of (15) then is

(i′) $\forall x\, (pf(Dx, \psi x))$

But in that case, we can derive

(iv) $pf(Da, \psi a)$

by universal instantiation. What we get from that, is not (iii), however, but

(iii′) $pf(Da, (\text{ii}))$

As far as I can tell, all Davidson's philosophical points are preserved by this way of formalizing prima facie inferences—most importantly, detachment remains impossible so that all conclusions from prima facie premises remain prima facie themselves.

An intention, however, cannot be a prima facie judgement, according to Davidson. An intention can only be what he calls an "all-out judgement": An "unconditional" judgement to the effect that an action is desirable. So, how do we ever get from (16) to the corresponding intention, i.e. to $(3')$?

$(3')$ Da

The inference from (16) to $(3')$, and that is precisely the point here, is *not logically valid*. That is why weakness of the will is so much as possible: The step from the all things considered judgement as to which action is best does not logically 'force' the agent to form the corresponding intention. She *can* form the intention to do something else. Doing so, however, is highly *irrational*.

Nevertheless, the inference is 'licensed'—not by logic, but by rationality. What licenses the inference thus is not logic, but rationality. More precisely, what licenses forming an intention is a *principle of rationality*, a principle that Davidson calls "the principle of continence" (Davidson 1970a, 41):

(P_{Cont}) Perform the action judged best on the basis of all available relevant reasons

The revised Davidsonian model of practical reasoning works with two basic kinds of pro-attitudes: On the one hand, there are the desires in all their variety. These are construed as prima facie judgements of desirability. On the other hand, there are the intentions. These are construed as all-out judgements of desirability. Getting from desires to intentions requires a complex process of weighing reasons. This process takes into account relevant beliefs (about the likely outcomes of one's actions), and it involves further prima facie judgements concerning the comparative desirability of actions of different types, including all things considered judgements as to which action is best (at a certain time). It can be described by means of the calculus of decision making under uncertainty. Since prima facie premises logically entail nothing but prima facie conclusions, however, the model crucially involves an informal step: The step from an all things considered judgement to an intention is not formally valid. Instead, it is licensed by a principle of rationality, the principle of continence.

Two more questions remain: What is the relation between intention and action on this model? And what about pure intentions? Even though distinct from actions, intentions remain very closely connected to actions, according to Davidson: "If someone forms an intention to act immediately, and nothing stops him, then he acts" (Davidson 1985d, 214f). There are, however, intentions that do not get acted on even though there is no outward force stopping the agent. The agent might simply change his mind. In order to allow for such intentions, Davidson argues, we need to distinguish between intentions to act immediately, and actions that are *future-directed*. If an intentions is sufficiently future-directed, the agent might reevaluate his reasons and thus come to change his mind.

Since they concern the future, these intentions cannot be directed at particular actions, however: The intended action does not yet exist, after all. Future-directed intentions therefore have to be general in content. Like all intentions, they are all-out judgements, but directed at types of action. In effect, future-directed intentions look quite a bit like desires did in the practical syllogism; they have the form 'Any action of mine at a certain time in the future that is of a certain type is desirable'. And Davidson explains how this can be:

It would be mad to hold that any action of mine in the immediate future that is the eating of something sweet would be desirable. But there is nothing absurd in my judging that any action of mine in the immediate future that is the eating of something sweet would be desirable given the rest of what I believe about the immediate future. I do not believe that I will eat a poisonous candy, and so that is not one of the actions of something sweet that my ... judgement includes (Davidson 1978, 99).[44]

In these ways, Davidson proposes to satisfy the three demands we started out with: The revised model of practical reasoning allows for the weighing of reasons, both in the form of weighing reasons for and against an action as well as of weighing reasons for different actions, it recognizes intentions, and it makes weakness of the will logically possible.

Some of the questions one might ask about the Davidsonian model are the following: Does it allow 'enough' practical irrationality? To what extent does it succeed in rendering irrationality intelligible? One might also more specifically ask whether Davidson really captures what is essential to weakness of the will, but we shall not pursue that issue here.[45]

The amount of practical irrationality allowed by this model is, of course, limited in principle: A minimal rationality is simply built into the Davidsonian notion of action. Moreover, this built-in rationality spreads to the whole process of action motivation and practical reasoning. The intelligibility of irrational

44. It would be a mistake, Davidson goes on to explain, to try and improve the statement of intention by including certain provisos, provisos like "provided the action is not of kind X, Y, or Z." There would be endless circumstances to be excluded.

45. For an overview and further literature, see S. Stroud 2008. Cf. also Lazar 1999; Glüer 2003b.

action therefore is limited, too. An irrational action will always be less intelligible than a fully rational one. Nevertheless, Davidson insists that for every intentional action there is a primary reason, and thus some intelligibility (Davidson 1982b, 173f). There is always something that spoke for the action in the eyes of the agent, and this something would have spoken for the action in our eyes, too. That holds even for the most irrational act—otherwise such 'acts' would not be actions at all, but things that merely happen to a person. But where an action is weak-willed, for instance, there at the same time are reasons against the action, reasons so strong that they should have outweighed what spoke for it. There will always be an element to such action that resists understanding—in case of weakness of the will, this can even be quite clear to the agent himself: "he recognizes, in his own intentional behavior, something essentially surd" (Davidson 1970a, 42).

There is an additional question here, however. We might agree that an event that has no reasons explanation whatsoever, and thus no subjective rationality at all, is not an action. We might even agree that there are limits to the overall irrationality we can intelligibly ascribe to an agent. Nevertheless, we might wonder whether the Davidsonian model in fact offers *any* room or explanation for irrationality.

Take wishful thinking. A wishful thinker believes something, for instance that she is not going to fail her driving test, despite much stronger evidence to the contrary. What makes her believe this is a very strong desire. The cause of her belief thus is another mental event, but a mental event that does not provide her with reasons for her belief. According to Davidson, it is this combination of elements that makes things like wishful thinking, self-deception, or akratic action irrational: What causes the irrational belief or action is a further mental state. That is why we are dealing with *irrationality*, not just some *arational* natural events. But the mental cause is *not* a reason (cf. Davidson 1982b, 179).

Nevertheless, Davidson insists, there still is something paradoxical about such irrationality:

> So, we introduce a mental description of the cause, which thus makes it a candidate for being a reason. But we still remain outside the only clear pattern of explanation that applies to the mental, for that pattern demands that the cause be more than a candidate for being a reason; it must *be* a reason, which in the present case it cannot be (Davidson 1982b, 180).

Davidson's suggestion for dealing with this paradox is Freudian in spirit:

> Mental phenomena may cause other mental phenomena without being reasons for them ... and still keep their character as mental, provided cause and effect are adequately segregated. The obvious and clear cases are those of social interaction. But I suggest that the idea can be applied to a single mind and person. Indeed, if we are to explain irrationality at all, it seems we must assume that the mind can be partitioned into quasi-independent structures (Davidson 1982b, 181).

Irrationality thus requires a certain degree of "compartmentalization".[46] This does not mean that each mental state of a person belongs to one and only one segment or compartment of that person's mind, Davidson explains: "The picture I want is one of overlapping territories" (Davidson 1982b, 181, fn. 6). In particu-

46. See also Davidson 1985b, 198.

lar, compartment borders are required where mental events cause other mental events without being reasons for them. Such causal relations are always border-crossings.

While the idea of a mental cause that is not a reason sits very well with wishful thinking, it is not quite as straightforwardly applied to weakness of the will. As Davidson points out, we can easily picture the acratic as compartmentalized, as "having two semi-autonomous departments of the mind, one that finds a certain course of action to be, all things considered, best, and another that prompts another course of action" (Davidson 1982b, 181). But even if desires from the wrong side win, these desires *are* reasons for the weak-willed action. So, where is the cause that is not a reason?

According to Davidson, the desire for the akratic act plays a double role in its generation: It is, indeed, a reason for the action, but at the same time this very desire causes the agent to ignore the principle of continence. And for this, the desire does *not* provide any reason (cf. Davidson 1982b, 178). This idea is rather elusive, however; in what sense is ignoring the principle of continence a mental event other than, or over and above, simply performing the akratic action?

Davidson's explanation has two steps: First, he argues that we need to describe the akratic as going "against his own second-order principle that he ought to act on what he holds best" (Davidson 1982b, 177). The principle of continence, that is, must be 'accepted' by the weak-willed subject, it must form part of his belief-desire system. Only then, Davidson argues, can we capture the sense in which weak-willed action is *objectively* irrational:

> If the agent does not have the principle that he ought to act on what he holds to be best, everything considered, then though his action

may be irrational from our point of view, it need not be irrational from his point of view (Davidson 1982b, 177).

Only if the akratic himself holds that he ought to act on his own best judgement, all things considered, is he *internally inconsistent* in a purely formal sense.

Once the principle of continence is construed as part of the akratic's system of mental states, Davidson can in a second step separate ignoring it from simply acting akratically. For now, preventing it from having its rightful effects is a mental event that needs explanation, and the desire for the akratic act provides precisely the right kind of explanation: A mental cause that is not a reason for ignoring or overriding the principle.

This account is quite problematic, however. In what sense does a subject 'accept', 'subscribe to', or 'have' a principle like that of continence? Davidson himself accepts that 'having' the principle cannot require being aware of, or able to formulate it. Rather, he suggests, 'accepting' such a principle "mainly consists in that person's pattern of thoughts [and actions] being in accordance with the principle" (Davidson 1985b, 203).

And in a sense that is very Davidsonian, indeed. Like other basic principles of rationality, continence is a principle any intentional creature acts—by and large—in accordance with. Together with the basic principles of decision theory, continence is, so to speak, the practical part of the principle of charity. Consequently, as Davidson himself puts it,

> the question whether a creature 'subscribes' to the principle of continence … is not an empirical question. For it is only by interpreting a creature as largely in accord with these principles that we can intelligibly attribute propositional attitudes to it, or that we can raise the question whether it is in some respect irrational. We see then that

my word 'subscribe' is misleading. Agents can't decide whether or not to accept the fundamental attributes of rationality: if they are in a position to decide anything, they have those attributes (Davidson 1985b, 196f).

All this strongly suggests that 'having' the principle does not require anything over and above being an intentional agent. But in that case, 'having' the principle does not require that the principle itself form the content of one of the agent's states of mind. And then, ignoring the principle and acting akratically need not at all be different things.

If this is right, weak-willed action cannot be explained by a mental cause that is not a reason. But that might not be a major disaster for the Davidsonian account of akrasia. If Davidson is right and the principle of continence is part of the basic rationality constitutive of being a minded creature, ignoring the principle of continence simply by acting against it is perfectly sufficient for being irrational. If Davidson is right, such an action is irrational from any point of view—there simply are no other points of view. When it comes to the mental, this is as objective as it gets.

These considerations very nicely bring us back to the more basic, overall concerns we were left with at the end of the last chapter: The place of action theory in Davidsonian interpretation.

We became interested in reasons explanations because the radical interpreter needs them for linking behavior and the propositional attitudes. Behavior provides his data, and the link allows for the determination of meanings and contents. And just as before, the best, and correct, theory of interpretation is that achieving the best overall fit with the data. Best fit, however, requires a standard or principle—and it is here that the principles of continence and decision theory play their role in Davidsonian interpretation, a role exactly analogous to that of the principle of charity. Desires, or preferences, together with beliefs, intentions and actions, form a (practically) rational structure governed by these principles. According to Davidson, this is as essential to all of these attitudes as by and large truth and coherence is to belief. As we just saw, Davidson argues—just as he does for charity—that these principles are not open to empirical testing, but constitutive of the attitudes (cf. also Davidson 1976a, 268ff, Davidson 1999b, 404). These principles thus are part of what we might call *charity in its widest sense*: The practical and theoretical rationality essential to the propositional attitudes and intentional action.

In the introduction, I said that the interpreter was the hero not only of Davidson's philosophy of language, but in a way of his whole philosophy. We have seen how the interpretation of linguistic utterances for Davidson becomes part and parcel of a larger foundational enterprise: the interpretation of whole persons or agents. At the end of the last chapter, we saw that the basic, non-individuative attitude the radical interpreter ultimately works with is that of preferring true uninterpreted sentences. By means of the principle of charity in its widest sense—including the principle of continence—the radical interpreter then determines the meanings of utterances such that beliefs, desires, intentions, and actions are optimally rational. For Davidson, minded creatures thus *essentially are rational animals*. And rational animals are interpretable animals. Their minds are essentially public; they are in principle accessible to their interpreters, to other rational animals understanding what they say, think, and do.

In this way, the principle of charity in its widest sense becomes the foundational principle of the mind. For Davidson, it is the principle relating the semantic to the non-semantic, attitude contents and action to mere behavior. Because charity constitutes the mental as essentially rational, the principle allows Davidson to combine the modern conviction that every difference ultimately is a physical difference and that the mental ultimately supervenes on the physical with a staunch humanistic belief in the irreducibility of the mental. We will look at Davidson's ideas about the mental and the physical in more detail in the last chapter.

Language, Mind, and World

In the preceding chapters, we have used the radical interpreter as our guide through the Davidsonian system of thought. In particular, we have been introduced to the basics of Davidson's philosophy of mind and language, and we have looked at the relevant parts of his action theory. In these final two chapters, I want to explore some of the most striking and important metaphysical and epistemological consequences Davidson draws from the core ideas of his philosophy. These can roughly be grouped by the following themes: *mind and world* and *mind and matter*. The present chapter is going to be the 'worldly' one, and in the next and final chapter, we'll get down to matters of matter.

5.1 The Third Dogma of Empiricism

5.1.1 Conceptual Schemes

A question that was more hotly debated in the 1970s than it is today concerns the possibility of alternative conceptual schemes.

With the idea that there are, or at least could be, conceptual schemes very different from our own came the thought that reality itself would somehow be different for those using a different conceptual scheme. If there are, or at least could be, *radically* different conceptual schemes—schemes consisting of concepts that we would not even be able to grasp—reality itself would thus be dependent on such schemes. This claim—that what is real depends on, or is relative to, a conceptual scheme—is called "conceptual relativism".

Conceptual relativism was powered by various sources. Some found inspiration in the writings of linguists or anthropologists such as Benjamin Lee Whorf (cf. Whorf 1956). Others, like Thomas Kuhn and Paul Feyerabend, got to similar conclusions from investigations in the philosophy and history of science (cf. Kuhn 1962; Feyerabend 1962). Chapter X of Kuhn's *The Structure of Scientific Revolutions* begins as follows:

Examining the record of past research from the vantage of contemporary historiography, the historian of science may be tempted to exclaim that when paradigms change, the world itself changes with them. Led by a new paradigm, scientists adopt new instruments and look in new places. Even more important, during revolutions scientists see new and different things when looking with familiar instruments in places they have looked before. It is rather as if the professional community had been suddenly transported to another planet where familiar objects are seen in a different light and are joined by unfamiliar ones as well. Of course, nothing of quite that sort does occur: there is no geographical transplantation; outside the laboratory everyday affairs usually continue as before. Nevertheless, paradigm changes do cause scientists to see the world of their research-engagement differently. In so far as their only recourse to that world is through what they see and do, we may want to say that after a revolution scientists are responding to a different world (Kuhn 1962, 111).[1]

But when Davidson in an influential article from 1974—*On the very Idea of a Conceptual Scheme*—launched a frontal attack on precisely the very idea of a conceptual scheme, he was probably most incensed by certain ideas in Quine's writings. Quine, Davidson contends, despite getting famously rid of two of the dogmas of empiricism, still subscribes to a third, and last, such dogma: The dualism of *scheme and content*.[2]

Here is a famous passage from *Word and Object* illustrating what Davidson objects to:

> We cannot strip away the conceptual trappings sentence by sentence and leave a description of the objective world; but we can investigate the world, and man as part of it, and thus find out what cues he could have of what goes on around him. Subtracting his cues from his world view, we get man's net contribution as the difference. This difference marks the extent of man's conceptual sovereignty—the domain within which he can revise theory while saving the data (Quine 1960, 5).

According to Quine, all our hypotheses and beliefs face the famous "tribunal of experience" only as holistic systems. Nevertheless, experience not only *is* a tribunal, it is so precisely because it lies outside the system. Experience thus is supposed to pro-

1. In how far the Davidsonian arguments to be outlined in what follows actually are on target when it comes to Kuhnian incommensurability is not immediately obvious, however. For more discussion, see Ramberg 1989, ch. 9.

2. The two dogmas Quine argued against in Quine 1951 are the belief in a fundamental difference between analytic and synthetic truths, and what Quine there calls "reductionism", i.e., "the belief that each meaningful statement is equivalent to some logical construct upon terms which refer to immediate experience" (20).

vide system-independent, 'raw' data or, to use a metaphor familiar from Sellars, the unconceptualized "given".[3] What is "given" in experience—be it thought of in terms of sensations, sense data, or patterns of what Quine calls "surface irritations"—thus provides the ultimate evidence for our beliefs and theories. At the same time, however, the given is not only independent of, but radically different from the content of our beliefs. There is, thus, a good and pressing question how these two things—experience or the given on the one hand, and our concepts, beliefs, and theories on the other—relate to one another.

It is with this question that the idea of a conceptual scheme might seem to help: "Conceptual schemes, we are told, are ways of organizing experience; they are systems of categories that give form to the data of sensation; they are points of view from which individuals, cultures, or periods survey the passing scene" (Davidson 1974b, 183).

And once the idea of such a scheme providing the interface for the experience-belief relation is in place, it might seem obvious that at least in principle there could be alternative schemes, alternative ways of organizing experience or carving up reality. Moreover, these schemes might be "incommensurable", that is, they might be so different that the beliefs or other propositional attitudes of one person "have no true counterparts for the subscriber to another scheme" (Davidson 1974b, 183). In that case, what a person can think, and what is real for them, would depend on what conceptual scheme they 'subscribe to'.

In the 1974 paper, Davidson is mainly concerned to show that once we manage to give precise, literal sense to the metaphors of a scheme organizing, systematizing, fitting, facing, or dividing up

---

3. Cf. Sellars 1963. Sellars, however, just like Davidson, does not believe in the existence of an unconceptualized given; his paper presents a forceful attack on what he calls the "myth of the given".

experience or reality, these claims are either obviously false—or entirely trivial: "Conceptual relativism is a heady and exotic doctrine, or would be if we could make good sense of it. The trouble is, as so often in philosophy, it is hard to improve intelligibility while retaining the excitement" (Davidson 1974b, 183).

To this end, Davidson in a first step investigates the relation between languages and conceptual schemes. It is clear, he thinks, that languages differ where conceptual schemes differ. But not the other way around: Linguistic differences do not necessarily show that the conceptual schemes associated with the languages in question are different. For instance, one language might have a handy, simple expression for a concept that requires a long and complex paraphrase in another language. Nevertheless, the concept is perfectly expressible in both. Such differences might very well reflect differences in interest or relevance, but, Davidson submits, they do not signal radical conceptual differences.

A real-world example would be the Swedish word 'lagom'. Something is lagom iff it is precisely the right amount of whatever it is, neither too little, nor—and that is at least equally important—too much. As far as I know, no other language has an equally short and frequently used expression for this concept. But as we have just seen that does not mean that it cannot be expressed in other languages.

Davidson concludes that in order to be associated with different conceptual schemes, languages would have to fail to be translatable. Consequently, "we may identify conceptual schemes with ... *sets of intertranslatable languages*" (Davidson 1974b, 185, emphasis added). The claim that there are, or could be, (different) conceptual schemes then amounts to the claim that there are, or could be, languages that cannot be translated into each other.

Regarding the possibility of translating one language into another, we must distinguish between *partial and total failure of translation*, however. In the second step, Davidson therefore argues against the possibility of either. When it comes to total failure, he argues that the metaphor of a scheme or language's 'fitting' experience or the evidence "adds nothing intelligible to the simple concept of being true" (Davidson 1974b, 193f). Thus, if there were alternative conceptual schemes, they would have to be "largely true but not translatable". But this is a dead end, according to Davidson: "The question whether this is a useful criterion is just the question how well we understand the notion of truth, as applied to language, independent of the notion of translation. The answer is, I think, that we do not understand it independently at all" (Davidson 1974b, 194). Why not? Because, according to Davidson, our best intuitions as to how to apply the concept of truth to sentences are formulated in Tarski's Convention T. And Convention T makes essential use of the concept of translation.

Davidson then discusses the idea of a partial failure of translation, but before we follow his train of thought, we should stop for a moment and reflect on the concept of *truth*. If nothing else, the argument just recounted might seem to generate a certain amount of internal tension for Davidson. For didn't he tell us earlier (see section 2.2.3.1) that the concept of truth is one of the clearest and most basic concepts we have? And that we therefore can quite legitimately use it to explain linguistic meaning without begging any meaning theoretical questions? In order to get a little clearer on these questions, we shall go on a short digression.

5.1.2 Truth: Beyond Realism and Anti-Realism

Contemporary theories of truth can roughly be categorized by means of their answers to the following two questions: First, is truth a substantive property? And second, if yes, is it an epistemic or a non-epistemic property? Redundancy theorists, disquotationalists, and deflationists deny that truth is a substantive property. Epistemic theories hold that it is a substantive, but in principle epistemically accessible property. Epistemicism about truth is often also called "anti-realism". Realists about truth hold that truth is a substantive property independent of our beliefs and cognitive abilities.[4]

Originally, Davidson thought that Tarski-theories in fact provided some sort of correspondence theories of truth (cf. Davidson 1969b)—a traditional kind of realism about truth. For a while, he then flirted with a sort of coherentism (cf. Davidson 1983), but realized quickly that his ideas were rather different from more traditional coherentisms (cf. Davidson 1987a). Eventually, he came to think of these traditional alternatives—coherence vs. correspondence, realism vs. epistemicism—as altogether mistaken (cf. Davidson 2005, 38ff, esp. fn 4). He argued that truth cannot be defined at all, and that the only way to say something revealing about the concept of truth is by tracing its relations to concepts equally fundamental and beyond definition (cf. Davidson 1996,

---

4. Epistemic conceptions of truth have typically been thought of as motivated by meaning theoretical concerns. Michael Dummett proposes to account for meaning in terms of verification instead of truth, and argues that, on such an account, the notion of truth must be explained "in terms of our capacity to recognize statements as true" (Dummett 1976, 75). Inspired by the later Wittgenstein, philosophers such as Crispin Wright have argued that, on pain of the kind of meaning Platonism attacked by Wittgenstein in the rule-following considerations (esp. PI 138-242), meaning has to be understood in terms of an epistemic concept of truth (cf. Wright 1980). Anti-realism about truth strikes many as having very counterintuitive consequences, however; Michael Dummett, for instance, argues that sentences about the past are made true not by past facts in themselves but by what is presently known or knowable. He is one of the few anti-realists who embrace this consequence; others, like Wright, argue against this actually being a consequence of anti-realism (cf. Wright 1986).

Dummett also argued that redundancy theorists and deflationists cannot understand meaning in terms of truth conditions (cf. Dummett 1959, 7). They hold that 'p is true' means the same as 'p'—a consequence of which may be that "the function of truth talk is wholly expressive, thus never explanatory" (Williams 1999, 547). Most deflationists agree with Dummett and take this to imply that meaning cannot be explained in terms of truth (cf. for instance Horwich 1998, 71ff. For a more precise formulation of the problem, cf. Patterson 2005).

20f). What we end up with from such a perspective combines vital insights of realism—such as the recognition-transcendence of truth—with equally vital insights of anti-realism—such as that truth nevertheless cannot be understood in total independence from our propositional attitudes, especially that of belief.

Davidson thus suggested that even though often beyond recognition, truth *is* essentially related to the propositional attitudes: The truth predicate gets interpreted only through the 'pattern' truth makes amongst the attitudes, including speech and action, and their causes. It has empirical content precisely because T-theories can be applied to intentional creatures, can be correct or incorrect for a speaker, or group of speakers: "If we knew in general what makes a theory of truth correctly apply to a speaker or group of speakers, we could plausibly be said to understand the concept of truth" (Davidson 2005, 37). Precisely at this point, however, Davidson must tread carefully in order not to beg any meaning theoretical questions. Given his overall meaning theoretical project, Davidson must be wary of taking meanings for granted in characterizing truth.

For that reason Davidson tries to find a way of relating truth to the very same non-semantic data about speakers' behavior in observable circumstances that according to him provide the determination base for meaning, or content in general: "I therefore see the problem of connecting truth with observable behavior as inseparable from the problem of assigning contents to all the attitudes" (Davidson 1996, 37).

Ultimately, then, he construes belief and truth as part of a set of basic, irreducible, and interdependent concepts capturing what's essential to intentional minds. Their empirical content derives from the metaphysics of content determination by means of the principle of charity. Because of its non-semantic determination base, content determination by charity thus allows us to say something revealing also about truth: "by relating it to concepts like belief, desire, cause and action" (Davidson 1996, 21).

5.1.3 More on Conceptual Schemes

Where does this leave us with respect to Davidson's argument against radically different conceptual schemes? Davidson argued that truth cannot be understood independently of meaning. Ergo, he concludes, we cannot understand the idea of a largely true, but untranslatable conceptual scheme, either. This, we suspected might create tension with a very fundamental claim in Davidson's account of meaning—the claim that truth is the basic semantic concept. Now, we saw that he later came to regard the concept of truth as part of a family of basic concepts. These concepts cannot be analyzed any further, but can nevertheless be illuminated by relating them to one another. Whether or not this relieves the tension would then seem to depend on whether meaning, and content, are part of that family of concepts or not.

If they are, the tension would seem to disappear: In this case, truth and meaning can be illuminated in terms of one another, and we can claim that we cannot understand either independently. Davidson's argument against radical translation failure then rests on the plausibility of the claim that truth cannot be understood independently of meaning.

There are, however, some both systematic and exegetical reasons to doubt that Davidson in fact included meaning, and content, within the basic circle of intentional concepts. For instance, Davidson always continued to insist that "truth is one of the clearest and most basic concepts we have" (Davidson 2005, 55) and that "meaning not only is a more obscure concept than that of truth; it clearly involves it: if you know what an utterance means, you know its truth conditions" (Davidson 1996, 37).

Insisting that truth has (some degree of) conceptual priority with respect to meaning is fully compatible with the claim that truth is one of a set of basic, interdependent concepts. According to Davidson, these concepts are endowed with empirical content *together*. They are part of a 'theory' that is interpreted by its relation to the non-semantic evidence, by its relation to observable behavior. This theory makes use of both the concepts of belief and of truth, but *not* those of meaning and content.[5] Moreover, the basic meaning theoretical project of understanding meaning and content in terms of truth—a project very much Davidson's—remains stronger and more informative or illuminating if truth has (a degree of) conceptual priority over meaning. More of the true spirit of analysis is preserved, so to speak, even though no reduction or definition is attempted.[6]

If meaning and content are not part of the basic cluster of concepts around truth and the propositional attitudes, the argument against radical translation failure does create a certain degree of internal tension for Davidson, however. To the extent that truth in fact is conceptually prior to meaning and content, understanding truth cannot depend on understanding meaning. Nevertheless, there might be an argument that is quite similar to Davidson's

5. The relevant concept of belief for instance is that of a propositional attitude individuated as an attitude in abstraction from any particular propositional content (cf. Davidson 2005, 67). And the same holds for the other elements of the basic intentional set—belief, desire, speech, and action.

6. Strawson distinguishes between reductive and what might be called "connective analysis" (cf. Strawson 1992, 17ff). A connective analysis investigates the relations between more or less basic concepts forming what one might call "wide hermeneutic circles". The wider the circle of only inter-definable concepts, the more illuminating the connective analysis. This is the kind of enterprise Davidson is into when it comes to the relations between truth and the propositional attitude. If meaning and content are not part of the hermeneutic circle of concepts around truth, however, the analytic project with respect to these concepts would be somewhat stronger. On a scale between the strictly reductive and the merely connective, its place would be somewhere in the middle.

original one, an argument he could have used without creating tension. This argument would use the connection between truth and the propositional attitudes, especially that of belief or holding true, to support the claim that any language associated with a largely true conceptual scheme by that very token also allows for translation. But we do not have the space here to elaborate on, or to assess the prospects of, such an argument.

What we might note, though, is that Davidson's argument against *partial failure of translation* is precisely one that turns on the principle of charity and its role in content determination (cf. Davidson 1974b, 195ff):

> We make maximum sense of the words and thoughts of others when we interpret in a way that optimizes agreement.... Where does this leave the case for conceptual relativism? The answer is, I think, that we must say much the same thing about differences in conceptual scheme as we say about differences in belief: we improve the clarity and bite of declarations of difference, whether of scheme or opinion, by enlarging the basis of shared (translatable) language or of shared opinion (Davidson 1974b, 197).

But don't some languages quite obviously contain parts that have no counterparts in others? Take two historical stages of English, one from around 1800 and one from today. Today's English contains the resources to talk about quantum mechanics. Can this part of today's English really be translated into 1800s English? A reply along the following lines, here reported as given by Jerry Katz, would seem to be available to Davidson, too:

> Katz replied that today's concepts could have been explained to people of two hundred years ago, given enough time, and our current language could be translated into that language by consider-

ing how such explanations would go. Although speakers of 200 years ago would have great difficulty in understanding translations of contemporary scientific theories, that would be because of the complexity of the theories, not because of a defect in the translations (Harman 2011, 17).

Davidson concludes that, whether failure of translation is supposed to be partial or total, there never could be good reason "to judge that others had concepts or beliefs radically different from our own" (Davidson 1974b, 197).[7] We should therefore give up not only the idea of possible alternative conceptual schemes, but the idea of a conceptual scheme in general.[8] And with the notion of a scheme, the notion of content that comes with it has to go: the notion of an uninterpreted sensory given, of unconceptualized experience. But wouldn't that be throwing out the baby with the bathwater? There might be no such thing as a conceptual scheme, but surely there is such a thing as reality, such a thing as the mind-independent world? Davidson does not think we need to worry on that count; it is precisely the dualism of scheme and content that results in relativism and the loss of objectivity. Giving it up thus actually means getting the world back:

7. This conclusion is not meant to be merely epistemic in character. Davidson's claim is not merely that we could never be in a position to know that there are alternative conceptual schemes. Rather, meaning and content are (metaphysically) determined in such a way that there are no differences that are in principle unknowable.

8. Quine concurred; he reacted to Davidson's attack by basically disowning conceptual schemes:

> A triad—conceptual scheme, language, and world—is not what I envisage. I think rather, like Davidson, in terms of language and the world. I scout the tertium quid as a myth of a museum of labeled ideas. Where I have spoken of a conceptual scheme I could have spoken of a language. Where I have spoken of a very alien conceptual scheme I would have been content, Davidson will be glad to know, to speak of a language awkward or baffling to translate. (Quine 1981, 41)

> Without the dogma, this kind of relativity goes by the board. Of course truth of sentences remains relative to language, but that is as objective as can be. In giving up the dualism of scheme and world, we do not give up the world, but re-establish unmediated touch with the familiar objects whose antics make our sentences and opinions true or false (Davidson 1974b, 198).

As always in philosophy, we need to be careful here. Davidson does not deny that experiences, sensations, or stimulations of nerve endings play a role in the formation of beliefs about the world around us. However, according to him, this role is *merely causal*. In particular, these things or states—often summarily called "intermediaries"—do *not* play any epistemic role.[9] According to Davidson, there are *no epistemic intermediaries* between ordinary material objects and perceptual beliefs about them: "No doubt meaning and knowledge depend on experience, and experience ultimately on sensation. But this is the 'depend' of causality, not of evidence or justification" (Davidson 1983, 146). The reasons for these claims are mostly to be found in his later papers. We shall look at Davidson's case against epistemic intermediaries in the course of the next two sections.

5.2 Reasons and Experience

Perceptual beliefs are beliefs we form on the basis of perception. They are, so to speak, the first belief states in the order of processing that runs from sensory inputs to the personal level cognitive states and beliefs of a subject. Intuitively, examples would be the

---

9. And here, Davidson does part company with Quine. In fact, Quine accuses Davidson of conflating the theory of truth with the theory of warranted belief here: "The proper role of experience or surface irritation is as a basis not for truth but for warranted belief" (Quine 1981, 39).

belief that there is something red and round in front of me, the belief that *this* bottle is green, or the belief that the screen on my desk is rectangular—if these are formed on the basis of perception. Most philosophers these days agree that such beliefs are 'about' ordinary material objects, and that they ascribe certain properties to them, properties called "observable" or "sensible" properties.[10]

According to Davidson, perceptual beliefs are epistemically basic in the following sense: There is nothing further, nothing epistemically more basic providing evidence or justification for them.[11] Moreover, these beliefs are often, especially in the most basic cases, about the very objects and events that cause them.

> Perception, once we have propositional thought, is direct and unmediated in the sense that there are no epistemic intermediaries on which perceptual beliefs are based, nothing that underpins our knowledge of the world (Davidson 1997a, 135).

> Many of my simple perceptions of what is going on in the world are not based on further evidence; my perceptual beliefs are simply caused directly by the events and objects around me (Davidson 1991, 205).

What are Davidson's objections to epistemic intermediaries, then? In 1999, Davidson summarizes them as follows:

10. There is much less agreement on the question which properties in fact are sensible. Everyone probably agrees that color properties and basic shape properties are sensible, but opinions differ on properties such as being a book, a car, or a cabbage.

11. This doesn't mean that these beliefs are incorrigible or infallible, quite the contrary: "the beliefs that are delivered by the senses, are always open to revision, in the light of further perceptual experience, in the light of what we remember, in the light of our general knowledge of how the world works" (Davidson 1999c, 106). Nor does it mean that perceptual beliefs don't derive justification from these other beliefs; they do get evidential support from "coherence with their fellows" (ibid.) That is precisely why conflict with further beliefs can lead us to revise perceptual beliefs, and justifiedly so.

I had, then, two objections to trying to base empirical knowledge on non-propositional "experience": first, that it couldn't be done, though many attempts had been made, and second, that if knowledge depended on something intermediate between its supposed object in the world and belief, skepticism was inevitable (Davidson 1999c, 105).

Skepticism is going to be the topic of the next section. In this section, we shall investigate Davidson's first objection: Perceptual experience, Davidson claims, cannot provide any epistemic base for perceptual belief. But why not? Here's the argument:[12]

> There is a simple explanation for the fact that sensations, percepts, and sense data cannot provide epistemic support for beliefs: reasons have to be geared conceptually to what they are reasons for. The relation of epistemic support requires that both relata have propositional content, and entities like sensations and sense data have no propositional content. Much of modern philosophy has been devoted to trying to arbitrate between an imagined unconceptualized given and what is needed to support belief. We now see that this project has no chance of success. The truth is, nothing can supply a reason for belief except another (or many another) belief (Davidson 1997a, 136).

Davidsonian epistemology is first and foremost subjective, or first person, epistemology: The epistemic relations he is interested in

---

12. An earlier, more dense formulation of basically the same point is this:

> The relation between sensation and belief cannot be logical, since sensations are not beliefs or other propositional attitudes. What then is the relation? The answer is, I think, obvious: the relation is causal. Sensations cause some beliefs and in this sense are the basis or ground of those beliefs. But a causal explanation of a belief does not show how or why the belief is justified (Davidson 1983, 143).

are relations accessible from the point of view of the epistemic subject. They are *reasons relations*, where reasons, too, are essentially subjective in the following two senses: They are 'possessed by', and accessible to, their subjects. As I explained before, these reasons are best thought of as the *contents* of their subjects' mental states, even though Davidson himself often refers to the states themselves as reasons (see chapter 3, section 3.1.1). Davidsonian reasons are subjective in the further sense that they do not have to be true.[13]

From this perspective, the idea that experience, sensation, or any other form of the given provides epistemic support for perceptual beliefs is the idea that experience provides *reasons* for perceptual belief. But this is impossible, since experience or the given at the same time is supposed to be the system-independent data coming from outside the belief-system, and therefore unconceptualized. We simply cannot have it both ways: According to Davidson, nothing can be both unconceptualized and provide reasons. What is unconceptualized lacks propositional content.[14] And propositional content is necessary for providing reasons.

13. Whether a particular belief that *p* does in fact provide a reason for believing that *q*, however, is not an entirely subjective matter, according to Davidson. In order to provide a reason for believing *q*, there needs to be a relation of inferential or evidential support between *p* and *q*, and this relation needs to be such that it is accessible, or appreciable, not only from the perspective of the subject, but from any rational creature's perspective. There is thus an objective, or at least inter-subjective, element to the Davidsonian conception of reasons.

14. Davidson held that in order to have a mental state with a certain propositional content, a creature needs to possess the concepts that would be used in ascribing that content to it. In one sense of the term, he thus did not think that there is such a thing as "nonconceptual content", even though it is not terribly clear how he thought of the conditions for concept possession. What is clear is that he thought that in order to have a concept, such as the concept *cloud*, a creature's cloud-beliefs would have to be part of a sufficiently large holistic system:

> I can believe a cloud is passing before the sun, but only because I believe there is a sun, that clouds are made of water vapour, that water can exist in liquid or gaseous form; and so on, without end. No particular list of further beliefs is required to give

When it comes to epistemic reasons, we cannot but conclude, Davidson submits, that the following principle holds:

(BP)   Nothing can supply a reason for belief except another (or many another) belief.
(Cf. Davidson 1997a, 136; Davidson 1983, 141)

Let's call (BP) the "belief principle". Needless to say, the belief principle is highly controversial.

One of its critics is John McDowell. In his *Mind and World* (1994) and related writings, he worries that on the belief principle, thinking of belief systems "can generate the spectre of a frictionless spinning in a void" (McDowell 1994, 18). It is not so much the coherentism he takes to be inherent in the principle that worries him here; rather, McDowell argues that without a "minimal empiricism" (McDowell 1996, 231), the beliefs in a belief system would not even have any empirical content (McDowell 1994, 17). To have empirical content, belief systems need to be constrained from the outside.

McDowell agrees with Davidson, however, that the desired constraint is supposed to both come from outside the belief system and be a *rational* constraint at the same time. What he disagrees with is the Davidsonian verdict that this cannot be done. It

substance to my belief that a cloud is passing before the sun, but some appropriate set of related beliefs must be there (Davidson 1977a, 200).

Moreover, to qualify as a propositional attitude, ascriptions of the attitude need to create intensional contexts:

How about the dog's supposed belief that the cat went up that oak tree? That oak tree, as it happens, is the oldest tree in sight. Does the dog think that the cat went up the oldest tree in sight? Or that the cat went up the same tree it went up the last time the dog chased it? It is hard to make sense of the questions (Davidson 1982c, 97).

Accordingly, Davidson notoriously denied cats and dogs (and all other higher animals) any beliefs. For a critical survey of notions of non-conceptual content and their uses, see Speaks 2005.

can be done, McDowell suggested in *Mind and World*, if we conceptualize the given. Experience, he submits, can provide rational constraint on belief systems because it is not true that experience is unconceptualized and non-propositional. Experience represents the world as being a certain way—as being thus-and-so, as McDowell would put it—and it therefore has content, is a kind of propositional attitude.[15] Nevertheless, experience is different from belief in that it is received passively "from without". Therefore, it can both provide reasons for, or—as McDowell later preferred to call them—"entitlements" to, belief and provide the external constraint required for securing empirical content.[16,17]

Whether a "minimal empiricism" is required for empirical content is a question we cannot attempt to settle here. Davidson did not think so; as we saw above, he prefers an account of content determination for basic perceptual beliefs in terms of shared, or common, typical causes. In reply to McDowell's criticism of the belief principle, he writes:

15. McDowell has recently qualified his position on this count. He still holds that experience has content, and provides what he calls "entitlements" to belief, but he now thinks that this content is of a special form. It is not propositional, but rather "intuitional" (McDowell 2008, 4). This position is at least superficially similar to the one Tyler Burge arrives at: According to Burge, experience has what he calls "representational content", but this content is not propositional in form (cf. Burge 2010, 430ff). Moreover, experience provides entitlement, but not reasons (cf. Burge 2003). Burgean entitlements, however, are different from McDowell's in at least this respect: According to Burge, but not to McDowell, experience can provide entitlements for *false* beliefs.

16. According to McDowell, experience is by its nature veridical. The contents of experience are facts. Experiences therefore entitle their subject to believing their contents, regardless of whether they conflict with the subject's background beliefs or not (cf. McDowell 1998; McDowell 2002; McDowell 2004). Illusions and hallucinations are not experiences; rather, they are "mere appearances", states that to their subject seem to be experiences, but aren't (McDowell 1982, 386). This position is one version of what is called "disjunctivism" in the theory of perception. Disjunctivisms of different kinds are defended, among others, by Paul Snowdon, Hilary Putnam, and Michael Martin.

17. For more on the Davidson-McDowell debate, see also Stroud 2002b; Glüer 2004; Ginsborg 2006; Glüer 2011.

John McDowell thinks this thesis leaves our beliefs without rational support or content. He is half right: I claim our perceptual beliefs require no more in the way of rational support than coherence with their fellows. But only half right, since I think I do have an account of how many of our perceptual beliefs come to have the contents they do, and I think this account also explains why we are justified in accepting them (Davidson 1999c, 106).

In the next section, we shall therefore return to the Davidsonian account of content determination and look, among other things, at those epistemological consequences Davidson here refers to.

One last reflection before we leave this section, however: Davidson's defense of the belief principle strongly relies on the claim that perceptual experience does not have any propositional content. Even though not implausible when it comes to mere sensations, 'sense data', and things like that, this claim is, I think, rather counterintuitive when it comes to full-fledged perceptual experiences—states such as an experience as of a red book on my desk, an experience as of a magnolia tree in full bloom outside my window, or an experience as of a vast expanse of blue sky and grey ocean in front of me. Experiences such as these intuitively represent the world as being a certain way. They pose conditions on the mind-independent outside world, conditions that the world has to fulfill in order for the experience to be true, correct, or accurate (cf., for instance, Peacocke 1992, 61). In this fairly uncontroversial sense, perceptual experiences intuitively have propositional contents. Moreover, these states represent the world as actually being the way it appears, they are 'committal' or 'assertive' states, states that—as a fashionable metaphor has it—'aim at truth'. It is thus intuitively very plausible to think of perceptual experience not only as a propositional attitude, but as a cognitive propositional attitude.

Does accepting that perceptual experience is a propositional attitude require rejecting the belief principle? Only, if we also hold that perceptual experiences supply their subjects with reasons for belief—*and* that they are not beliefs themselves. In that case, however, perceptual experience would be a propositional attitude *sui generis*, a propositional attitude, as Davidson puts it, "for which we have no word" (Davidson 1999c, 107). What is more, we not only lack a word, but also an explanation "of why an attitude which has no subjective probability whatever can provide a reason for a positive belief" (ibid.). In this cursory remark, Davidson actually provides the seeds of a completely different argument for the belief principle, an argument independent of the counterintuitive claim that experiences lack propositional content.

For Davidson, any state of holding a proposition true is a belief. Holding trues, or beliefs, come in degrees. If experience is a propositional attitude sui generis, it therefore does not involve any degree of holding true—"no subjective probability whatever". But then, how can a proposition that you do not hold true to any degree, a proposition as to whose truth value you have no opinion whatsoever, be a reason for you to believe something? This, I think, it is an excellent question. Developed in the right way, it might provide the grounds for arguing that belief, or holding true, is the only attitude that provides its subject with epistemic reasons for belief.[18]

---

18. For more on this, see Glüer 2011. See also Stroud 2002b; Ginsborg 2006. Noteworthy is, too, that it is an argument like this that provides one of the main motivations for McDowell's retraction of the claim that experiences do have propositional content. Cf. McDowell 2008, 11. One might, however, use the very same argument in order to defend a belief theory of experience, a theory, that is, according to which experiences are beliefs (of a special kind) (cf. Glüer 2009).

As we saw earlier, Davidson had another reason for keeping perceptual experience from providing reasons, from being epistemically significant at all: He thought this would inevitably lead to *skepticism*. We should not allow any epistemic intermediaries, he argued, because "they may be lying. The moral is obvious. Since we can't swear intermediaries to truthfulness, we should allow no intermediaries between our beliefs and their objects in the world" (Davidson 1983, 144). No, we can't swear intermediaries to truthfulness—but can we swear anything else to truthfulness? Most importantly, can we swear *(perceptual) belief* to truthfulness? The passage just quoted strongly indicates that Davidson thought so. In the next section, we'll see why.

5.3 Triangulation

The skepticism Davidson is mainly concerned with is skepticism about our knowledge of the external world. An external world skeptic holds that we might be radically mistaken about the world around us, more precisely, that all (or at least most) of our beliefs about the external world might be false.[19] What is important here, is that such a skeptic holds not only that each and every such belief, taken individually, could be false—that might well be true according to Davidson—but that they could all be false *at the same time*. This, Davidson emphasized, is a different claim—and it does not follow from the first (cf. Davidson 1990a, 194f).

Let's focus on perceptual belief. Is it possible that our perceptual beliefs are radically mistaken? That most, or even all, of them are false at one and the same time? As we saw in the last section,

---

19. Even though he focused on external world skepticism, Davidson thought that his arguments also extended to skepticism about other minds as well as our own mind. Cf. Davidson 1991.

Davidson claims that perceptual beliefs often, or in the most basic cases, are directly caused by objects, or events, in the subject's environment. And not by any old objects or events; according to Davidson, perceptual belief is such that it is typically caused by the very objects, or events, it is *about*. "What stands in the way of global skepticism of the senses is, in my view, the fact that we must, in the plainest and methodologically most basic cases, take the objects of a belief to be the causes of that belief" (Davidson 1983, 151).[20]

But every single belief has many causes. Each and every event of belief formation is located on a long, long chain of causally linked events. Each of these events is, in some sense, a cause of that belief. And not only that, there is probably more than one such causal chain for each and every belief, too. So, what does Davidson mean when he talks about "*the* causes of that belief"?

As we saw in chapter 3, section 3.1.2, on Davidson's (later) account of content determination the objects of perceptual beliefs are their *typical, common (or shared) causes*. This combination of social and causal elements comes to play a more and more important role for Davidson; it is a theme central to many of his later writings.[21] In these writings, Davidson explores and expounds a type of argument that we shall call a *triangulation argument*. These arguments come in quite a number of subtly different versions in these writings. Not all of these can be explored here; rather, their presentation will be significantly streamlined and somewhat simplified.[22]

---

20. This is not meant to completely exclude the possibility of illusion or even outright hallucination, but it is meant to establish the "veridical" nature of belief (cf. Davidson 1983, 146). 'Veridical'—as used by Davidson—means something like *mostly true*.)

21. The most important of these writings are: Davidson 1982c; Davidson 1990a; Davidson 1991; Davidson 1992; Davidson 1994.

22. For a handbook article specifically on triangulation, see Glüer 2006b.

All along, we have seen Davidson argue for claims like this: "It follows from the nature of correct interpretation that an interpersonal standard of consistency and correspondence to the facts applies to both the speaker and the speaker's interpreter, to their utterances and to their beliefs" (Davidson 1991, 211). And we have seen how he anchors the principle behind this, the principle of charity, in the very nature of belief: According to Davidson, belief is by its very nature such that it comes in coherent and mostly true clusters. But while he earlier focused more on coherence and on agreement between speaker and interpreter, Davidson now perceives a need to dig deeper when it comes to truth. Agreement might be necessary for communication, but, he asks, "why should an interpersonal standard be an objective standard, that is, why should what people agree on be true?" (Davidson 1991, 211f).

But Davidson is concerned with more than skepticism when it comes to triangulation. Another crucial element of his thought is the idea that language, meaning and content are essentially public. We can, in principle, know what others say and think. Intuitive as this is, Davidson now wants to dig deeper here, too. Triangulation is supposed to provide us with an argument for the publicness of language. Moreover, it is supposed to provide us with an argument for the claim that not only interpret*ability* is necessary for meaning, but actual interpretation. And the same is supposed to hold for thought. The relevant question here is the following: "Even if it is the case that communication assumes an objective standard of truth, why should this be the only way such a standard can be established?" (Davidson 1991, 212).

The answers to these questions, Davidson argues, are no longer to be had from considering interpretation, be it ever so radical: "If we are to establish the essentially public character of language, we need an entirely different sort of argument" (Davidson

1992, 117). The triangulation argument is supposed to be such an argument, an argument supporting claims about the conditions necessary for propositional thought. As the name suggests, it is an argument for the claim that *triangulation is necessary for propositional thought.*

In real life, triangulation is a technique for the precise determination of for instance a ship's position or the direction of a road or tunnel. It is based on the laws of plane trigonometry, which state that, if one side and two angles of a triangle are known, the other two sides and angle can be readily calculated. In his 1982 paper *Rational Animals*, Davidson for the first time used the analogy with triangulation to argue that actual linguistic communication is necessary for propositional thought. After that, he used a number of more or less different versions of the triangulation idea to argue for such controversial claims as that propositional thought requires language, that there cannot be a solitary thinker or speaker, and that epistemological foundationalism is untenable. Here, we shall focus on two of the main versions of the triangulation argument and their anti-skeptical potential.

The first of these arguments I shall call the *argument from content determination.* In this argument, triangulation is used to support externalism about the content of perceptual belief. More precisely, it is an argument for a specifically Davidsonian *social-perceptual externalism.* Its main claim is that the content of perceptual belief is determined by a triangle formed by two sentient creatures and an object (or event) in the world. The argument concludes that without such a triangle, perceptual beliefs would not have any determinate objects. In other words: For perceptual belief to have determinate objects, the existence of, and interaction with, other sentient creatures and external objects is required. Why?

If we consider one creature in isolation, Davidson argues, there simply is no answer to the question what that creature is thinking about. More precisely, there is not even any answer to the question what such a creature is *reacting to* in its environment. Let's call our creature Alf. Clearly, the notion of the cause of Alf's reaction isn't sufficient for determining what Alf is reacting to: For any of Alf's reactions, there is a whole chain of causes. Imagine Alf reacting to a scene in front of him. Imagine, too, that this reaction is triggered by means of a visual apparatus very similar to ours. Now trace the causal chain leading to a particular such reaction backwards: It reaches through the most proximal stimuli—such as patterns of irradiation on Alf's retina—via more and more "distal" ones—such as a table standing right in front him or a rabbit scurrying by in plain view—all the way to the most distal of them all, the Big Bang. Which of these objects or events is the relevant cause of Alf's reaction?

We can make the question more concrete by asking: What is it Alf sees? If we put ourselves in his place, intuition starts kicking in: Intuitively, what we see in such a situation is not a pattern of irradiation on our own retina, nor is it the Big Bang. Rather, it is a table (or a rabbit). But first of all, creatures such as Alf might well react to other things than we do. And second, even for us, the notion of a cause just by itself does not deliver this intuitive result. What about a *typical* cause, then? What precisely Alf reacts to, the idea would be, is not determined by a single occasion; rather, it is the cause that is common to a certain kind of occasion.[23]

But according to Davidson, not even the typical cause will do. A plausible externalism needs to combine a perceptual with

---

23. The idea that mental representations represent those objects that typically cause them to be 'tokened' is one of the basic ideas in informational semantics. Teleosemantics has it that mental representations represent those typical causes that it is the representational mechanism's biological function to 'track' (for an overview, see Papineau 2006).

a *social* element, it needs to bring a second creature into the picture, a creature sufficiently like the first in terms of its sense apparatus and similarity responses. The problem this is supposed to help with is solving for a certain "ambiguity of the concept of cause":

> In the present case the cause is doubly indeterminate: with respect to width, and with respect to distance. The first ambiguity concerns how much of the total cause of a belief is relevant to content. The brief answer is that it is the part or aspect of the total cause that typically causes relevantly similar responses. What makes the responses relevantly similar in turn is the fact that others find those responses similar. . . . The second problem has to do with the ambiguity of the relevant stimulus, whether it is proximal (at the skin, say) or distal. What makes the distal stimulus the relevant determiner of content is again its social character; it is the cause that is shared (Davidson 1997a, 130).

Let us here focus on Davidson's second problem. This is a problem about the 'location' of the stimulus, that is, the event or object that is the typical cause of a reaction of a certain type R. 'Where' on the causal chain is this object? If we just look at a series of chains leading to Rs in a single creature such as Alf, we might well find that there is a whole segment of each of these chains that is typical, a segment, that is, that is longer than is intuitively right. Assume, for instance, that Alf has visual beliefs, more precisely, visual table-beliefs. What is typical in the causation of Alf's visual table beliefs might well include both the table *and* the pattern of retinal stimulation. What's worse, the retinal patterns might be even more typical than tables themselves. Davidson concludes: "If we consider a single creature by itself, its responses, no matter how complex, cannot show that it is reacting to, or thinking

about, events a certain distance away rather than, say, on its skin"
(Davidson 1992, 119).

Rather, the answer is supposed to derive from the reactions of
a second creature. A second creature observing Alf reacts to two
things: Alf's reactions and the objects causing Alf's reactions. The
question which of its typical causes determines the content of a
perceptual belief can then be answered in the following way, here
with a child in place of Alf:

> The relevant stimuli are the objects or events we naturally find
> similar (tables) which are correlated with responses from the child
> we find similar. It is a form of triangulation: one line goes from
> the child in the direction of the table, one line goes from us in the
> direction of the table, and the third line goes between us and the
> child. Where the lines from child to table and us to table converge,
> 'the' stimulus is located. Given our view of child and world, we can
> pick out 'the' cause of the child's responses. It is the common cause
> of our response and the child's response (Davidson 1992, 119).

More precisely, the principle of content determination for perceptual belief Davidson advocates is this: "The stimulus that matters
is *the nearest mutual cause*" (1998: 84, emphasis added). This is
the mutual, or common, cause that is closest to Alf (or the child)
and us on the respective causal chain. And what holds for determining the objects sentient creatures react to, Davidson seems to
assume, holds mutatis mutandis for determining the objects the
perceptual beliefs of sapient creatures are about.[24]

---

24. Føllesdal argues that there is no such thing as a causal chain: "The events with which I
am familiar have a multitude of causes. One should rather talk about causal trees" (Føllesdal
1999, 725). If this is true, typical segments of causes not only are longer, but also 'wider', than
is intuitively right. Moreover, it would also be more difficult to locate the object of a thought
or reaction at 'the' intersection of two such trees—there might be many such.

However, this kind of triangulation is not yet fully interactive: To determine the nearest mutual cause, and thus the object, of Alf's perceptual state, we do not need to interact with Alf in any way. More precisely: In the triangle described so far, Alf reacts to the object, and we react to Alf and to the object. But Alf does not need to react to us. Therefore, it remains unclear why our actual presence should be required at all. Even in our absence, the table is the closest share*able* object on the chain leading to Alf's reaction. What remains unclear, that is, is why actual sharing is required—where shareability seems to do just as well.

To see why Davidson thinks that the actual presence of a second, sufficiently similar creature is required for propositional thought, we need to look at other versions of the triangulation argument. Here, I shall focus on what I shall call the *argument from objectivity*. In this argument, triangulation is used to support the claim that interaction with a second creature is necessary for having beliefs or propositional thoughts in general. Beliefs—at least most of them—have what Davidson calls "objective contents". Davidson argues as follows:

> Thought, propositional thought, is objective in the sense that is has a content which is true or false independent . . . of the existence of the thought or the thinker. Furthermore, this is a fact of which a thinker must be aware; one cannot believe something, or doubt it, without knowing that what one believes or doubts may be either true or false and that one may be wrong. Where do we get the idea that we may be mistaken, that things may not be as we think they are? (Davidson 1997b, 129.)

Having beliefs, or propositional thoughts in general, Davidson claims, requires a subject to possess a whole family of concepts including the concepts of belief, of objective truth and of mistake.

There is no point in ascribing beliefs to a creature who does not appreciate that what it thinks might be false, that the world might be otherwise from what it believes: "Error is what gives belief its point," Davidson writes as early as 1975 (Davidson 1975, 168).[25] But as long as we are concerned with a single creature—Alf, say—and his reactions to his environment, not even the notion of a deviation from the pattern of his reactions gets any grip. To establish as much as that someone is deviating from a pattern of reactions, we need at least two sets of reactions. If these reactions show a lot of overlap otherwise, but differ from time to time with respect to the same stimulus, it becomes plausible to say that (at least) one of these different reactions constitutes a deviation from a pattern. This, Davidson argues, does not establish *which* of the reactions deviates from the pattern, nor does it establish yet *what* the pattern, or the "norm" is. Nevertheless, it allows us "to make sense of there being a norm" (Davidson 2001b, 7). Davidson concludes that a necessary condition for a reaction's being a deviation from a pattern is that there are (at least) two sufficiently similar creatures reacting to the same object or event. And what holds for deviation mutatis mutandis also holds for propositional thought and belief.

Again, however, the triangle is not fully interactive yet; so far, all we need is two creatures reacting to the same object or event. But here is the crux: As we saw, Davidson thinks that in order to have any *beliefs* a creature needs to have the *concept of belief*,

25. In Davidson 1975, we already find the seeds of what later develops into the triangulation arguments:

> Can a creature have a belief if it does not have the concept of belief? It seems to me it cannot, and for this reason. Someone cannot have a belief unless he understands the possibility of being mistaken, and this requires grasping the contrast between truth and error—true belief and false belief. But this contrast ... can emerge only in the context of interpretation, which alone forces us to the idea of an objective public truth (Davidson 1975, 170).

of objective truth or mistake. So, where does that come from? In addition to the possibility of deviation from a pattern of reaction, what is required for (mistaken) belief?

It is here that true interaction enters the triangulation picture. For Davidson's idea is that possession of the concept of truth requires that the triangulating creatures are aware of the triangulation: "The basic triangle of two people and a common world is one of which we must be aware if we have any thoughts at all" (Davidson 1998, 86). Propositional thought, that is, requires the triangulating creatures to be aware of each other *as parts of the same triangle*, as reacting to the same object or event. This does *not* mean that for each particular thought, its thinker needs to be aware of triangulating with another thinker. Nor does it mean that we cannot have any thoughts while alone. Rather, triangulation is a condition on having the general capacity for thinking propositional thoughts.[26] Nevertheless, the requirement of mutual awareness or knowledge of the triangle is a tall order. Much, very much, is required for such knowledge to be possible. According to Davidson, nothing less than linguistic communication will do: "For two people to know of each other that they are so related, that their thoughts are so related, requires that they be in communication. Each of them must speak to the other and be understood by the other" (Davidson 1992, 121). To sum up this line of argument: Davidson argues that triangulation is a necessary condition both on propositional thought in general, and on propositional thought's having any determinate object.

The triangulation arguments have been criticized from a number of different directions. That possession of the concept of belief is necessary for belief has not only been argued to involve

---

26. Because it is aiming at necessary conditions on such a general capacity, Bridges—in obvious and fairly appropriate reference to Kant—calls Davidson's externalism "transcendental" (cf. Bridges 2006).

"hyper-intellectualization" (cf. Burge 2010, 281ff), but to be empirically false (cf. Glüer and Pagin 2003). Even if possession of the concept of belief is necessary for having beliefs, however, one might doubt that triangulation is the only way it could be acquired (cf. Child 1996, 19). The arguments for the necessity of linguistic communication for propositional thought have been charged with circularity (cf. Pagin 2001), and the argument against solitary speakers or thinkers has been found less than persuasive for a variety of additional reasons (cf. Føllesdal 1999; Pagin 2001; Bridges 2006; Glüer 2006b). As far as I can tell, many, but by no means all of these criticisms are on target. But of course, triangulation has staunch defenders, too (cf. Yalowitz 1999; Lasonen and Marvan 2004; Verheggen 2006, 2007; Bouma 2006). We cannot decide these discussions one way or another here. I leave it to interested readers to further pursue the matter on their own.

To round this chapter off, we shall rather return to the question of skepticism. Let's grant that the triangulation arguments do establish at least some of what Davidson takes them to establish: In order to have any beliefs with determinate objects there need to be other people around. Moreover, for these beliefs to have determinate contents, in the most basic cases they need to be typically caused by the very objects or events they are about. What would all of this accomplish with respect to external world skepticism? Here's one thought: Maybe the existence of the external world, and even the truth of most of our most fundamental beliefs about it are, in fact, a condition on having any beliefs. But does it follow from this that there is an external world? Or that it fundamentally is as we believe it is? This follows only if we actually do have beliefs. But what if we don't? It might thus seem as if the specter of external world skepticism has been banned only to invite another form of skepticism: skepticism about our own mental states.

Davidson once commented on a rather similar consequence for more mainstream forms of externalism:

> In the present case, ordinary skepticism of the senses is avoided by supposing that the world itself more or less correctly determines the contents of thoughts about the world.... But skepticism is not defeated; it is only displaced onto knowledge of our own minds. Our ordinary beliefs about the external world are (on this view) directed onto the world, but we don't know what we believe (Davidson 1987b, 22).

But he thought that his own version of externalism, with its characteristic combination of social and perceptual elements, is as inhospitable to skepticism about our own mental states as it is to external world skepticism (and skepticism about other minds):

> The conclusion does not follow, at least for the kind of externalism I have described.... My reasoning can be summarized as follows. An interpreter must discover, or correctly assume on the basis of indirect evidence, what the external factors are that determine the content of another's thought; but since these factors determine both the contents of one's thought and the contents of the thought one believes one has (these being one and the same thought), there is no room for error about the contents of one's own thought of the sort that can arise with respect to the thoughts of others (Davidson 1990a, 197f).[27]

But these considerations do not speak to the skeptic who does not, or not only, claim that we might be subject to radical error about the *contents* of our own beliefs, but that we simply might

---

27. See also Davidson 1984a; Davidson 1987b.

not have any beliefs at all. Of course, it would be self-defeating to actually believe that we do not have any beliefs. We cannot truly believe that we don't have any beliefs. But it does not follow that we in fact have beliefs. If this is enough for a skeptic, we might well suspect that not even the most successful triangulation argument could ever completely close the door to skepticism.[28]

28. For more on Davidsonian anti-skepticism, see B. Stroud 2002a.

Chapter 6

The Mental and the Physical

Ever since the rise of materialism in early modern thought, finding a place for the mind and the mental in the material world has exercised philosophers. Descartes famously espoused a rather radical form of dualism: substance dualism. According to substance dualism, mental 'things' or substances do not even share any attributes or properties with material 'things' or substances. One notorious difficulty for such a position is accommodating the powerful intuition that minds and material objects interact.

The reductive naturalism that dominated twentieth century Anglo-American philosophy opposed any form of dualism: The mental, reductive naturalists hold, can be reduced to, and fully explained in terms of, the physical. The model for such reduction came from the natural sciences. Examples would be the identification of lightning with electrical discharge or that of heat with molecular movement. Such reductions do not proceed by definition or conceptual analysis, but via so-called "bridge-laws" nomologically tying two types, or 'typings', of phenomena together.

With respect to the mental and the physical, the discussion now focused on states or events, and the basic idea was that mental states or events ultimately *are* physical states or events. Positions of this kind came to be known as *identity theories*. Identity theories came in various forms; one popular idea was that mental states or events such as being in pain, believing that *p*, or forming the intention to ϕ are identical with neurophysiological states or events. Thus J. J. C. Smart famously suggested that pain might be identical to C-fiber stimulation (cf. Smart 1959). Specification of the right neurophysiological states was mostly left to future science, but identity theorists held that ultimately, such identifications would be forthcoming.

Typically, identity theorists considered the claim that mental states or events are nomologically reducible to physical ones as an empirical hypothesis. And most were optimistic that this hypothesis was correct. But not everyone; early on, Quine argued that our vocabulary for the mental, especially the intentional terminology of folk psychology, was not up to snuff. This vocabulary, he held, simply wasn't acceptable by scientific standards (Quine 1960, 216ff). Eliminative materialists such as Patricia and Paul Churchland (cf. Churchland 1984) also held that there is virtually no chance of ever finding the mental states and events of everyday life and its folk psychology amongst the detailed descriptions of brain activity available to any future neuroscience. Like Quine's, their stance towards this was firmly materialist: So much the worse for mental events and folk psychology. What neuroscience would ultimately show is that such events—just like phlogiston—never really existed.

Substance dualism and eliminative materialism are extreme positions. In between, there is quite a bit of logical space. This space, however, has more than one dimension. A lot depends on how we think of reduction, for instance. And on how we think of events.[1] We do not have the space here to map out this territory in satisfying detail. What I shall do instead is look more closely at how Davidson conceives of it. We are already familiar with Davidson's account of events (see chapter 4, section 4.2.1.2): Events are dated particulars whose existence is independent of their descriptions. This view is crucial to the Davidsonian take on reduction. Here are the basics:

Take two different vocabularies V_1 and V_2, for instance a mental and a physical vocabulary. These vocabularies contain, among other things, predicates, descriptions, and singular terms that we take to be satisfied by, or referring to, certain entities (objects, states, or events). Accordingly, associated with each vocabulary V_i, there is a domain D_i: a domain of mental entities and a domain of physical objects, for instance. The predicates of each such vocabulary V_i partition the associated domain D_i into sets or classes. V_i-predicates thus *classify* D_i-entities as belonging to certain *types*, more precisely as belonging to certain V_i-types. Mental predicates classify events as belonging to mental types, for instance as being pains or beliefs that p. The particular entities so classified, however, are simply there—they exist in complete independence of how they are described. This is crucial to the Davidsonian picture: Ontology is independent of description, but classification is not. Particular objects are just there, and can, in principle, be described and classified in a multitude of different ways.

Reduction then concerns the precise relations between V_1, V_2, D_1, and D_2. Davidson distinguishes between three more or less

---

1. As we shall see shortly, Davidsonian token-identity, for instance, requires construing events in a way that allows mental events to fall under physical descriptions without being type-identical with physical events. Not all accounts of events allow this; for instance, Kim's account in terms of property exemplifications (cf. chapter 4, section 4.2.1.2, fn. 10) does not. Cf. Davidson 1970b, 213; McLaughlin 1985, 339.

interesting kinds of reduction: conceptual or definitional, nomological, and ontological (cf. Davidson 1985d, 242f). *Ontological reduction* of V_1 to V_2 demands only that each individual entity in D_1 is identical to an entity in D_2: Here, D_1 either is identical to D_2, or a proper part of it. The result is ontological *monism*: V_1 does not require any entities over and above those already contained in D_2.

Conceptual reduction requires that all (essential) concepts of V_1 can be *analyzed* or *defined* in terms of V_2. Consequently, all V_1-types of entities can be identified with V_2-types. If the mental could be conceptually reduced to the neurophysiological, types of mental states or events—such as pains or beliefs that p—would be identical to types of brain states or events, such as C-fiber firings. Moreover, this identity would be a matter of *conceptual necessity*. Along with almost everyone else in the twentieth-century debate, Davidson did not think the mental was conceptually reducible to the physical, or any part thereof.

Nomological reduction also requires type-identities. But here, the tie between V_1-types and V_2-types is weaker. It holds as a matter of the laws of nature: by *nomological necessity*. What links types from different vocabularies (or theories) are "bridge laws". This is the type of identity that those believing in reduction of the mental to the neurophysiological had in mind. Neurophysiology is not the only candidate, however. Still, any nomological reduction of the mental to the physical requires psycho-physical bridge laws of some kind.

Both conceptual and nomological reduction of V_1 to V_2 thus demand identity between V_1-types and V_2-types. Here, the vocabularies not only share an ontology, they also share ways of classifying the entities in this ontology. More precisely, what is required is that all (essential) V_1-types are identical to V_2-types.

The corresponding identity theories therefore are often called "type-identity theories". Identity theories espousing monism, but not type-identity, are called "token-identity theories": According to a mental-physical token-identity theory, every particular mental state or event, every token m of a mental type M, is identical to a particular physical state or event, a token p of some physical type P—but there is no conceptual or nomological connection between M and P.

As we already saw, it was generally thought to be an empirical question whether the mental is nomologically reducible to the physical, or to some specific part of it. This is were Davidson went into sharp opposition: He held that we have very good reasons of a strongly a priori character for thinking that nomological reduction of the mental to the physical is impossible. He held that the mental is strictly anomalous: There are no strict laws for mental events. This includes the claim that there are no strict psychophysical laws, and hence no strict psychophysical bridge laws. Nevertheless, Davidson was a monist. He held that there is token-identity between the mental and the physical. The resulting position is known as *anomalous monism*.

This combination might seem unusual, but there is nothing obviously inconsistent about it. It allows Davidson to preserve the irreducibly sui generis character of our self-conception as rational animals—while at the same time being adamant that ontology is not made by description. But what's most intriguing about anomalous monism might well be the way Davidson argued for it: According to him, *monism actually is a consequence of anomalism*—together with some further assumptions, of course. If the mental cannot be nomologically reduced to the physical, it must be identical to it. Token-identical, to be sure, but still. It is this argument that we shall turn to now.

6.1 Anomalous Monism

Anomalous monism is a combination of claims about mental events:

(AM) Mental events are
  (ID)   identical to physical events, but
  (A_M) there are no strict laws on the basis of which mental events can be predicted or explained.[2]

So, what are mental events? And what are physical events? Events, we already know from Davidson's action theory, are to be construed as dated particulars whose existence does not depend on whether, or how, they are described. "Events are mental only as described" (Davidson 1970b, 215), Davidson holds, and the same holds for an event's being physical. Events are mental, or physical, only insofar as they (uniquely) satisfy, or are referred to by, certain descriptions. For Davidson, the characteristics of the mental and the physical thus first and foremost concern two vocabularies for events, two ways of describing and explaining events.

What is a mental description, then? Earlier, we saw that Davidson thinks of the formation of beliefs, desires and intentions as mental events. And indeed, the vocabulary of the propositional attitudes is paradigmatically mental for him. Consequently, one criterion for counting a predicate ψ as a "mental verb" is creating non-extensional contexts when used in sentences of the form $\ulcorner S \ \psi s \ that \ p \urcorner$. An event then can be characterized as mental iff it has a mental description, that is, a description that is true of

---

2. As we shall see in a moment, (AM) strictly speaking holds for those mental events that causally interact with physical events. There is little doubt, however, that Davidson thought that no mental event was causally isolated from the physical; cf. Davidson 1970b, 208.

that event and contains at least one mental verb essentially (cf. Davidson 1970b, 210ff).[3] "It is less important," Davidson originally wrote, "to characterize a physical vocabulary because relative to the mental it is, so to speak, recessive in determining whether a description is mental or physical" (Davidson 1970b, 211). In other words: Any description that isn't mental is physical.

Later, Davidson was less inclusive; in *Representation and Interpretation* he explains:

> A particular physical event, state, or disposition is one that can be picked out—described uniquely—using a vocabulary drawn from some physical science. A particular mental event, state, or disposition is one that can be picked out—described uniquely—in the vocabulary that we reserve for the intentional. So if mental events and states are identical with physical events and states, the very same events and states must have descriptions in both the mental and physical vocabularies (Davidson 1990c, 92).

The question then is: Why should we think that mental events are identical with physical events? As already hinted, the rather

---

3. One might worry that this characterization does not include certain kinds of events more traditionally considered paradigmatic of the mental, events such as feeling pain or having an after-image. As Davidson observes, the real worry is the opposite: The characterization of the mental just given not only can be made to include these events, but probably any event whatsoever. The trick is to uniquely describe some clearly physical event such as the collision of two distant stars as *the P*-event that took place at the same time at which some mentally described event occurred. This description turns events such as the collision of distant stars into mental events—according to the criterion provided above. Davidson does not think this a serious problem, however: "It would be instructive to try to mend this trouble, but it is not necessary for present purposes. We can afford Spinozistic extravagance with the mental since accidental inclusions can only strengthen the hypothesis that all mental events are identical with physical events. What would matter would be failure to include bona fide mental events, but of this there seems to be no danger" (Davidson 1970b, 212). One might also have the opposite worry: One might worry, that is, that the existence of a physical description is a very *weak* condition on a mental event's being a physical event—too weak, for instance, to amount to a substantive form of materialism. Cf. Latham 2003.

surprising answer Davidson gives is: Because the mental is anomalous. Anomalism, the second component of anomalous monism, thus is one of the premises in Davidson's argument for identity, its first component.

Anomalism of the mental is the claim that

(A_M)　There are no strict laws on the basis of which mental events can be predicted or explained.

The anomalism of the mental takes the claim that there are no strict psychological laws—a claim that we already are familiar with from Davidson's theory of action—one step further: Now, Davidson argues that there are *no strict laws whatsoever* for events described as mental. In particular, there are no strict *psychophysical* laws, that is, no strict laws connecting events described as mental with events described as physical.

It is important here to keep in mind what Davidson means by a "strict law". Quite generally, he holds that all "laws are linguistic" (Davidson 1970b, 215). Laws are true *lawlike* statements:

(LL)　Lawlike statements are
　　　i)　universally quantified statements
　　　ii)　that support counterfactual and subjunctive claims, and are supported by their instances.

Strict laws, then, are a particular kind of true, lawlike statement. Strictly lawlike statements do *not* contain singular terms referring to particular objects, locations, or times. Nor do they contain so-called ceteris paribus clauses—hedge or escape clauses insulating them to a certain extent from counterexamples (cf. Davidson 1970b, 217; Davidson 1995b, 265f). Strict laws are exceptionless. As we saw above (p. 194f), Davidson does not dispute that there

[252]

are interesting psychological generalizations that are hedged by ceteris paribus clauses. Nor does he deny that there are interesting psychophysical generalizations of this sort (cf. Davidson 1993b, 9; Davidson 1995b, 266).[4] But he claims that these generalizations cannot be sharpened into strict laws.

Why not? Davidson has over the years suggested a number of considerations supporting the anomalism of the mental.[5] The basic suggestion, already offered in *Mental Events*, is that the principles constitutive of our mental and physical concepts are of a radically different nature. This difference immediately excludes conceptual reduction, and it also provides us with very good reasons (of a rather a priori kind) for thinking that nomological reduction is impossible.

Originally, Davidson supported this claim mainly by means of a suggestive comparison (cf. Davidson 1970b, 219ff). Take a principle such as the *transitivity of length*: If A is longer than B and B is longer than C, then A is longer than C. This principle certainly is among the principles constitutive of physical objects. Now, compare principles like the transitivity of length to what is constitutive of the mental: the *principle of charity*. Charity identifies mental events in a holistic way, maximizing or optimizing overall truth and rationality. The radical interpreter and the physicist thus try to understand the world and the phenomena it contains in radically different ways. As Davidson later emphasizes, the relevant difference is *not* that the radical interpreter employs norms while the physicist does not. Insofar as these constitutive principles can

---

4. Probabilistic or indeterministic laws, on the other hand, may well be strict, according to Davidson (cf. Davidson 1970b, 219; Davidson 1995b, 266): "The point that distinguishes strict laws is not so much the guaranteeing of the effect by satisfaction of the antecedent as the inclusion, in the antecedent, of all conditions and events that can be stated that could possibly *prevent* the occurrence of the effect" (Yalowitz 2005, 12).

5. For an overview see Yalowitz 2005. See also McLaughlin 1985.

be called norms, both employ norms or, maybe better, standards. The point is that these standards are *very different*: "When we try to understand the world as physicists, we necessarily employ our own norms, but *we do not aim to discover rationality in the phenomena*" (Davidson 1991, 215, emph. added). As interpreters, however, we *do*.

Suggestive as the comparison may be, it certainly falls short of being a conclusive argument. And Davidson never really provided all the elements required for such an argument, either. What exactly is it about rationality and the mental that prevents mental and physical types from being connected by strict laws? One quite clear line of thought crystallizing in Davidson's later writings in fact focuses less on rationality than on the *causal nature* of mental concepts.[6] Physics, Davidson explains, aims at strict, exceptionless laws. We might not know these laws yet, but an ideal, fully developed physics consists of a closed system of strict laws. And such laws do *not* employ causal concepts. Mental concepts, by contrast, "are *irreducibly causal*" (Davidson 1991, 216, emphasis added). Generalizations employing irreducibly causal concepts cannot be sharpened into strict laws. Their ceteris paribus clauses defy conversion into precise specifications of the appropriate circumstances. Moreover, dropping those causal concepts would amount to changing the subject. This sets them apart, Davidson argues, from other causal concepts such as those of elasticity or solubility:

---

6. For Davidson these things are of course intimately connected: As we saw in more detail in chapter 4, section 4.2, it is precisely *because* of their causal nature that the intentional concepts can be used in reasons explanations—explanations that rationalize action, belief formation, etc. For Davidson, it is thus "part of the concept of an intentional action that it is caused and explained by beliefs and desires" and "it is part of the concept of a belief or a desire that it tends to cause, and so explain, actions of certain sorts" (Davidson 1991, 217).

In the case of causal properties like elasticity, slipperiness, malleability, or solubility, we tend to think, rightly or wrongly, that what they leave unexplained can be (or already has been) explained by the advance of science. We would not be changing the subject if we were to drop the concept of elasticity in favor of a specification of the microstructure of the materials in the airplane wing that cause it to return to its original shape when exposed to certain forces. Mental concepts and explanations are not like this. They appeal to causality because they are designed, like the concept of causality itself, to single out from the totality of circumstances with conspire to cause a given event just those factors that satisfy some particular explanatory interest. When we want to explain an action, for example, we want to know the agent's reasons, so we can see for ourselves what it was about the action that appealed to the agent. But it would be foolish to suppose that there are strict laws that stipulate that whenever an agent has certain reasons he will perform a given action (Davidson 1991, 216).

Psychological explanations, the idea is, are essentially interest-relative: They aim at rationalization, at bringing out the reasons for which someone did or believed something. This interest-relativity is built into them by means of the concepts of the intentional, concepts that are irreducibly causal. Generalizations employing such concepts therefore *have* to be hedged by ceteris paribus clauses: No matter in how much detail we have spelled out a person's reasons (and other psychological events, states, or traits), there can always be yet further reasons (or other psychological events, states, or traits) keeping them from performing a given action. Moreover, the more precise we make such generalizations, the less they will serve our original explanatory interests:

The more precise and general laws are, the less likely it is that we will be in a position to employ them in predicting the outcomes of our ordinary actions. ... Our intense interest in the explanation and understanding of intentional behavior commits us irrevocably to such concepts as belief, desire, intention and action; yet these are concepts that cannot, without losing the explanatory power they have which binds us to them, be reduced to an all-encompassing physics (Davidson 1995b, 276).

And what holds for psychological explanations and generalizations also holds for psycho*physical* explanations and generalizations—as well as for any other explanations and generalizations mixing the psychological with something non-psychological. If there are no strict laws connecting reasons with actions, there are no strict laws connecting reasons with, for instance, physically described bodily movements, either.[7]

Even if these considerations go some way towards closing the gaps in the argument for the anomalism of the mental, they might not reach all the way. Davidson himself, for one, seems to have considered them insufficient: "Much of what I have said about what distinguishes mental concepts from the concepts of

---

7. Even if it is plausible that there are no strict laws explaining mental events as *effects* of physical events, or vice versa, we might still wonder why precisely this prevents psychophysical *bridge laws*. After all, these are *not about successive events* at all; rather, they identify two types of events. To see the connection, assume the following (for reductio ad absurdum): There are no strict *causal* psychophysical laws, but we both have a ceteris paribus causal psychophysical generalization (i) and a strict psychophysical bridge law (ii):

(i) Ceteris paribus, events of type M_1 cause events of type P_2.
(ii) $\forall x \, (M_1 x \text{ iff } P_1 x)$.

We could then substitute P_1 for M_1 in (i), resulting in a ceteris paribus physical generalization. Which would be 'backed' by a strict law belonging to an ideal physics. Such a law would specify the conditions under which an event of type P_1 nomologically necessitates one of P_2. Applying (ii) once more, M_1 would be substituted for P_1 in the formulation of this law. The result of such substitution—counter to assumption—a strict causal psychophysical law.

a developed physics could also be said to distinguish the concepts of many of the special sciences such as biology, geology, and meteorology," he admits (Davidson 1991, 217). And even though he thinks that these special sciences cannot be nomologically reduced to an ideal physics, either, he nevertheless insists on another deep division between the special sciences and psychology. Therefore, "it may seem that there must be something more basic or foundational that accounts for this division" (ibid.). At this point, Davidson mostly falls back on those suggestive, but inconclusive considerations to do with rationality (cf. Davidson 1990c, 98f, Davidson 1987c, 114f). In one place, however, he goes further and connects this line of thought with the idea of triangulation as the origin, and ultimate foundation, of all our knowledge:

> Communication, and the knowledge of other minds that it presupposes, is the basis of our concept of objectivity, our recognition of a distinction between false and true belief. There is no going outside this standard to check whether we have things right. . . . It is here, I suggest, that we come to the ultimate springs of the difference between understanding minds and understanding the world as physical. A community of minds is the basis of knowledge; it provides the measure of all things. It makes no sense to question the adequacy of this measure, or to seek a more ultimate standard (Davidson 1991, 217f).

The ambition of reducing the mental to the physical somehow amounts to seeking a more ultimate standard for describing the world, the idea seems to be, but that would be reversing the metaphysical order of things—and is therefore doomed to failure. Again, this is suggestive, but hardly conclusive.

We shall leave the arguments for the anomalism of the mental now and proceed on the assumption that the mental is, indeed, anomalous.[8] Even for those skeptical of anomalism, the idea of deriving identity from it should be intriguing.[9]

So, how does Davidson get to monism from anomalism? Two more premises are required. The first, Davidson calls "the Principle of Causal Interaction" (Davidson 1970b, 208) and takes to be evident:

(PCI)   There are causal relations between events described as physical and events described as mental.

(Davidson 1995b, 266.)

Beliefs, desires, and intentions cause bodily movements, and physical events cause perceptions, beliefs, and desires; thus, "perception and action provide the most obvious cases where mental and physical events interact" (Davidson 1970b, 208).

The second premise required is more controversial. It is a principle we have met before: "the Principle of the Nomological Character of Causality" (Davidson 1970b, 208):

(NCC)   If two events are related as cause and effect, there is a strict law covering the case.   (Davidson 1995b, 266.)

This is part of the broadly Humean conception of causality adopted by Davidson. Both Hume and Davidson hold that every

8. For further discussion, see McLaughlin 1985; Yalowitz 2005. For an instructive list of considerations that Davidson did *not* think provided good reasons for the irreducibility of the mental to the physical, see Davidson 1973c, 251ff. These include the multiple realizability of the causal role that, according to mainstream functionalism at the time, characterizes a mental state, externalism about mental content, as well as a certain kind of normativism.

9. As far as anomalous monism is concerned, we might moreover ask why the mental even has to be categorically divided not only from (ideal) physics, but also from the special sciences? To be sure, the mental is rather different from the weather, but the reason why neither can be reduced to the physical might still be the same.

true singular causal statement entails the existence of a strict law covering the case.[10] This much, Davidson argues, is simply part of our concept of a physical object. According to him, the validity of the principle of the nomological character of causality is a matter of the connections between the concepts of physical objects, their changes, and laws:

> The causal powers of physical objects are essential to determining what sorts of objects they are by defining what sorts of changes they can undergo while remaining the same objects and what sorts of changes constitute their beginnings or ends. Our concept of a physical object is the concept of an object whose changes are governed by law (Davidson 1995b, 274).

Moreover, Davidson argues, these laws are exceptionless, strict laws. Why? What counts as an event or change in a physical object or system determines what counts as a state of such an object or system. But "once we decide what constitutes a state, we have decided what counts as a causal law" (Davidson 1995b, 277). And as long as there are exceptions to a causal generalization, we are going to conclude that we haven't yet precisely described the relevant initial state of the physical system we are concerned with. It is thus part of our concept of physical objects that their states and changes are governed by strict (physical) laws.[11]

It has been objected that we in fact use singular causal statements all the time even though we know the associated univer-

---

10. Hume, however, also holds that singular causal statements can be *analyzed* in terms of universal generalizations: a true singular causal statements entails a law. Davidson on the other hand insists all that is entailed is *that there is such a law* (Davidson 1967a, 159f).

11. According to Davidson, quantum mechanics does not provide a counterexample to these claims; quite on the contrary: "Quantum mechanics sacrifices determinism as the cost of gaining universality.... Far from challenging the cause-law thesis, quantum physics exemplifies it" (Davidson 1995b, 278).

sal generalizations to be false (cf. E. Anscombe 1971). Thus, we might say that Oblomov's lack of exercise caused his heart failure even though we know perfectly well that not all couch potatoes will have heart attacks. As already seen above, Davidson has a good answer to such worries: True singular causal statements entail that there is a strict law covering the case. But these statements are extensional. The law whose existence they entail does not have to be formulated in the vocabulary used in the singular causal statement. For instance, the law covering a true action explanation does not have to be formulated in the intentional vocabulary used in that explanation. Consequently, the relevant strict law might be a physical law.[12] And now, we only need to understand why Davidson thinks that it *has to be* physical to complete the case for anomalous monism.

It is here that the principle of causal interaction comes in. Take a particular mental event e_m that causes a particular physical event e_p. If we know that the singular causal statement

(1) e_m caused e_p

is true, we also know that there is a strict law covering the case. Moreover, we know that this law can neither be a psychological, nor a psychophysical law. Consequently, it must be a physical

---

12. But does anyone know *any* law, physical or otherwise, that literally is strict in Davidson's sense? The answer seems to be negative. Moreover, "science seems to have done well without any apparent use of them" (Yalowitz 2005, 22). Davidson does not think this is a good objection, either. His idea has been all along that the formulation of strict laws belongs to a future, maybe only ideal, complete physics. All that is required for the truth of a singular causal statement is the *existence* of a law covering the case—*knowledge* of this law is not required. It is not completely clear, however, that this response is really open to him. After all, he construes laws as *linguistic*. And while it seems intuitively right to say that (at least some) *truths* exist whether they are known or not it is much less clear that there is any sense in which the *sentences* expressing some unknown law belonging to an ideal, complete physics exist right now, an ideal physics presumably operating with concepts for which we do not even have any linguistic expressions yet.

law.[13] And if there is a physical law covering (1), then there is a physical description true of, or referring to, e_m. Which means that e_m is identical to a physical event. And this generalizes:

> So every mental event that is causally related to a physical event is a physical event. In order to establish anomalous monism in full generality it would be sufficient to show that every mental event is cause or effect of some physical event; I shall not attempt this (Davidson 1970b, 224).

Thus, the principles of causal interaction and the nomological character of causality allow Davidson to derive psychophysical monism—psychophysical token identity—from the anomalism of the mental.

6.2 Explanation, Supervenience, and the Irreducibility of the Mental

Despite his monism, Davidson did not think of himself as a materialist or a physicalist. For one thing, he observed: "Identity is a symmetrical relation" (Davidson 1987b, 33). If a mental event is identical with a physical event, this does not make it more physical than mental.[14] This much, of course, can be said of all identity

---

13. Cf. Davidson 1970b, 224. As far as I can see, Davidson leaves it open whether there are strict laws that are not physical. There are passages where he seems to suggest that there might be (cf. Davidson 1995b, 266). If so, there might be non-physical strict laws covering our case, too. Nevertheless, there *must* be one that is physical: One of the events concerned is a physical event, and as such it must be covered by a physical law. That is all that is required for Davidson's argument, and it follows from his claim that our concept of a physical object is one of an object governed by strict physical laws.

14. It doesn't help to call the physicalism "non-reductive physicalism" (cf. Rorty 1987).

theories. But there are deeper reasons for not considering anomolous monism a form of materialism, Davidson explains:

> Anomalous monism resembles materialism in its claim that all events are physical, but rejects the thesis, usually considered essential to materialism, that mental phenomena can be given purely physical explanations. Anomalous monism shows an ontological bias only in that it allows the possibility that not all events are mental, while insisting that all events are physical. Such a bland monism, unbuttressed by correlating laws or conceptual economies, does not seem to merit the term 'reductionism'; in any case it is not apt to inspire the nothing-but reflex ('Conceiving the *Art of the Fugue* was nothing but a complex neural event', and so forth) (cf. Davidson 1970b, 214).

According to anomalous monism, every mental event is identical with a physical event. This identity holds precisely because there is a strict physical law subsuming both events. Nevertheless, Davidson insists, mental events cannot be given purely physical *explanations*. This is the very heart of anomalous monism—the reason why we'll never give up on the intentional vocabulary: Nothing else allows us to explain and understand intentional action. It is therefore important to see in some detail how Davidson manages to combine these elements.

Let's start with what we might call a psychophysical explanation: An explanation of a mental event by a physical one. Here are some examples: He wanted an ice cream because of the heat. Dehydration made him drink what he knew to be poisoned water. The suit hanging in front of the closet made him believe there was a burglar in the bedroom. According to Davidson, such explanations have the basic form of singular causal statements:

(2) e_p caused e_m.

Singular causal statements are extensional: Their truth value does not depend on the way the individual events involved are described or classified. Thus, there can be a strict physical law L_p covering these cases. This law subsumes both events under physical types, e_p, let's say, under P_1 and e_m under P_2. Explanations, however, are *not* extensional; explanatory force does depend on how the events involved are described or classified (cf. Davidson 1990c, 91ff). To have explanatory force, a generalization has to type the events involved in the right way. To explain e_m, that is, the generalization has to subsume e_m under a mental type. But anomalism prevents this; if anomalism holds, there is no mental type identical to P_2. Therefore, citing L_p will not provide an *explanation* of e_m.

To illustrate his point, Davidson offers the following analogy:

Suppose, following folk advice, I am attempting to go to sleep by counting sheep. Every now and then, at random, a goat slips into the file. In my drowsy state I find I cannot remember the classificatory words 'sheep' and 'goat'. Nevertheless, I have no trouble identifying each animal: there is animal number one, animal number two, and so on. In my necessarily finite list, I can specify the class of sheep and the class of goats: the sheep are animals 1, 2, 4, 5, 6, 7, 8, and 12; the goats are animals 3, 9, 10, and 11. But these classifications are no help if I want to frame interesting laws or hypotheses that go beyond the observed cases, for example, that goats have horns. I can pick out any particular sheep or goat in my animal numbering system, but I cannot, through conceptual poverty, tell the sheep from the goats generally. So it may be with the mental and the physical. Each mental event, taken singly, may have (must have, if I am right) a physical description, but the mental classifications may elude the physical vocabularies. If so, no physical or non-mental science could be expected to explain thinking, the formation of intentions, or the states of belief, desire, hope, and fear that characterize our mental lives and explain our actions (Davidson 1990c, 92).

It is important here to be clear about the analogy: The animal numbering system is supposed to be analogous to the language of physics, the goat-and-sheep language to the terminology of the intentional. So, even though the former is the language that will supply the strict laws required by the truth of any singular causal statements in the area, it will not provide any interesting laws or hypotheses about mental events (sheeps and goats). These—that is, interesting laws or hypotheses about mental events—need to be couched in intentional vocabulary. Once more, Davidson does not deny that there are interesting laws or hypotheses about mental events. Indeed, it would be hard to see how singular causal statements formulated in intentional vocabulary could so much as have any explanatory force if there weren't any such laws. Indeed, as Davidson himself protests,

> it is not even slightly plausible that there are no important general causal connections between the mental and physical properties of events. I have always held that there are such connections; indeed much of my writing on action is devoted to spelling out the sort of general causal connections that are essential to our ways of understanding, describing, explaining, and predicting actions, what causes them, and what they cause (Davidson 1993b, 14).

Davidson's claim is that these generalities necessarily have ceteris paribus character. They cannot be sharpened into strict laws (see also chapter 4, section 4.2.3).

This means, however, that two things come apart here that it is prima facie rather natural to to think go together: Explanatory force and strict covering laws. Intuitively, causal explanations need to be backed or 'covered' by projectible generalities. In Davidsonian parlance: Singular causal statements need to be covered by true lawlike statements to have any explanatory force. And Davidson's picture accommodates this requirement; as we just saw, he holds—plausibly—that it can be met by ceteris paribus laws.[15] But then, explanatory force cannot be what motivates the further requirement that true singular causal statements be covered by strict laws. Yet, according to Davidson, the existence of strict covering laws is entailed by the truth of any singular causal statement. Ingenious as the Davidsonian construction is, the support for the principle of the nomological character of causality rests entirely on those conceptual considerations regarding the concepts of physical object, change, and law. One might worry whether the support they provide really is sufficiently strong.

Another worry that has exercised people over anomalous monism concerns *epiphenomenalism*. Doesn't, they ask, anomalous monism render the mental a mere epiphenomenon? A phenomenon, that is, that makes no causal difference? Another way of putting this worry is: Does not anomalous monism render the mental *causally inert*? For isn't it the case that according to anomalous monism, it is not *qua* mental events that mental events cause

---

15. On the assumption that we don't know any strict laws yet, not even within physics, this holds there, too: Even within physics, explanatory force can be secured by ceteris paribus covering laws.

other events, but *qua* physical events? According to anomalous monism, isn't it in virtue of its physical properties, not its mental properties, that an event causes what it does?[16]

Davidson had no patience for things like the *'qua'*—or the 'in virtue of'—locution. More precisely, he "couldn't put things this way" (cf. Davidson 1993b, 13). The reason for this is his extensionalist view of causation. According to Davidson, it is events that stand in relations of cause and effect. These events are mental or physical only in the sense that certain descriptions are true of them. But how they are described is irrelevant to the truth of singular causal statements about them. So, yes, it is irrelevant to the causal efficacy of mental events that they can be described as mental. But, and this is crucial,

> it is also irrelevant to the causal efficacy of physical events that they can be described in the physical vocabulary. It is *events* that have the power to change things, not our various ways of describing them. Since the fact that an event is a mental event, i.e. that it can be described in a psychological vocabulary, can make no difference to the causes and effects of that event, it makes no sense to suppose that describing it in the psychological vocabulary might deprive the event of its potency. An event, mental or physical, by any other name smells just as strong (Davidson 1993b, 12).

But that does not mean that there is no good question to be asked here. The question to be asked, according to Davidson is the following: "Might it not happen that the mental properties of an event make no difference to its causal relations?" (Davidson

---

16. Anomalous monism has been criticized along these lines by, among others, Honderich 1982, Sosa 1984, Dretske 1989, Kim 1989a.

1993b, 13.)[17] The answer is that anomalous monism just by itself does not exclude this possibility. Nor is it excluded by the combination of anomalous monism with the principle of causal interaction and the principle of the nomological character of causality. But that these claims are *consistent* with the inertness of the mental does not mean that they *imply* it. Since they do not imply this, it is perfectly open to him, Davidson maintains, to construe the relation between the mental and the physical in such a way that the mental properties of an event do make a difference to its causal relations. For indeed, if they did not make such a difference, that would amount to a refutation of anomalous monism (cf. Davidson 1993b, 14). On any plausible picture of the relation between the mental and the physical, the mental makes a causal difference.

In order to provide us with a plausible view of the relation between the mental and the physical, anomalous monism thus needs to be supplemented with a more precise characterization of that relation. Intuitively, Davidson submits, "there is a sense in which the physical characteristics of an event (or object or state) *determine* the psychological characteristics" (Davidson 1973a, 253). This is perfectly consistent with the anomalism of the mental: "Although, as I am urging, psychological characteristics cannot be reduced to others, nevertheless they may be (and I think they are) strongly dependent on them" (ibid.). The way to combine these ideas, according to Davidson, is to think of mental predicates as *supervenient* on physical predicates (cf. Davidson 1970b, 214, Davidson 1973a, 253, Davidson 1993b, 4ff, Davidson 1995b, 266). Here is how Davidson originally characterized supervenience:

17. Note, that the problem is not that the critics talk about properties. Davidson is quite happy to phrase the problem in terms of properties, even though he did not think properties formed a basic ontological category.

Although the position I describe denies there are psychophysical laws, it is consistent with the view that mental characteristics are in some sense dependent, or supervenient, on physical characteristics. Such supervenience might be taken to mean that *there cannot be two events alike in all physical respects but differing in some mental respect*, or that an object cannot alter in some mental respect without altering in some physical respect (Davidson 1970b, 214, emphasis added).

More precisely, Davidsonian supervenience is a relation holding between a predicate and a set of predicates:

(SV)   A predicate p is supervenient on a set of predicates S iff p does not distinguish any entities that cannot be distinguished by S.

(Davidson 1993b, 4.)

As Davidson points out, supervenience as just defined holds in a number of cases that he deems uninteresting: It trivially holds where p belongs to S, for instance. It also holds where p can be explicitly defined in terms of S, and where there is a law to the effect that p is coextensive with a predicate definable in terms of S. Supervenience, that is, does not exclude reduction. The point is that it does not require the possibility of reduction: "The interesting cases," Davidson continues, "are those where p resists any of these forms of reduction" (Davidson 1993b, 5). And clearly, he thinks that the relation between the mental and the physical is one of these interesting cases: The mental supervenes on the physical, but resists conceptual or nomological reduction. It is nomological reduction that is particularly interesting here, of course. What exactly does supervenience amount to if it does not allow for nomological reduction? In what sense does the physical determine the mental?

As Davidson initially put it, the idea is that two events that share all physical properties *cannot* differ in mental properties. He does not elaborate on the kind of necessity he has in mind. However, since he seems to consider supervenience a matter of very strong intuitive plausibilty—he never even argues for it—I would think it safe to think that the necessity is (if not conceptual then at least) metaphysical. For present purposes, that does not matter, however. The following considerations do not require anything stronger than nomological necessity. So, lets assume that Davidson holds that as a matter of (at least) nomological necessity any two events sharing all physical properties share all mental properties, too—if they have any. Why doesn't this imply that, after all, there are strict psychophysical laws?

To see why one might think so, and also why this would be a mistake, think about two events e_1 and e_2. Assume that they share a set of physical properties P, and that these are all the physical properties of e_1 and e_2. Assume further that P is some sort of "maximal set", that is, that no event having P has any physical properties not in P. From supervenience, it follows that e_1 and e_2 must be of the same mental type. And so must any other event e_i that has P. Let's say that e_1 is a belief that water is wet. Then so is e_2 and any other event e_i that has P. One might think that this amounts to there being a law to the effect that any event that has P is a belief that water is wet. Such a law might not yet be a bridge law—there might be other sets of physical properties also having nomological connections with beliefs that water is wet. But its existence would be sufficient to show that anomalous monism is false. It would be sufficient to show that the mental is not anomalous.[18]

18. See Yalowitz 2005, 43ff.

This line of reasoning is mistaken, however. Davidsonian supervenience implies only that events having P necessarily are of the *same* mental type. It does *not* imply that there is a particular mental type M such that events having P *necessarily* are Ms. For each nomologically possible world w, that is, there has to be a mental type that all the P-events belong to. But this type does not have to be the same across all nomologically possible worlds. Let's say that P-events are beliefs that water is wet in the actual world @. Supervenience is consistent with there being a nomologically possible world w_1 where P-events are desires to eat a piece of chocolate, and a nomologically possible world w_2 where P-events are intentions to scare a burglar. It is even consistent with there being a nomologically possible world w_3 in which P-events aren't mental at all. All that is required by supervenience is that whatever variation there is across nomologically possible worlds, the P-events 'vary together', so to speak. This form of supervenience has been called "weak supervenience" (Kim 1984a), a terminology sometimes adopted by Davidson himself (cf. Davidson 1993b, 7, where it occurs in what might well be scare quotes). Weak supervenience of the mental on the physical is consistent with there being no strict psychophysical laws.

Jaegwon Kim, in his controversy with Davidson on these matters, remained dissatisfied with the Davidsonian setup.[19] He objected to the idea that weak supervenience is sufficient for drawing that "plausible picture of the relation between the mental and the physical" (Davidson 1993b, 7) that Davidson had promised. According to Kim, weak supervenience is not enough to satisfy our metaphysical intuitions. These intuitions have it that there is a strong dependence of the mental on the physical. Or, as Davidson

19. Cf. Kim 1984a; Kim 1984b; Kim 1987; Kim 1989a; Kim 1989b; Kim 1993.

himself put it, that the physical *determines* the mental. But, Kim argues,

> determination or dependence is naturally thought of as carrying *a certain modal force*; if being a good man is dependent on, or is determined by, certain traits of character, then having these traits must insure or guarantee being a good man.... The connection between these traits and being a good man must be more than a *de facto* coincidence that varies from world to world (Kim 1984a, 160, first emphasis added).

We only get a reasonably intuitive notion of dependence or determination here, Kim maintains, if we assume strong supervenience (cf. Kim 1984a, 163ff, Kim 1987). Believing that water is wet, for instance, strongly supervenes on P iff it is (nomologically) necessary that any P-event is a belief that water is wet.

Davidson remained unmoved. He insisted that "clearly supervenience gives a sense to the notion of dependence here, enough sense anyway to show that mental properties make a causal difference" (Davidson 1993b, 14). We shall get back to the causal difference issue soon. There is a point to Kim's complaint, however, and we shall have a look at that first. Intuitively, there *is* rather little substance to the claim that the physical determines the mental if that is compatible with there being *no* mental type M such that there are any two possible worlds where all P-events are of mental type M. *Some* such cross-world identity of supervenient type—"supervenient cross-world identity", for short—does seem to be required if the physical determines the mental. Now, Davidsonian supervenience does not *imply* that there is no supervenient cross-world identity or that all counterfactual conditionals of a certain kind, conditionals like (3) below, are false—even though it is *consistent* with both. Again, it thus looks like we need to put more constraints on the relation between the mental and the physical to get a plausible picture. Mere weak supervenience isn't quite enough yet.

One idea would precisely be to require certain counterfactual conditionals to come out true, conditionals like (3):[20]

(3)   Had there been an event e such that e was P, e would have been M.

We don't have the space here to go into much further detail, but the idea roughly is the following: According to a popular and plausible account of counterfactuals, counterfactual conditionals are true iff the consequent is true in all the possible worlds closest, or most similar, to the actual world in which the antecedent is true (or the antecedent is true at no such world, but we shall abstract from that here).[21] Strict laws are such that they are true at all nomologically possible worlds. But determining the nomologically possible worlds is not sufficient for determining the truth value of a counterfactual like (3) (if M is a predicate that does not occur in any strict law). To determine (3)'s truth value, we need to put a similarity order on the nomologically possible worlds—so that we can see which of them are closest to the actual world. To be true, (3) only needs to be true at these closest worlds.

Anomalism thus is compatible with the truth of counterfactuals like (3) as long as their consequents are true in *the closest* possible worlds in which their antecedents are true—but nevertheless not in *all* such nomologically possible worlds. In other words, there need to be nomologically possible worlds in which

---

20. Cf. Lepore and Loewer 1987.

21. This understanding of counterfactual conditionals is due to Stalnaker 1968 and Lewis 1973. There are differences between their accounts, but they do not matter here.

the antecedent is true, but the consequent is not. As long as these worlds are 'far enough out', the counterfactuals will remain true.

The question is whether the truth of such counterfactuals would give sufficient modal force to the claim that the mental depends on, or is determined by, the physical. These counterfactuals are not supported by any strict laws. Is there any explanation of their truth? Or does it ultimately remain a mere coincidence?

An idea that Davidson himself at least hinted at has it that these counterfactuals *are* supported by laws—not by strict laws, but by ceteris paribus laws (see above, p. 129; 130).[22] The question then is whether this supplies Davidsonian supervenience with the modal force required for an intuitive notion of determination.

But even if Kim's point holds in its full strength, that is, even if strong supervenience is required by a plausible picture of the relation between the mental and the physical, the question of nomological *reduction* has not been settled yet. For even though the claim that the mental is anomalous would be false if there were laws to the effect that physical type P determines mental type M—let's call them "PM laws"—it is by no means obvious that the existence of such laws implies the existence of *bridge laws*. For nomological reduction, we need bridge laws *identifying* mental types with physical types. Identity is bi-directional. But PM laws are one-way streets, so to speak. And it is far from obvious that the existence of PM laws guarantees the existence of laws going in the other direction ("MP laws"). Most of Davidson's remarks on the issue of supervenience, laws, and reduction target this issue. Here is a rather typical passage:

22. Cf. Lepore and Loewer 1987, 640f. See also Kim 1995, 135f; Kim 1993; Yalowitz 2005, 5.3.

Supervenience does not imply the existence of psycho-physical laws. To see this, it is only necessary to recognize that although supervenience entails that any change in a mental property p of a particular event e will be accompanied by a change in the physical properties of e, it does not entail that a change in p in other events will be accompanied by an identical change in the physical properties of those other events. Only the latter entailment would conflict with $AM + P$ [anomalous monism in conjunction with the causal efficacy of the mental and the nomological character of causality] (Davidson 1993b, 7).

Prima facie, this seems quite wrong. Matters improve, however, when taking into account that this passage occurs in a paper that starts with the following characterization of anomalous monism: "AM holds that mental entities (particular time- and space-bound objects and events) are physical entities, but that mental concepts are not reducible by definition or natural law to physical concepts" (Davidson 1993b, 3). That is, what Davidson calls "AM" in this paper does not contain the claim that the mental is anomalous tout court, but only that there are no bridge laws. Therefore, the only relevant psychophysical laws are psychophysical bridge laws. Davidson's claim is that supervenience does not imply the existence of such laws because it does not imply the existence of MP laws. For instance, even if all P-events are beliefs that water is wet, it obviously does not follow that all beliefs that water is wet are P-events. And the latter would not follow even if the former were a law. Simply because it would not be excluded that there are (tons of) other (maximal) physical types Q, R, S, and so on—all of which are different from P and from one another, but all of which nevertheless also are beliefs that water is wet.

This observation is hardly conclusive, however. If the list of physical types instantiating belief that water is wet consists of types *P*, *Q*, *R*, and *S*, wouldn't that imply pretty straightforwardly that there is a bridge law connecting belief that water is wet to physical events of type *P or Q or R or S*? Settling this question depends on answering tricky questions about the identity of types: Is there such a thing as a disjunctive type? Intuitively, the answer might seem to be yes—at least for short disjunctions like the one just considered. But what happens if there is an infinite number of disjuncts? This is not excluded even by strong supervenience, and here, it might seem more intuitive to say that there simply is no physical type that all instantiations of belief-that-water-is-wet belong to. This does not seem to be the line Davidson would have taken, however. He explicitly acknowledges that "even if finitude is not assumed, there seems no compelling reason to deny that there could be coextensive predicates, one mental and one physical" (Davidson 1970b, 216). Such predicates, he continues, could be used to form *true general statements* about the mental and the physical. What Davidson denies is only that such statements would be *strictly lawlike*.

But what could prevent true MP generalizations from being strictly lawlike? The Davidsonian line of thought here might be the following: Strict laws are true in all nomological possible worlds. MP generalizations do not have to be. To be true, they only have to be true—in the actual world. So, even if there are true MP generalizations, the supervenience of the mental on the physical, be it ever so strong, is entirely silent regarding the modal profile of these generalizations. After all, the assumption is only that the mental supervenes on the physical, not the other way around. Consequently, such a generalization could be true without being a strict law.

To illustrate this possibility, let's assume that across the space of all possible worlds, there are only two physical types instantiating belief that water is wet: P and Q. But the actual world @ is such that there are no Q-events in @. In that case, the MP generalization 'an event e is a belief that water is wet iff e is a P-event' is true, but not a strict law. There are possible worlds in which (some) beliefs that water is wet are Q-events.

But that there are true MP generalizations that aren't strict laws does not show that there can't be true MP generalizations that are. On the assumption of strong supervenience of the mental on the physical, it would still seem to hold that we do get strict laws once we take the disjunction of *all* physical types on which a given mental type supervenes *in some world or other*. In our toy example, taking the disjunction of P and Q would seem to suffice. This line of thought thus seems to drive us back to the idea that strict bridge laws, and nomological reduction, can only be avoided if supervenience does not amount to nomological necessitation.

Another idea would be to distinguish between basic physical types and non-basic physical types, where only basic physical types occur in fundamental physical laws. Disjunctive types, especially those involving very long or even infinite disjunctions, it could then be argued, are non-basic (cf. Lepore and Loewer 1989a, 180). If bridge laws are fundamental physical laws they, too, require basic types. Consequently, even strong supervenience of the mental on the physical would not imply MP laws.

It's time to round off these explorations. We have seen that Davidsonian supervenience is weak supervenience: Even if it requires enough supervenient cross-world identity to support the truth of counterfactuals, this identity does not have to hold across all nomological possible worlds. Two last questions need to be answered. For one, we need to get back to the question of the causal efficacy of the mental: Does Davidsonian supervenience ensure that the mental makes a causal difference? For another, we need to know a little more about on precisely what the mental is supposed to supervene: Is there *any particular kind* of physical property that suffices for determining mental properties? Or is the supervenience supposed to be completely *global*?

Let's start with the latter question. The supervenience of the mental on the physical would be "local" if the (minimal) supervenience base for the mental was a proper subclass of the class of physical properties. For instance, if the mental supervened on the neurophysiological, this would be an instance of local supervenience. If, however, there is no supervenience base smaller than the the set of all physical properties the supervenience is global. According to Davidson, the latter is the case. The physical difference required by any mental difference can, in principle, be *anywhere* in the physical world. Most importantly, the required difference need not be 'internal' to the relevant subject: "we are," Davidson claims, "free to hold that people can be in all relevant physical respects identical (identical in the 'necktie sense') while differing psychologically" (cf. Davidson 1987b, 33). Mere externalism about mental content thus is no reason to deny (token) identity between the mental and the physical.

That leaves the causal efficacy of the mental. As we saw above (p. 181), for Davidson this is the question whether the mental properties of an event make a difference to its causal relations. And according to him, supervenience ensures that they do:

> For supervenience as I have defined it does, as we have seen, imply that if two events differ in their psychological properties, they differ in their physical properties (which we assume to be causally efficacious). If supervenience holds, psychological properties make

a difference to the causal relations of an event, for they matter to the physical properties, and the physical properties matter to causal relations. It does nothing to undermine this argument to say 'But the mental properties make a difference not *as* mental but only because they make a difference to the physical properties'. Either they make a difference or they don't; if supervenience is true, they do (Davidson 1993b, 14).

Again, however mere weak supervenience might seem too thin, too weak to give a plausible picture of causal efficacy. Intuitively, we require there to be some counterfactual force to the difference the mental makes. Consider the following example: Someone is killed by a loud shot. It seems intuitively quite plausible to say that its loudness was irrelevant to the shot's causing the death. After all, a counterfactual like the following does seem to be true:

(4)   Had the gun been equipped with a silencer the shot would have killed the victim just the same.   (Sosa 1984, 278.)[23]

Davidson's answer to this example is this:

> The crucial counterfactual is fatally (sorry) ambiguous. Had the gun been equipped with a silencer, a quiet shot, if aimed as the fatal shot was and otherwise relevantly similar, would no doubt have resulted in *a* death. But it would not have been the same shot as the fatal shot, nor could the death it caused have been the same death (Davidson 1993b, 17).

23. For similar examples, see Anscombe 1969, Honderich 1982, Dretske 1989, and for more discussion see Lepore and Loewer 1987, Lepore and Loewer 1989a, Fodor 1989, Yalowitz 2005, 53ff.

This is funny, but intuitively false. For any particular event, we can consider what would have been true of *that very event* under counterfactual circumstances.[24] The question relevant here then is whether the loudness and the deathliness of *that particular shot* come apart in any of the closest nomologically possible worlds. Assume that they do. In that case, it seems plausible to say that its loudness is causally irrelevant to the shot's deathliness.

If anomalous monism is true, doesn't the same hold for mental and physical properties? Not necessarily. To get a plausible picture of the relation between the mental and the physical, weak supervenience must be combined with enough supervenient cross-world identity to support counterfactuals, we saw earlier. If that can be done, there is no analogy with the shot's loudness and deathliness. If the relevant counterfactuals are true, that is, the physical analogue of the shot's deathliness would *not* have occurred without the supposed mental analogue of the shot's loudness. An event's mental properties thus would not be irrelevant to its causal relations in the way loudness is irrelevant to our shot's deathliness (cf. Lepore and Loewer 1987). And this would seem quite sufficient to ensure that an event's mental properties do make a difference to its causal relations. Whether we can ultimately draw a plausible enough picture of the relation between

---

24. Consequently, and contrary to what Davidson claims, the counterfactual intuitively seems to be true even if 'the shot' is construed as referring to the shot that actually was fired. That "the same shot cannot be both both loud and silent" (Davidson 1993b, 17) is true, but irrelevant. The question is whether that particular loud shot *could have been* silent, i.e., whether there is a possible world in which that very same shot is not loud, but silent. Answering this question in the affirmative, however, conflicts with the Davidsonian idea that events are identical iff their causes and effects are—at least on the assumption that that also holds across possible worlds.

the mental and the physical along these lines is a question we have to leave open here.

And with that, our tour of the Davidsonian metaphysics of mind concludes. So does our tour of the Davidsonian philosophy as a whole. We have used the radical interpreter as our guide through a vast theoretical edifice, one of the last grand systems to be constructed in philosophy. Our tour has not led us into every room and corner—in fact, there are whole sidewings left to be explored. Those, readers will have to venture into by themselves. My hope is to have provided them with a guide to the most basic and important lines of Davidsonian thought—thus equipping them for further exploration. Along the way, we have encountered open questions and tensions in Davidson's philosophy. But that there are open questions and tensions threatening its foundations does not diminish the grandeur of the Davidsonian structure. What is more, as with any philosophy, open questions only prove that it is still standing strong—to be admired and attacked.

APPENDIX

A T-theory for a Fragment of English[1]

We shall now consider a very simple fragment of English that we shall call 'QE', and show how to construe a T-theory for it. The vocabulary of QE contains the following:

1. Proper names: 'Elsa', 'John', 'Mary', 'Paul'
2. Predicates: 'sleeps', 'loves', 'envies', 'helps'
3. Logical particles: 'and', 'or', 'it is not the case that', and 'if, then'
4. Quantifiers: 'everyone', 'someone'

The grammar is very simple, too. Proper names and quantifiers are both noun phrases (NPs). The category S is that of sentences. The rules are then:

1.   NP + 'sleeps' is an S
2. NP_1 + 'loves'—'envies'—'helps' + NP_2 is an S
3.   'it is not the case that' + S is an S
4. S_1 + 'and'—'or'—'if, then' + S_2 is an S

---

1. Special thanks to Peter Pagin for helping me make this appendix.

By these rules we can e.g. form the following sentences:

(5)   Mary sleeps or John loves Mary.
(6)   Everyone loves someone.
(7)   If Elsa helps Paul, then Paul loves Elsa and John envies Paul.

Even though this fragment is very simple, the examples show that it has ambiguous sentences. (6) can mean that there is some person such that everyone loves that person, or that for each person there is some person, not necessarily the same, that the first person loves. And (7) can mean either that *John envies Paul* (unconditionally) *and if Elsa helps Paul, then Paul loves Elsa*, and it can mean that *If Elsa helps Paul, then Paul loves Elsa and* (under this condition) *John envies Paul*. These ambiguities matter semantically. So we need to disambiguate the sentences before they can be interpreted.

We disambiguate by means of bracketing sentences and indexing the quantifiers for scope relations. Using these devices we get the following readings corresponding to the readings just specified:

(6′)   Everyone$_2$ loves someone$_1$.
(6″)   Everyone$_1$ loves someone$_2$.
(7′)   (If Elsa helps Paul, then Paul loves Elsa) and John envies Paul.
(7″)   If Elsa helps Paul, then (Paul loves Elsa and John envies Paul).

In order to apply the Tarskian semantics, the fragment needs to be regimented into the apparatus of quantifiers and variables. Thus we will have

1. Proper names:	'Elsa', 'John', 'Mary', 'Paul'
2. Predicates:	'sleeps', 'loves', 'envies', 'helps'
3. Logical connectives:	'&', '∨', '¬', '→'
4. Quantifiers:	'∀', '∃'
5. Individual variables:	$x_1, x_2, \ldots$

The grammar is the usual formation rules for a first-order language. The translation rules are again very simple (we will not spell them out). What we need to take account of is the relative scope of simple sentences containing (different) quantifiers. Corresponding to $(6')$ and $(6'')$ we have

(6^*) $\quad \exists x_1 \forall x_2 (x_2 \text{ loves } x_1)$
(6^*) $\quad \forall x_1 \exists x_2 (x_1 \text{ loves } x_2)$

One must also take care that when a new variable is introduced in the translation, it does not already occur in the scope of the new quantifier.

It should be noted at this point that the first-order language is expressively richer than the QE fragment. For instance, a first-order sentence such as

(8) $\quad \forall x_1 (\exists x_2 (x_1 \text{ loves } x_2) \;\rightarrow\; \exists x_3 (x_3 \text{ loves } x_1))$

does not have a counterpart in QE. It would need forms such as

$(8')$ $\quad$ Everyone who loves someone is loved by someone.
$(8'')$ $\quad$ Everyone is such that if he/she loves someone, then he/she is loved by someone.

In $(8')$ we use a subordinate relative clause, and in $(8'')$ bound pronouns, to express the same proposition, and QE does not contain either of these devices. Adding them to QE would complicate the grammar considerably. It is not needed in order to exemplify the basic features of T-theories. Still, the T-theory that we give below, applied to just the regimented language, does provide an interpretation of (8) (after going through the example derivation below, you could try it as an exercise).

We can now set out the basic clauses for the **T-theory for QE**. We shall use 's' as a meta-language variable for infinite sequences ($s = \langle s_1, s_2, \ldots \rangle$), and '$a_1$', '$a_2$', ... as meta-language individual variables. The axioms and axiom schemata are the following:

1. Singular terms: $\vdash \text{Ref}(\text{'Elsa'}) = \text{Elsa}$

                                $\vdash \text{Ref}(\text{'Mary'}) = \text{Mary}$

                                $\vdash \text{Ref}(\text{'John'}) = \text{John}$

                                $\vdash \text{Ref}(\text{'Paul'}) = \text{Paul}$

2. Predicates: $\vdash \forall s \, (\text{sat}(s, \ulcorner x_i \text{ sleeps} \urcorner \text{ iff } s_i \text{ sleeps})$

                                $\vdash \forall s \, (\text{sat}(s, \ulcorner x_i \text{ loves } x_j \urcorner) \text{ iff } s_i \text{ loves } s_j)$

                                $\vdash \forall s \, (\text{sat}(s, \ulcorner x_i \text{ helps } x_j \urcorner) \text{ iff } s_i \text{ helps } s_j)$

                                $\vdash \forall s \, (\text{sat}(s, \ulcorner x_i \text{ envies } x_j \urcorner) \text{ iff } s_i \text{ envies } s_j)$

3. Connectives: $\vdash \forall s \, (\text{sat}(s, \ulcorner S_1 \ \& \ S_2 \urcorner) \text{ iff sat}(s, S_1) \text{ and sat}(s, S_2))$

                                $\vdash \forall s \, (\text{sat}(s, \ulcorner \neg S \urcorner) \text{ iff it is not the case that sat}(s, S)$

                                $\vdash \forall s \, (\text{sat}(s, \ulcorner S_1 \ \lor \ S_2 \urcorner \text{ iff sat}(s, S_1) \text{ or sat}(s, S_2)))$

                                $\vdash \forall s \, (\text{sat}(s, \ulcorner S_1 \ \to \ S_2 \urcorner) \text{ iff: if sat}(s, S_1), \text{ then sat}(s, S_2))$

4. Quantifiers: $\vdash \forall s \, (\text{sat}(s, \ulcorner \exists x_i P x_i \urcorner) \text{ iff for some } a_i \, (sat(s[a_i/s_i], \ulcorner P x_i \urcorner)))$

                                $\vdash \forall s \, (\text{sat}(s, \ulcorner \forall x_i P x_i \urcorner) \text{ iff for every } a_i \, (sat(s[a_i/s_i], \ulcorner P x_i \urcorner)))$

                                where $\ulcorner x_i \urcorner$ etc. is schematic, with instances like 'x_{13}',

                                and where $s[b/s_i]$ is the sequence differing from s at most by having b in its i:th position.[2]

5. Terms in formulas: $\vdash \text{sat}(s, \ulcorner Pt \urcorner) \text{ iff sat}(s[\text{Ref}(t)/s_i], P x_i)$,

                                provided $\ulcorner x_i \urcorner$ does not already occur in $\ulcorner P \urcorner$.

We will also need rules of inference in order to derive the right theorems. But we don't want the full power of first-order logic, since that would have the consequence, for instance, that if $\vdash A$ iff B is a theorem, so is $\vdash A$ iff (B or (p and not p)). But the latter would not be interpretive if the former is. Therefore, we limit ourselves to a few more specialized rules of inference. They provide one alternative for capturing what Davidson had in mind when speaking of "canonical derivations" (see above, p. 65).

---

2. The method of quantifying over individual meta-language variables applied in the quantifier clauses is suggested in Wiggins 1980, 325.

Rule 1: If $\vdash a = b$ and $\vdash X(a)$, then $\vdash X(b)$

Rule 2: If $\vdash \forall s(A \text{ iff } B)$ and $\vdash \forall s(X(A))$, then $\vdash \forall s(X(B))$

Rule 3: If $\vdash \forall s(A(s) \text{ iff } B)$ and 's' does not occur in B,
then $\vdash \forall s(A(s)) \text{ iff } B$

Rule 4: If $\vdash A \text{ iff } B$ and $\vdash B \text{ iff } C$,
then $\vdash A \text{ iff } C$

Rule 5: $\vdash$ True (s) iff True (s'), if s' is the regimentation of s

Rule 6: $\vdash$ for all $s, a, i \,(s[a/s_i]_i = a)$

In Rules 1 and 2 'X' is schematic for the sentential context. We can now define truth:

Rule 7: $\vdash$ True S iff for all $s \,(\text{sat}(s, S))$

To get a bit of a feeling for how this works, let's run through a derivation. Below, for the sake of readability, we shall use italics instead of quote marks for expressions that are mentioned.

(9) i) $\vdash$ True(*If someone sleeps, then Paul sleeps*) iff
True($\exists x_1(x_1$ *sleeps*) $\rightarrow$ *Paul sleeps*) (rule 5)

ii) $\vdash$ True($\exists x_1(x_1$ *sleeps*) $\rightarrow$ *Paul sleeps*) iff
for all $s(\text{sat}(s, \exists x_1(x_1$ *sleeps*) $\rightarrow$ *Paul sleeps*)) (rule 7)

iii) $\vdash$ For all $s \,(\text{sat}(s, \exists x_1(x_1$ *sleeps*) $\rightarrow$ *Paul sleeps*) iff
if sat($s, \exists x_1(x_1$ *sleeps*)), then sat($s, Paul$ *sleeps*)) (Connectives)

iv) $\vdash$ For all $s \,(\text{sat}(s, \exists x_1(x_1$ *sleeps*)) iff
for some $a_1(\text{sat}(s[a_1/s_1], x_1$ *sleeps*))) (quantifiers)

v) $\vdash$ For all s (for some $a_1(\text{sat}(s[a_1/s_1], x_1$ *sleeps*)) iff
for some $a_1(s[a_1/s_1]_1$ *sleeps*)) (predicates, rule 2)

vi) $\vdash$ For all s (for some $a_1(s[a_1/s_1]_1$ *sleeps*)) iff
for some $a_1(a_1$ *sleeps*)) (rule 6, rule 1)

vii) $\vdash$ For all s (sat($s, Paul$ *sleeps*) iff
sat($s[\text{Ref}(Paul)/s_2], x_2$ *sleeps*)) (terms in formulas)

viii) $\vdash$ For all s (sat($s[\text{Ref}(Paul)/s_2], x_2$ *sleeps*) iff
$s[\text{Ref}(Paul)/s_2]_2$ *sleeps*) (predicates)

ix) ⊢ For all s ($s[\text{Ref}(Paul)/s_2]_2$ *sleeps* iff
    Ref(*Paul*) sleeps)   (rule 6, rule 1)

x) ⊢ For all s (Ref(*Paul*) sleeps iff
    Paul sleeps)   (singular terms, rule 1)

xi) ⊢ For all s (if sat($s, \exists x_1(x_1$ *sleeps*)), then sat($s, Paul$ *sleeps*) iff
    if for some $a_1(a_1$ sleeps), then Paul sleeps)
                                  ((9iv)-(9x), rule 2)

xii) ⊢ For all s (sat($s, \exists x_1(x_1$ *sleeps*) $\rightarrow$ *Paul sleeps*) iff
    if for some $a_1(a_1$ sleeps), then Paul sleeps)
                                ((9iii), (9xi), rule 2)

xiii) ⊢ For all s (sat($s, \exists x_1(x_1$ *sleeps*) $\rightarrow$ *Paul sleeps*)) iff
    if for some $a_1(a_1$ sleeps), then Paul sleeps
                                     ((9xii), rule 3)

xiv) ⊢ True($\exists x_1(x_1$ *sleeps*) $\rightarrow$ *Paul sleeps*) iff
    if for some $a_1(a_1$ sleeps), then Paul sleeps
                              ((9ii), (9xiii), rule 4)

xv) ⊢ True(*If someone sleeps, then Paul sleeps*) iff
    if for some $a_1(a_1$ sleeps), then Paul sleeps.
                                     ((9i), (9xiv), rule 4).

BIBLIOGRAPHY

Anscombe, Elizabeth (1957). *Intention*. Oxford: Blackwell.

—— (1969). "Causality and Extensionality." In: *Journal of Philosophy* 66, pp. 152–59.

—— (1971). *Causality and Determination*. Cambridge: Cambridge University Press.

Anscombe, Elizabeth Anscombe (1979). "Under a Description." In: *Nous* 13, pp. 219–33.

Bar-On, Dorit and Mark Risjord (1992). "Is There Such a Thing as a Language." In: *Canadian Journal of Philosophy* 22, pp. 163–90.

Bennett, Jonathan (1985). "Adverb-Dropping Inferences and the Lemmon-Criterion." In: *Actions and Events. Perspectives on the Philosophy of Donald Davidson*. Ed. by Ernest Lepore and Brian McLaughlin. Oxford: Basil Blackwell, pp. 193–206.

Boghossian, Paul (1996). "Analyticity Reconsidered." In: *Nous* 30, pp. 360–91.

—— (2003). "Epistemic Analyticity: A Defense." In: *Grazer Philosophische Studien* 66, pp. 15–35.

Borg, Emma (2004). *Minimal Semantics*. Oxford: Oxford University Press.

Bouma, Hanni K. (2006). "Radical Interpretation and High-Functioning Autistic Speakers: A Defense of Davidson on Thought and Language." In: *Philosophical Psychology* 19, pp. 639–62.

Bratman, Michael (1987). *Intention, Plans, and Practical Reasoning*. Cambridge, Mass.: Harvard University Press.

Bridges, Jason (2006). "Davidson's Transcendental Externalism." In: *Philosophy and Phenomenological Research* 73, pp. 290–315.

Burge, Tyler (1986). "On Davidson's 'Saying That.'" In: *Truth and Interpretation: Perspectives on the Philosophy of Donald Davidson*. Ed. by Ernest Lepore. Oxford: Basil Blackwell, pp. 190–210.

———(2003). "Perceptual Entitlement." In: *Philosophy and Phenomenological Research* LXVII, pp. 503–48.

———(2010). *Origins of Objectivity*. Oxford: Oxford University Press.

Cappelen, Herman and Ernest Lepore (2004). *Insensitive Semantics*. Oxford: Blackwell.

Carnap, Rudolf (1947). *Meaning and Necessity. A Study in Semantics and Modal Logic*. Chicago: University of Chicago Press.

Casati, Roberto and Achille Varzi (1997). *50 Years of Events. An Annotated Bibliography 1947 to 1997*. URL: http://www.pdcnet.org/pages/Products/electronic/eventsbib.htm.

Castañeda, Hector-Neri (1975). *Thinking and Doing*. Dordrecht: D. Reidel.

Casullo, Alberto (1988). "Revisability, Reliabilism, and A Priori Knowledge." In: *Philosophy and Phenomenological Research* 49, pp. 187–213.

———(2002). "A Priori Knowledge." In: *The Oxford Handbook of Epistemology*. Ed. by Paul Moser. Oxford: Oxford University Press, pp. 95–143.

Child, William (1996). *Causality, Interpretation, and the Mind*. Oxford: Oxford University Press.

Chisholm, Roderick (1970). "Events and Propositions." In: *Nous* 4, pp. 15–24.

Churchland, Paul (1984). *Matter and Consciousness*. Cambridge, Mass.: MIT Press.

Davidson, Donald (1963). "Actions, Reasons, and Causes." In: *Essays on Actions and Events*. Oxford: Clarendon Press 1980, pp. 3–19.

———(1965). "Theories of Meaning and Learnable Languages." In: *Inquiries into Truth and Interpretation*. Oxford: Clarendon Press 1984.

———(1967a). "Causal Relations." In: *Essays on Actions and Events*. Oxford: Clarendon Press 1980, pp. 149–62.

———(1967b). "The Logical Form of Action Sentences." In: *Actions and Events*. Oxford: Clarendon Press 1980, pp. 105–21.

———(1967c). "Truth and Meaning." In: *Inquiries into Truth and Interpretation*. Oxford: Clarendon Press 1984, pp. 17–36.

———(1968). "On Saying That." In: *Inquiries into Truth and Interpretation*. Oxford: Clarendon Press 1984, pp. 93–108.

———(1969a). "The Individuation of Events." In: *Actions and Events*. Oxford: Clarendon Press 1980, pp. 163–80.

————— (1969b). "True to the Facts." In: *Inquiries into Truth and Interpretation.* Oxford: Clarendon Press 1984, pp. 37–54.

————— (1970a). "How is Weakness of the Will Possible?" In: *Actions and Events.* Oxford: Clarendon Press 1980, pp. 21–42.

————— (1970b). "Mental events." In: *Essays on Actions and Events.* Oxford: Clarendon Press 1980, pp. 207–25.

————— (1971a). "Agency." In: *Actions and Events.* Oxford: Clarendon Press 1980, pp. 43–62.

————— (1971b). "Eternal vs. Ephemeral Events." In: *Actions and Events.* Oxford: Clarendon Press 1980, pp. 189–203.

————— (1973a). "Freedom to Act." In: *Actions and Events.* Oxford: Clarendon Press 1980, pp. 63–81.

————— (1973b). "Radical Interpretation." In: *Inquiries into Truth and Interpretation.* Oxford: Clarendon Press 1984, pp. 125–39.

————— (1973c). "The Material Mind." In: *Essays on Actions and Events.* Oxford: Clarendon Press 1980, pp. 245–59.

————— (1974a). "Belief and the Basis of Meaning." In: *Inquiries into Truth and Interpretation.* Oxford: Clarendon Press 1984, pp. 141–54.

————— (1974b). "On the Very Idea of a Conceptual Scheme." In: *Inquiries into Truth and Interpretation.* Oxford: Clarendon Press 1984, pp. 183–98.

————— (1974c). "Psychology as Philosophy." In: *Essays on Actions and Events.* Oxford: Clarendon Press 1980, pp. 229–39.

————— (1974d). "Replies to David Lewis and W. V. Quine." In: *Synthese 27,* pp. 345–49.

————— (1975). "Thought and Talk." In: *Inquiries into Truth and Interpretation.* Oxford: Clarendon Press 1984, pp. 155–70.

————— (1976a). "Hempel on Explaining Action." In: *Essays on Actions and Events.* Oxford: Clarendon Press 1980, pp. 261–75.

————— (1976b). "Reply to Foster." In: *Inquiries into Truth and Interpretation.* Oxford: Clarendon Press 1984, pp. 171–79.

————— (1977a). "Reality without Reference." In: *Inquiries into Truth and Interpretation.* Oxford: Clarendon Press 1984, pp. 215–25.

————— (1977b). "The Method of Truth in Metaphysics." In: *Inquiries into Truth and Interpretation.* Oxford: Clarendon Press 1984, pp. 199–214.

————— (1978). "Intending." In: *Actions and Events.* Oxford: Clarendon Press 1980, pp. 83–102.

————— (1979). "The Inscrutability of Reference." In: *Inquiries into Truth and Interpretation.* Oxford: Clarendon Press 1984, pp. 227–41.

———— (1980a). "A Unified Theory of Thought, Meaning and Action." In: *Problems of Rationality*. Oxford: Clarendon Press 2004, pp. 151–66.

———— (1980b). *Essays on Actions and Events*. Oxford: Clarendon Press.

———— (1982a). "Communication and Convention." In: *Inquiries into Truth and Interpretation*. Oxford: Clarendon Press 1984, pp. 265–80.

———— (1982b). "Paradoxes of Irrationality." In: *Problems of Rationality*. Oxford: Clarendon Press 2004, pp. 169–87.

———— (1982c). "Rational Animals." In: *Subjective, Intersubjective, Objective*. Oxford: Clarendon Press 2001, pp. 95–105.

Davidson, Donald (1983). "A Coherence Theory of Truth and Knowledge." In: *Subjective, Intersubjective, Objective*. Oxford: Clarendon Press 2001, pp. 137–53.

———— (1984a). "First Person Authority." In: *Subjective, Intersubjective, Objective*. Oxford: Clarendon Press 2001, pp. 3–14.

———— (1984b). *Inquiries into Truth and Interpretation*. Oxford: Clarendon Press.

———— (1985a). "A New Basis for Decision Theory." In: *Theory and Decision* 18, pp. 87–98.

———— (1985b). "Deception and Devision." In: *Problems of Rationality*. Oxford: Clarendon Press 2004, pp. 199–212.

———— (1985c). "Incoherence and Irrationality." In: *Problems of Rationality*. Oxford: Clarendon Press 2004, pp. 189–98.

———— (1985d). "Replies." In: *Essays on Davidson. Actions and Events*. Ed. by Bruce Vermazen and Merrill B. Hintikka. Oxford: Clarendon Press, pp. 242–52.

———— (1985e). "Reply to Quine on Events." In: *Actions and Events. Perspectives on the Philosophy of Donald Davidson*. Ed. by Ernest Lepore and Brian McLaughlin. Oxford: Basil Blackwell, pp. 162–71.

———— (1986). "A Nice Derangement of Epitaphs." In: *Truth, Language and History*. Oxford: Clarendon Press 2005, pp. 89–108.

———— (1987a). "Afterthoughts." In: *Subjective, Intersubjective, Objective*. Oxford: Clarendon Press 2001, pp. 154–57.

———— (1987b). "Knowing One's Own Mind." In: *Subjective, Intersubjective, Objective*. Oxford: Clarendon Press 2001, pp. 15–38.

———— (1987c). "Problems in the Explanation of Action." In: *Problems of Rationality*. Oxford: Clarendon Press 2004, pp. 101–16.

———— (1989). "James Joyce and Humpty Dumpty." In: *Truth, Language and History*. Oxford: Clarendon Press 2005, pp. 143–57.

———— (1990a). "Epistemology Externalized." In: *Subjective, Intersubjective, Objective*. Oxford: Clarendon Press 2001, pp. 193–204.

———— (1990b). "Meaning, Truth, and Evidence." In: *Truth, Language and History*. Oxford: Clarendon Press 2005, pp. 47–62.

———— (1990c). "Representation and Interpretation." In: *Problems of Rationality*. Oxford: Clarendon Press 2004, pp. 87–99.

———— (1991). "Three Varieties of Knowledge." In: *Subjective, Intersubjective, Objective*. Oxford: Clarendon Press 2001, pp. 205–20.

———— (1992). "The Second Person." In: *Subjective, Intersubjective, Objective*. Oxford: Clarendon Press 2001, pp. 107–121.

———— (1993a). "Locating Literary Language." In: *Truth, Language and History*. Oxford: Clarendon Press 2005, pp. 167–81.

———— (1993b). "Thinking Causes." In: *Mental Causation*. Ed. by John Heil; Alfred Mele. Oxford: Clarendon Press, pp. 3–17.

———— (1994). "The Social Aspect of Language." In: *Truth, Language and History*. Oxford: Clarendon Press 2005, pp. 109–25.

———— (1995a). "Could There be a Science of Rationality?" In: *Problems of Rationality*. Oxford: Clarendon Press 2004, pp. 117–34.

———— (1995b). "Laws and Cause." In: *Dialectica* 49, pp. 263–79.

———— (1995c). "The Problem of Objectivity." In: *Problems of Rationality*. Oxford: Clarendon Press 2004, pp. 3–18.

———— (1996). "The Folly of Trying to Define Truth." In: *Truth, Language and History*. Oxford: Clarendon Press 2005, pp. 19–37.

———— (1997a). "Seeing Through Language." In: *Truth, Language and History*. Oxford: Clarendon Press 2005, pp. 127–41.

———— (1997b). "The Emergence of Thought." In: *Subjective, Intersubjective, Objective*. Oxford: Clarendon Press 2001, pp. 123–34.

———— (1998). "The Irreducibility of the Concept of the Self." In: *Subjective, Intersubjective, Objective*. Oxford: Clarendon Press 2001, pp. 85–92.

———— (1999a). "Reply to Andrew Cutrofello." In: *The Philosophy of Donald Davidson*. Ed. by Lewis Edwin Hahn. Chicago and La Salle, Ill.: Open Court, pp. 342–44.

———— (1999b). "Reply to Ariela Lazar." In: *The Philosophy of Donald Davidson*. Ed. by Lewis Edwin Hahn. Chicago and La Salle, Ill.: Open Court, pp. 402–05.

———— (1999c). "Reply to John McDowell." In: *The Philosophy of Donald Davidson*. Ed. by Lewis Edwin Hahn. Chicago and La Salle, Ill.: Open Court, pp. 105–08.

———— (1999d). "Reply to Pascal Engel." In: *The Philosophy of Donald Davidson*. Ed. by Lewis Edwin Hahn. Chicago and La Salle, Ill.: Open Court, pp. 460–62.

———— (2001a). "Comments on Karlovy Vary Papers." In: *Interpreting Davidson*. Ed. by Petr Kotatko, Peter Pagin, and Gabriel Segal. Stanford: Center for the Study of Language and Information (CSLI), pp. 285–307.

———— (2001b). "Externalisms." In: *Interpreting Davidson*. Ed. by Petr Kotatko, Peter Pagin, and Gabriel Segal. Stanford: CSLI, pp. 1–16.

———— (2005). *Truth and Predication*. Cambridge, Mass.: The Belknap Press of Harvard University Press.

Davidson, Donald and Kathrin Glüer (1995). "Relations and Transistions. An Interview with Donald Davidson." In: *Dialectica* 49, pp. 75–86.

Dennett, Daniel C. (1990). *The Intentional Stance*. Cambridge, Mass.: MIT Press.

Dretske, Fred (1989). "Reasons and Causes." In: *Philosophical Perspectives 3: Philosophy of Mind and Action Theory*, pp. 1–15.

Dummett, Michael (1959). "Truth." In: *Truth and Other Enigmas*. Cambridge, Mass: Harvard University Press 1978, pp. 1–24.

———— (1974). "What is a Theory of Meaning (I)." In: *The Seas of Language*. Oxford: Oxford University Press 1993, pp. 1–33.

———— (1976). "What is a Theory of Meaning (II)." In: *The Seas of Language*. Oxford: Oxford University Press 1993, pp. 34–93.

———— (1986). "A Nice Derangement of Epitaphs: Some Comments on Davidson and Hacking." In: *Truth and Interpretation: Perspectives on the Philosophy of Donald Davidson*. Ed. by Ernest Lepore. Oxford: Basil Blackwell, pp. 459–76.

———— (1991). *The Logical Basis of Metaphysics*. Cambridge, Mass.: Harvard University Press.

Etchemendy, John (1988). "Tarski on Truth and Logical Consequence." In: *Journal of Symbolic Logic* 53, pp. 51–79.

Evans, Gareth (1975). "Identity and Predication." In: *Journal of Philosophy*, 72, pp. 343–63.

Evnine, Simon (1991). *Donald Davidson*. Key Contemporary Thinkers. Stanford: Stanford University Press.

Feyerabend, Paul (1962). "Explanation, Reduction, and Empiricism." In: *Realism, Rationalism and Scientific Method. Philosophical Papers Vol. 1*. Cambridge: Cambridge University Press 1981, pp. 44–96.

Fodor, Jerry (1987). *Psychosemantics*. Cambridge, Mass.: Harvard University Press.

——— (1989). "Making Mind Matter More." In: *Philosophical Topics* 17, pp. 59–79.

Fodor, Jerry and Ernest Lepore (1991). "Why Meaning (Probably) Isn't Conceptual Role." In: *Mind and Language* 6, pp. 328–43.

——— (1992). *Holism: A Shopper's Guide*. Oxford: Basil Blackwell.

Føllesdal, Dagfinn (1973). "Indeterminacy of Translation and Under-Determination fo the Theory of Nature." In: *Dialectica* 27, pp. 289–301.

——— (1975). "Meaning and Experience." In: *Mind and Language: Wolfson College Lectures 1974*. Ed. by Samuel Guttenplan. Oxford: Oxford University Press, pp. 25–44.

——— (1990). "Indeterminacy and Mental States." In: *Perspectives on Quine*. Ed. by Robert Barrett and Roger Gibson. Oxford: Blackwell, pp. 98–109.

——— (1999). "Triangulation." In: *The Philosophy of Donald Davidson*. Ed. by Lewis Edwin Hahn. Chicago and La Salle, Ill.: Open Court, pp. 719–28.

Frege, Gottlob (1884a). *Die Grundlagen der Artithmetik*. Breslau: Wilhelm Koebner.

——— (1884b). *The Foundations of Arithmetic: A logico-mathematical enquiry into the concept of number*. Ed. by J. L. Austin. 2nd ed. Evanston: Northwestern University Press 1980.

——— (1892). "Über Sinn und Bedeutung." In: *Zeitschrift für Philosophie und philosophische Kritik* 100, pp. 25–50.

——— (undated [1914]). "Letter to Jourdain." In: *Meaning and Reference*. Ed. by A. W. Moore. Oxford: Oxford University Press 1993.

——— (undatiert [1914]). "Frege an Jourdain." In: *Wissenschaftlicher Briefwechsel*. Ed. by Gottfried Gabriel et al. Hamburg: Felix Meiner, 1976.

Gallois, Andre and John O'Leary-Hawthorne (1996). "Externalism and Scepticism." In: *Philosophical Studies* 81, pp. 1–26.

George, Alexander (1990). "Whose Language is it Anyway? Some Notes on Idiolects." In: *Philosophical Quarterly* 40, pp. 275–98.

——— (2004). "Linguistic Practice and Its Discontents: Quine and Davidson on the Source of Sense." In: *Philosophers' Imprint* 4. URL: http://hdl.handle.net/2027/spo.3521354.0004.001.

Ginet, Carl (1990). *On Action*. Cambridge: Cambridge University Press.

Ginsborg, Hannah (2006). "Reasons for Belief." In: *Philosophy and Phenomenological Research* 72, pp. 286–318.

Glüer, Kathrin (2000). "Wittgenstein and Davidson on Agreement in Judgment." In: *Wittgenstein Studies* 2, pp. 81–103.

—— (2001). "Dreams and Nightmares. Conventions, Norms, and Meaning in Davidson's Philosophy of Language." In: *Interpreting Davidson.* Ed. by Petr Kotatko, Peter Pagin, and Gabriel Segal. Stanford: CSLI, pp. 53–74.

—— (2003a). "Analyticity and Implicit Definition." In: *Grazer Philosophische Studien* 66, pp. 37–60.

—— (2003b). "Is There Such a Thing as Weakness of the Will?" In: *A philosophical smorgasbord: essays on action, truth and other things in honour of Fredrick Stoutland.* Ed. by Krister Segerberg and Rysiek Sliwinski. Uppsala: Dept. of Philosophy, pp. 65–83.

—— (2004). "On Perceiving That." In: *Theoria* 70, pp. 197–212.

—— (2006a). "The Status of Charity I: Conceptual Truth or Aposteriori Necessity?" In: *International Journal of Philosophical Studies* 14, pp. 337–59.

—— (2006b). "Triangulation." In: *The Oxford Handbook of Philosophy of Language.* Ed. by Ernest Lepore and Barry Smith. Oxford: Oxford University Press, pp. 1006–019.

—— (2007). "Critical Notice: Donald Davidson's Collected Essays." In: *Dialectica* 61, pp. 275–84.

Glüer, Kathrin (2009). "In Defence of a Doxastic Account of Experience." In: *Mind and Language* 24, pp. 297–373.

—— (2011). "Theories of Meaning and Truth Conditions." In: *The Continuum Guide to the Philosophy of Language* Ed. by Max Kölbel and Manuel García-Carpintero. London: Continuum (forthcoming).

Glüer, Kathrin and Peter Pagin (2003). "Meaning Theory and Autistic Speakers." In: *Mind and Language* 18, pp. 23–51.

—— (2006). "Proper Names and Relational Modality." In: *Linguistics & Philosophy* 29, pp. 507–35.

—— (2008). "Relational Modality." In: *Journal of Logic, Language, and Information* 17. An earlier version appeared in: H. Lagerlund, S. Lindström and R. Sliwinski (eds), *Modality Matters. Twentyfive Essays in Honour of Krister Segerberg,* Uppsala 2006, 123–48., pp. 307–22.

—— (2011). "General Terms and Relational Modality." In: *Nous* (forthcoming).

Glüer, Kathrin and Åsa Wikforss (2009a). "Against Content Normativity." In: *Mind* 118, pp. 31–70.

——— (2009b). "The Normativity of Meaning and Content." In: *The Stanford Encyclopedia of Philosophy*. Ed. by Edward N. Zalta. Summer 2009. URL: http://plato.stanford.edu/archives/sum2009/entries/meaning-normativity/.

Goldman, Alvin (1989). "Interpretation Psychologized." In: *Mind and Language* 4, pp. 161–85.

Grandy, Richard E. (1990). "Understanding and the Principle of Compositionality." In: *Philosophical Perspectives* 4, pp. 557–72.

Grandy, Richard E. and Richard Warner (2009). "Paul Grice." In: *The Stanford Encyclopedia of Philosophy*. Ed. by Edward N. Zalta. Summer 2009. URL: http://plato.stanford.edu/archives/sum2009/entries/grice/.

Grice, Paul (1957). "Meaning." In: *Studies in the Ways of Words*. Cambridge, Mass.: Harvard University Press 1987, pp. 213–23.

——— (1971). "Intention and Certainty." In: *Proceedings of the British Academy* 57, pp. 263–79.

——— (1989). *Studies in the Ways of Words*. Cambridge, Mass.: Harvard University Press.

Hacking, Ian (1975). *Why does Language Matter to Philosophy?* Cambridge: Cambridge University Press.

Hare, Richard M. (1952). *The Language of Morals*. Oxford: Clarendon Press.

Harman, Gilbert (2011). "Davidson's Contribution to the Philosophy of Language." In: *Davidson's Philosophy. A Reappraisal*. Ed. by Gerhard Preyer. Oxford: Oxford University Press (forthcoming).

Heck, Richard G. (1997). "Tarski, Truth, and Semantics." In: *Philosophical Review* 106, pp. 533–54.

Heck, Richard G. and Robert May (2006). "Frege's Contribution to Philosophy of Language." In: *The Oxford Handbook of Philosophy of Language189-*. Ed. by Ernest Lepore and Barry Smith. Oxford University Press, pp. 3–39.

Higginbotham, James (1992). "Truth and Understanding." In: *Philosophical Studies* 65, pp. 3–16.

Honderich, Ted (1982). "The Argument for Anomalous Monism." In: *Analysis* XLII, pp. 59–64.

Hornsby, Jennifer (2008). "Davidson and Dummett on the Social Character of Language." In: *Knowledge, Language, and Interpretation. On the Philosophy of Donald Davidson*. Ed. by Maria Cristina Amoretti and Nicla

Vassalo. Schriften zur Erkenntnis- und Wissenschaftstheorie. Heusenstamm: ontos, pp. 107–22.

Horwich, Paul (1998). *Meaning*. Oxford University Press.

Jackman, Henry (2003). "Charity, Self Interpretation, and Belief." In: *Journal of Philosophical Research* 28, pp. 145–70.

Jacob, Pierre (1991). "Are Mental Properties Causally Efficacious?" In: *Grazer Philosophische Studien* 39, pp. 51–73.

Kim, Jaegwon (1976). "Events as Property Exemplifications." In: *Action Theory*. Ed. by M. Brand; D. Walton. Dordrecht: D. Reidel, pp. 159–77.

——— (1984a). "Concepts of Supervenience." In: *Philosophy and Phenomenological Research* XLV, pp. 153–76.

——— (1984b). "Epiphenomenal and Supervenient Causation." In: *Midwest Studies in Philosophy* 9, pp. 257–70.

——— (1987). "'Strong and 'Global Supervenience Revisited." In: *Philosophy and Phenomenological Research* XLVIII, pp. 315–26.

——— (1989a). "Mechanism, Purpose, and Explanatory Exclusion." In: *Philosophical Perspectives* 3, pp. 77–108.

——— (1989b). "The Myth of Nonreductive Materialism." In: *Proceedings and Addresses of the American Philosophical Association* 63, pp. 31–47.

——— (1993). "Can Supervenience and 'Non-Strict Laws' Save Anomalous Monism?" In: *Mental Causation*. Ed. by John Heil; Alfred Mele. Oxford: Clarendon Press 1993, pp. 19–26.

——— (1995). "Explanatory Exclusion and the Problem of Mental Causation." In: *Philosophy of Psychology*. Ed. by Cynthia McDonald and Graham McDonald. Oxford: Basil Blackwell, pp. 121–41.

King, Jeffrey C. (2006). "Formal Semantics." In: *The Oxford Handbook of Philosophy of Language*. Ed. by Ernest Lepore and Barry Smith. Oxford: Clarendon Press Press, pp. 557–73.

Kölbel, Max (2001). "Tow Dogmas of Davidsonian Semantics." In: *Journal of Philosophy* 98, pp. 613–35.

Kripke, Saul (1972). *Naming and Necessity*. Cambridge, Mass.: Harvard University Press.

——— (1982). *Wittgenstein on Rules and Private Language*. Cambridge, Mass.: Harvard University Press.

——— (2008). "Frege's Theory of Sense and Reference: Some Exegetical Notes." In: *Theoria*, pp. 181–218.

Kuhn, Thomas (1962). *The Structure of Scientific Revolutions*. Chicago: University of Chicago Press.

Künne, Wolfgang (1981). "Verstehen und Sinn." In: *Allgemeine Zeitschrift für Philosophie* 6, pp. 1–16.

——— (1990). "Prinzipien der wohlwollenden Interpretation." In: *Intentionalität und Verstehen*. Ed. by Siegfried Blasche et al. Frankfurt a. M.: Surhkamp, pp. 212–36.

——— (1991). "Handlungs- und andere Ereignissätze. Davidsons Frage nach ihrer logischen Form." In: *Grazer Philosophische Studien* 39, pp. 27–49.

Larson, Richard and Gabriel Segal (1995). *Knowledge of Meaning: An introduction to semantic theory*. Cambridge, Mass.: MIT Press.

Lasonen, Maria and Tomasz Marvan (2004). "Davidson's Triangulation: Content-Endowing Causes and Circularity." In: *International Journal of Philosophical Studies* 12, pp. 177–95.

Latham, Noa (2003). "What is Token-Physicalism?" In: *Pacific Philosophical Quarterly* 84, pp. 270–90.

Lazar, Ariela (1999). "Akrasia and the Principle of Continence or What the Tortoise Would Say to Achilles." In: *The Philosophy of Donald Davidson*. Ed. by Lewis Edwin Hahn. Chicago and La Salle, Ill.: Open Court, pp. 381–401.

Lemmon, E. J. (1967). "Comments." In: *The Logic of Decision and Action*. Ed. by Nicholas Rescher. Pittsburgh: University of Pittsburgh Press, pp. 96–103.

Lenman, James (2010). "Reasons for Action: Justification vs. Explanation." In: *The Stanford Encyclopedia of Philosophy*. Ed. by Edward N. Zalta. Spring 2010. URL: http://plato.stanford.edu/archives/spr2010/entries/reasons-just-vs-expl/.

Lepore, Ernest (1985). "The Semantics of Action, Event, and Singular Causal Sentences." In: *Actions and Events. Perspectives on the Philosophy of Donald Davidson*. Ed. by Ernest Lepore and Brain McLaughlin. Oxford: Basil Blackwell, pp. 151–61.

Lepore, Ernest and Barry Loewer (1987). "Mind Matters." In: *Journal of Philosophy* 84, pp. 630–42.

——— (1989a). "More on Making Mind Matter." In: *Philosophical Topics* XVII, pp. 175–91.

——— (1989b). "You Can Say That Again." In: *Midwest Studies in Philosophy* 14, pp. 338–56.

Lepore, Ernest and Kirk Ludwig (2005). *Donald Davidson. Meaning, Truth, Language, and Reality*. Oxford: Oxford University Press.

——— (2007a). *Donald Davidson's Truth-Theoretic Semantics*. Oxford: Clarendon Press.

———— (2007b). "The Reality of Language. On the Davidson/Dummett Exchange." In: *The Philosophy of Michael Dummett*. Ed. by Randall E. Auxier and Lewis Edwin Hahn. The Library of Living Philosophers Volume 31. Chicago and La Salle, Ill.: Open Court, pp. 185–214.

Lepore, Ernest and Brian McLaughlin (1985). "Actions, Reasons, Causes, and Intentions." In: *Actions and Events. Perspectives on the Philosophy of Donald Davidson*. Ed. by Ernest Lepore and Brian McLaughlin. Oxford: Basil Blackwell, pp. 3–13.

Lewis, David (1972). "Psychophysical and theoretical identifications." In: *Australasian Journal of Philosophy* 50, pp. 249–58.

———— (1973). *Counterfactuals*. Oxford: Basil Blackwell.

———— (1974). "Radical Interpretation." In: *Synthese* 27, pp. 331–44.

———— (1975). "Languages and Language." In: *Language, Mind, and Knowledge*. Ed. by Keith Gunderson. Minnesota Studies in the Philosophy of Science 7. Minneapolis: University of Minnesota Press.

Malpas, Jeff E. (1988). "The Nature of Interpretative Charity." In: *Dialectica* 42, pp. 17–32.

Matthews, Robert J. (2007). *The Measure of Mind*. Oxford: Oxford University Press.

McDowell, John (1982). "Criteria, Defeasibility, and Knowledge." In: *Meaning, Knowledge, and Reality*. Cambridge, Mass.: Harvard University Press 1998, pp. 369–94.

———— (1994). *Mind and World*. Cambridge, Mass.: Harvard University Press.

———— (1996). "Précis of Mind and World." In: *Philosophical Issues 7: Perception*. Ed. by E. Villanueva. Atascadera, Calif.: Ridgeview Publishing Company, pp. 231–40.

———— (1998). "Reply to Commentators." In: *Philosophy and Phenomenological Research* 58, pp. 403–31.

———— (2002). "Responses." In: *Reading McDowell: On Mind and World*. Ed. by Nicholas H. Smith. London and New York: Routledge, pp. 269–305.

———— (2004). "Reply to Kathrin Glüer." In: *Theoria* LXX, pp. 213–15.

McDowell, John (2008). "Avoiding the Myth of the Given." In: *John McDowell: Experience, Norm, and Nature*. Ed. by Jakob Lindgaard. Oxford: Wiley-Blackwell, pp. 1–14.

McGinn, Colin (1977). "Charity, Interpretation, and Belief." In: *Journal of Philosophy* 74, pp. 521–35.

——— (1986). "Radical Interpretation and Epistemology." In: *Truth and Interpretation: Perspectives on the Philosophy of Donald Davidson*. Ed. by Ernest Lepore. Oxford: Basil Blackwell, pp. 356–68.

McLaughlin, Brian (1985). "Anomalous Monism and the Irreducibility of the Mental." In: *Actions and Events. Perspectives on the Philosophy of Donald Davidson*. Ed. by Ernest Lepore and Brian McLaughlin. Oxford: Basil Blackwell, pp. 331–68.

Melden, A. I. (1961). *Free Action*. London: Routledge and Kegan Paul.

Mele, Alfred (2003). *Motivation and Agency*. New York: Oxford University Press.

Montague, Richard (1969). "On the Nature of Certain Philosophical Entities." In: *The Monist* 53, pp. 159–94.

Pagin, Peter (1997). "Is compositionality compatible with holism?" In: *Mind and Language* 12, pp. 11–33.

——— (2000). "Publicness and Indeterminacy." In: *Knowledge, Language and Logic: Questions for Quine*. Ed. by Peter Kotatko and Alex Orenstein. Boston Studies in the Philosophy of Science. Kluwer, pp. 163–80.

——— (2001). "Semantic Triangulation." In: *Interpreting Davidson*. Ed. by Peter Kotatko; Peter Pagin; Gabriel Segal. Stanford: CSLI, pp. 199–212.

——— (2003). "Communication and Strong Compositionality." In: *Journal of Philosophical Logic* 32, pp. 287–322.

——— (2005). "Compositionality and Context." In: *Contextualism in Philosophy*. Ed. by Gerhard Peter and Gerhard Preyer. Oxford: Oxford University Press, pp. 303–48.

——— (2006). "Meaning Holism." In: *Oxford Handbook of the Philosophy of Language*. Ed. by Ernest Lepore and Barry Smith. Oxford: Clarendon Press, pp. 213–32.

——— (2008). "Indeterminacy and the Analytic-Synthetic Distinctions: A Survey." In: *Synthese* 164, pp. 1–18.

——— (2011a). "Laws of Pragmatics." Unpublished manuscript.

——— (2011b). "Truth Theories, Competence, and Semantic Computation." In: *Davidson's Philosophy. A Reappraisal*. Ed. by Gerhard Preyer. Oxford: Oxford University Press (forthcoming).

Pagin, Peter and Jeffrey Pelletier (2007). "Content, Context and Composition." In: *Content and Context. Essays on Semantics and Pragmatics*. Ed. by Gerhard Peter and Gerhard Preyer. Oxford: Oxford University Press, pp. 25–62.

Pagin, Peter and Dag Westerståhl (2010a). "Compositionality I: Definitions and Variants." In: *Philosophy Compass* 5, pp. 250–64.

—— (2010b). "Compositionality II: Arguments and Problems." In: *Philosophy Compass* 5, pp. 265–82.

—— (2011). "Pure Quotation, Compositionality, and the Semantics of Linguistic Context." In: *Linguistics and Philosophy* (forthcoming).

Papineau, David (2006). "Naturalist Theories of Meaning." In: *The Oxford Handbook of Philosophy of Language*. Ed. by Ernest Lepore; Barry Smith. Oxford: Clarendon Press, pp. 175–88.

Parsons, Terence (1990). *Events in the Semantics of English. A Study in Subatomic Semantics*. Cambridge, Mass: MIT Press.

Patterson, Douglas (2005). "Deflationism and the Truth-Conditional Theory of Meaning." In: *Philosophical Studies* 124, pp. 271–94.

Peacocke, Christopher (1978). "Necessity and Truth Theories." In: *Journal of Philosophical Logic* 7, pp. 473–500.

—— (1992). *A Study of Concepts*. Cambridge, Mass: MIT Press.

Perry, John (1993). "Thought without Representation." In: *The Proboem of the Essential Indexical and Other Essays*. Oxford: Oxford University Press, pp. 171–88.

Pietroski, Paul (1994). "A Defense of Derangement." In: *Canadian Journal of Philosophy* 24, pp. 95–118.

—— (2005). *Events and Semantic Architecture*. Oxford: Oxford University Press.

Quine, Willard Van Orman (1951). "Two Dogmas of Empiricism." In: *From a Logical Point of View*. Cambridge, Mass.: Harvard University Press, 1980, pp. 20–46.

—— (1958). "Speaking of Objects." In: *Ontological Relativity & Other Essays*. New York: Columbia University Press 1969, pp. 1–25.

—— (1960). *Word and Object*. Cambridge, Mass.: MIT Press.

—— (1968). "Existence and Quantification." In: *Ontological Relativity & Other Essays*. New York: Columbia University Press 1969, pp. 91–113.

—— (1976). "Wither Physical Objects?" In: *Boston Studies in the Philosophy of Science* 39, pp. 497–507.

—— (1981). "On the Very Idea of a Third Dogma." In: *Theories and Things*. Cambridge, Mass.: The Belknap Press of Harvard University Press, pp. 38–42.

—— (1985). "Events and Reification." In: *Actions and Events. Perspectives on the Philosophy of Donald Davidson*. Ed. by Ernest Lepore; Brian McLaughlin. Oxford: Basil Blackwell, pp. 162–71.

—— (1992a). *Pursuit of Truth* revised edition. Cambridge, Mass.: Harvard University Press.

Quine, Willard Van Orman (1992b). "Structure and Nature." In: *Journal of Philosophy* 89, pp. 5–9.

Ramberg, Bjørn T. (1989). *Donald Davidson's Philosophy of Language. An Introduction*. Oxford: Basil Blackwell.

—— (2003). "Illuminating Language: Interpretation and understanding in Gadamer and Davidson." In: *A House Divided. Comparing Analytic and Continental Philosophy*. Ed. by C. G. Prado. New York: Prometheus, pp. 213–34.

Ramsey, Frank P. (1931). "Truth and Probability." In: *Philosophical Papers*. Ed. by D. H. Mellor. Cambridge: Cambridge University Press 1990, pp. 52–94.

Rawling, Piers (2001). "Davidson's Measurement Theoretic Reduction of the Mind." In: *Interpreting Davidson*. Ed. by Peter Kotatko; Peter Pagin; Gabriel Segal. Stanford: CSLI, pp. 237–55.

Recanati, Francois (2004). *Literal Meaning*. Oxford: Oxford University Press.

—— (2007). "It is raining (somewhere)." In: *Linguistics & Philosophy* 30, pp. 123–46.

Reimer, Marga (2004). "What Malapropisms Mean: A Reply to Donald Davidson." In: *Erkenntnis* 60, pp. 317–34.

Rorty, Richard (1987). "Non-reductive Physicalism." In: *Objectivity, Relativism and Truth*. Cambridge: Cambridge University Press 1991, pp. 113–25.

Rumfitt, Ian (1993). "Content and Context: The paratactic theory revisited and revised." In: *Mind* 102, pp. 429–54.

Russell, Bertrand (1905). "On Denoting." In: *Mind* 14, pp. 479–93.

Schiffer, Stephen (1987). *Remnants of Meaning*. Cambridge, Mass.: MIT Press.

Schroeder, Timothy (2003). "Donald Davidson's Theory of Mind is Non-Normative." In: *Philosophers' Imprint* 3. http://hdl.handle.net/2027/spo.3521354.0003.001.

Searle, John (1978). "Literal Meaning." In: *Erkenntnis* 13, pp. 207–24.

—— (1983). *Intentionality*. Cambridge: Cambridge University Press.

Segal, Gabriel (1999). "How a Truth Theory Can Do Duty as a Theory of Meaning." In: *Donald Davidson: Truth, Meaning, and Knowledge*. Ed. by Urszula Zeglen. New York: Routledge, pp. 48–58.

—— (2006). "Truth and Meaning." In: *The Oxford Handbook of Philosophy of Language*. Ed. by Ernest Lepore and Barry Smith. Oxford: Oxford University Press, pp. 189–212.

Sellars, Wilfrid (1963). "Empiricism and the Philosophy of Mind." In: *Science, Perception and Reality*. London: Routledge and Kegan Paul, pp. 127–96.

——— (1966). "Thought and Action." In: *Freedom and Determinism*. Ed. by Keith Lehrer. New York: Random House, pp. 105–39.

Smart, J. J. C. (1959). "Sensations and Brain Processes." In: *The Philosophical Review* 68, pp. 141–56.

Smith, Michael (1987). "The Humean Theory of Motivation." In: *Mind*, pp. 36–61.

——— (2003). "Humeanism, Psychologism and the Normative Story." In: *Ethics and the A Priori*. Cambridge: Cambridge University Press 2004, pp. 146–54.

Soames, Scott (1992). "Truth, Meaning, and Understanding." In: *Philosophical Studies* 65, pp. 17–35.

——— (2008). "Truth and Meaning: In Perspective." In: *Midwest Studies in Philosophy* 32, pp. 1–19.

Sosa, Ernest (1984). "Mind-body Interaction and Supervenient Causation." In: *Midwest Studies in Philosophy* IX, pp. 271–83.

Speaks, Jeff (2005). "Is There a Problem about Nonconceptual Content?" In: *Philosophical Review* 114, pp. 359–98.

——— (2006). "Truth theories, translation manuals, and theories of meaning." In: *Linguistics & Philosophy* 29, pp. 487–505.

Spitzley, Thomas (1990). "Davidson and Hare on Evaluations." In: *Ratio* 3, pp. 48–63.

Stalnaker, Robert (1968). "A Theory of Conditionals." In: *Studies in Logical Theory*. Ed. by Nicholas Rescher. New York: Oxford University Press, pp. 98–112.

——— (1997). "Reference and Necessity." In: *A Companion to the Philosophy of Language*. Ed. by Bob Hale and Crispin Wright. Basil Blackwell.

Stoutland, Fred (1970). "The Logical Connection Argument." In: *American Philosophical Quarterly* 4, pp. 117–29.

Strawson, Peter F. (1992). *Analysis and Metaphysics. An Introduction to Philosophy*. Oxford: Oxford University Press.

Stroud, Barry (2002a). "Radical Interpretation and Philosophical Scepticism." In: *Understanding Human Knowledge—Philosophical Essays*. Oxford: Oxford University Press, pp. 177–202.

——— (2002b). "Sense-Experience and the Grounding of Thought." In: *Reading McDowell: On Mind and World*. Ed. by Nicholas H. Smith. London and New York: Routledge, pp. 79–91.

Stroud, Sarah (2008). "Weakness of Will." In: *The Stanford Encyclopedia of Philosophy*. Ed. by Edward N. Zalta. Fall 2008. http://plato. stanford.edu/archives/fall2008/entries/weakness-will/.

Talmage, Catherine (1994). "Literal Meaning, Conventional Meaning and First Meaning." In: *Erkenntnis* 40, pp. 213–25.

—— (1996). "Davidson and Humpty Dumpty." In: *Nous* 30, pp. 537–44.

Tarski, Alfred (1933). "The Concept of Truth in Formalized Languages." In: *Logic, Semantics, Metamathematics*. Ed. by John Corcoran. Trans. by J. H. Woodger. 2nd ed. Indianapolis: Hackett Publishing Company, 1983.

—— (1944). "The Semantic Conception of Truth." In: *Philosophy and Phenomenological Research* 4, pp. 341–76.

Tersman, Folke (1998). "Stimulus Meaning Debunked." In: *Erkenntnis* 49, pp. 371–85.

Thompson, Judith Jarvis (1971). "The Time of a Killing." In: *Journal of Philosophy* 68, pp. 115–32.

Travis, Charles (1989). *The Uses of Sense*. Oxford: Oxford University Press.

Varzi, Achille and Fabio Pianesi (2000). "Events and Event Talk: An Introduction." In: *Speaking of Events*. Ed. by James Higginbotham, Fabio Pianesi, and Achille Varzi. Oxford: Oxford University Press, pp. 3–47.

Velleman, J. David (1989). *Practical Reflection*. Princeton: Princeton University Press.

—— (2000). *The Possibility of Practical Reason*. Oxford: Oxford University Press.

Verheggen, Claudine (2006). "How Social Must Language Be?" In: *Journal for the Theory of Social Behavior* 36, pp. 203–19.

—— (2007). "Triangulating with Davidson." In: *Philosophical Quarterly* 57, pp. 96–103.

Weir, Alan (2006). "Indeterminacy of Translation." In: *The Oxford Handbook of Philosophy of Language*. Ed. by Ernest Lepore and Barry Smith. Oxford: Oxford University Press, pp. 233–49.

Whorf, Benjamin Lee (1956). *Language, Thought, and Reality: Selected Writings of Benjamin Lee Whorf*. Ed. by J. Carroll. Cambridge, Mass.: MIT Press.

Wiggins, David (1980). "'Most' and 'All': Some Comments on A Familiar Programme." In: *Reference, Truth and Reality: Essays on the Philosophy of Language*. Ed. by Mark Platts. London: Routledge and Kegan Paul, pp. 318–46.

—— (1997). "Meaning and truth conditions: from Frege's grand design to Davidson's." In: *A Companion to the Philosophy of Language*. Ed. by Bob Hale and Crispin Wright. Basil Blackwell, pp. 3–28.

Williams, Michael (1999). "Meaning and Deflationary Truth." In: *Journal of Philosophy* 96, pp. 545–64.

Williamson, Timothy (2004). "Philosophical 'Intuitions' and Scepticism about Judgement." In: *Dialectica* 58, pp. 109–53.

——— (2006). "Conceptual Truth." In: *Proceedings of the Aristotelian Society, Supplementary Volume* 80, pp. 1–41.

——— (2007). *The Philosophy of Philosophy*. Oxford: Blackwell.

Wilson, George (1989). *The Intentionality of Human Action*. Stanford: Stanford University Press.

——— (2009). "Action." In: *The Stanford Encyclopedia of Philosophy*. Ed. by Edward N. Zalta. Fall 2009. http://plato.stanford.edu/archives/fall2009/entries/action/.

Wilson, Neil L. (1959). "Substances Without Substrata." In: *Review of Metaphysics* 12, pp. 521–39.

Wittgenstein, Ludwig (1922). *Tractatus Logico-Philosophicus (Deutsch/English)*. Trans. by F. P. Ramsey and C. K. Ogden. London: Routledge and Kegan Paul.

——— (1958). *The Blue and Brown Books. Preliminary Studies for the "Philosophical Investigations."* Oxford: Basil Blackwell.

Wright, Crispin (1980). *Wittgenstein on the Foundations of Mathematics*. London: Duckworth.

——— (1986). *Realism, Meaning and Truth*. Oxford: Blackwell.

Yalowitz, Steven (1999). "Davidson's Social Externalism." In: *Philosophia* 27, pp. 99–136.

——— (2005). "Anomalous Monism." In: *The Stanford Encyclopedia of Philosophy*. Ed. by Edward N. Zalta. Spring 2009. Stanford: CSLI. http://plato.stanford.edu/archives/spr2009/entries/anomalous-monism/.

INDEX

action, 4
  definition of intentional,
    195–196
  explanation of, 147–148, 152,
    154, 157, 159–160, 162–166
    (*see also* reasons explanation)
  individuation of, 166–167,
    178–183
  and intentional states, 4, 147–148,
    210–211
  as intentional under a description,
    179–181, 187
  non-intentional, 166–167, 181
  sentences, logical form of,
    168–178, 188
  theory of, 13, 153–211
agreement, maximizing or
    optimizing of, 77–81, 113, 119,
    127–132, 222 (*see also* charity,
    principle of)
akrasia, *see* weakness of the will
analysis, conceptual, 19, 19 n. 1,
    143–146, 221–222, 245,
    248

analytic-synthetic distinction, 131,
    141
animals, rational, 4, 5, 118, 210, 249
anomalous monism, 14, 15–16, 190,
    249, 250–261, 267, 272, 279
Anscombe, Elisabeth, 168 n. 9, 259,
    278 n. 23
anti-reductivism, *see* reduction (*see*
    also mental, irreducible
    nature of)
a priori, 140–144
Aristotle, 140, 154–155, 157, 160

Bar-On, Dorit, 97 n. 65
behaviorism, semantic, 8, 27
belief,
  coherent and veridical nature of,
    5, 112, 116, 119, 121, 142, 234
  contexts, *see* propositional attitude
    contexts
  interdependence of meaning and,
    see meaning
  and the notions of mistake and
    truth, 239–241